Thinking Clearly

◆ A GUIDE TO ◆

CRITICAL REASONING

Jill LeBlanc MCMASTER UNIVERSITY

Thinking Clearly

◆ A GUIDE TO ◆

CRITICAL REASONING

 W. W. NORTON & COMPANY NEW YORK LONDON

The text of this book is composed in Minion with the
display set in Bodoni Campanile and Perpetua.
Composition by Willow Graphics
Book design by Jack Meserole

PRINTED IN THE UNITED STATES OF AMERICA

First Edition

Library of Congress Cataloging-in-Publication Data

LeBlanc, Jill (Jill E.)
    Thinking clearly : a guide to critical reasoning / Jill LeBlanc.
      p. cm.
    Includes index.
    ISBN 0-393-97218-6 (pbk.)
    1. Critical thinking.   2. Logic.   I. Title.
  BC177.L43   1998
  160—dc21   97-24969

W. W. Norton & Company, Inc., 500 Fifth Avenue, New York, N.Y. 10110
http://www.wwnorton.com

W. W. Norton & Company Ltd., 10 Coptic Street, London WC1A 1PU

2 3 4 5 6 7 8 9 0

Contents

3 Categorical Logic   54

4 Necessary and Sufficient Conditions   85

5 Language   115

Introduction

Everyone knows to some extent how to reason—to think, argue, recognize evidence and weigh it—because this is one of the main things that humans do. So in this book, you won't be learning something completely new to you; you'll be learning to do a familiar thing better. The skills you learn here will help you communicate better, both in and out of school. Many of you won't go on to careers directly related to your present major, but reasoning skills will be valuable whatever you pursue.

Every example in this book is a real one: it was an argument that someone made, in conversation or in writing. Some examples are trivial and some are profound, but it's important to recognize the scope of topics that arguments can cover. Arguments aren't something we come up with only for school, or only when the topic is "worthy." We construct and evaluate arguments many times every day. As you work through this book and become more sensitive to arguments, you'll be surprised where, and how frequently, you find them.

1

Identifying Arguments

OUR ULTIMATE GOAL in studying critical thinking is to learn to evaluate arguments—other people's arguments and our own. Arguments can be about topics that are trivial or profound; academic or personal; political, ethical, or aesthetic. In a sociology course, for example, you might encounter an argument that drug use causes poverty. You might counter with a paper arguing that it's poverty that causes drug abuse. You could give your roommate several reasons to go to a movie with you on Friday night rather than to a party; standing in line at the movie, you might argue that Quentin Tarantino is a better director than Ron Howard. In the newspaper, editorials and letters to the editor present you with arguments. During elections, each candidate offers arguments that you should vote for him or her rather than for the opposing candidate. Advertisements are arguments that you should buy that product.

Arguments matter: many arguments have important consequences. For example, if you buy a car, you'll have to make payments on it for years, as well as rely on it for transportation, so you'd better be sure that the argument in the advertisement urging you to choose that car is a good one. And if you accept a candidate's argument to vote for her, you cannot forget that her policies will affect the lives of many citizens. Will the policy change their lives for the worse?

Before we can evaluate arguments, though, we need to be able to recognize them. In this chapter, we'll learn to identify arguments and to distinguish them from some other kinds of discourse.

1

◼ ARGUMENTS

An **argument** is an attempt to justify or prove a conclusion. In other words, an argument tries to make you believe something, and gives you reasons to believe it. What the argument is trying to make you believe is called the **conclusion**. The reasons that it gives are called the **premises**. There can be one premise given to support a conclusion, or there can be many: there is no standard length for an

> **REVIEW BOX 1.1**
>
> **Arguments**
>
> An argument is an attempt to justify or prove a conclusion.

argument. An argument can be stated in one sentence, or it can take a whole book. The premises can be implicit or explicit. They can be given in the form of words or even pictures.

If you say you had an argument with a friend, you generally mean that you had a quarrel. That meaning of "argument" is not the one that we'll use. For us, "argument" means an attempt to justify a conclusion. Sometimes arguments take place when people disagree. For example, two people may debate opposing positions by supporting their own positions, and perhaps criticizing and attempting to refute the other view. In such cases, each person is trying to convince the other by giving reasons. Arguments can also take place where there is no disagreement—someone can try to convince you of something about which you have no opinion. In these instances, refutation plays no part. An argument does not require two people, since you can also use an argument to convince yourself.

Arguments can be good or bad. Later, we'll learn to recognize the difference, but before we can do that, we need to be able to identify arguments when we see them. There are two questions to ask about every passage: [1] Is there an attempt to convince me of something? [2] Are reasons given to convince me? If we answer "yes" to both questions, the passage is an argument.

Indicator words can help you recognize arguments. Words like "thus" and "therefore" may indicate a conclusion; words like "since" and "because" may signal a premise. (A partial list of indicator words is contained in Review Box 1.2.) It is important to remember indicator words so that you can recognize them—but some arguments do not contain any of these words; some nonarguments do contain them. Ultimately, you must make your decision on the basis of the content and context of the passage. Let's look at some examples.

> [1] Eyed needles have been found on Paleolithic sites from 40,000 years ago. It is believed that Paleolithic people used them to sew animal skins into protective suits. Thus tailoring is a very old practice.

Example [1] is an argument. You'll probably notice at once that it contains the word "thus"—possibly indicating a conclusion. So ask yourself two questions: [1] Does the passage try to make me believe something? Yes—that tailoring is a very old invention. [2] Are reasons to believe this provided? Yes—needles from long ago have been found. Answering "yes" to both questions tells you that this passage is an argument. These needles from long ago are *evidence* for the conclusion that tailoring is a very old practice. They help to prove that the conclusion is true. Here is another example.

REVIEW BOX   1.2

Indicator words

FOR CONCLUSIONS:
thus, therefore, hence, so , it follows that, shows that, indicates that, proves that, then

FOR PREMISES:
for, since, because, for the reason that, on the grounds that, follows from

> [2] Financial and human resources have been directed too much toward finding a cure for AIDS, and not enough toward education. We have heard for many years that education is the most effective weapon against AIDS, and this is still the case. In fact, education will continue to be crucial even if a cure is found; it is not merely a temporary solution. Even if drugs and vaccines are developed, AIDS will not just disappear, especially among the underprivileged, any more than any other infectious disease has just disappeared.

Example [2] does not contain any indicator words. We can recognize it as an argument only by considering its meaning. Is the passage trying to make us believe something? Yes—that resources should go into education as well as toward finding a cure. Does the passage give us reasons to be convinced? Yes—education will still be important even if a cure is found, as a comparison with other infectious diseases would show.

Strategies and Conventions

Questions for arguments

A passage is an argument if you anser "yes" to both of these questions:
• Is it trying to convince me of something?
• Are reasons given to convince me?

To say that reasons are given to believe a conclusion is not to say that the reasons are good. Supporting a conclusion with bad reasons makes for a bad argument; however, a bad argument is still an argument. Only after we have determined that a passage offers reasons to believe something can we determine whether those reasons are good ones.

Compare examples [1] and [2] with the following:

> [3] Rimbaud claimed that the only way an artist could arrive at the truths he wanted was to experience every form of love, suffering, and madness, and that he might prepare for this by a planned disordering of all the senses, for example, by drunkenness.

Example [3] is not an argument. It reports what Rimbaud thought an artist must do to arrive at truths. It makes no attempt to convince us of anything, and gives no reasons to believe that what it says is true. Though there may be an assumption that we will accept the information it contains, example [3] is not *about* accepting it.

Here is one more example, before we try some exercises.

> [4] Real numbers can be thought of as points on the number line. Real numbers include rational numbers, which

can be expressed as decimal expansions that either terminate or repeat some pattern endlessly; and irrational numbers, like π, whose decimal expansion neither terminates nor contains a fixed repeating pattern. Real numbers are not closed under algebraic functions.

Example [4] is not an argument. It's a description or definition of real numbers. Again, we may want to say that the passage is intended to be believed. If we read this in a math textbook we'd probably have no reason to doubt it. (We'll consider this issue in Chapter 6.) But it does not offer reasons to believe what it says. The passage simply presents the information, which may or may not be new to us.

EXERCISE 1.1

Determine whether each of the following passages is or is not an argument and give reasons for your decision.

Example

Ever-growing suburban populations suck the life out of cities. Suburbs make good public transit almost impossible. Riders are not concentrated along a few main roads; rather, they are scattered over many smaller ones. Thus it becomes expensive to carry them, resulting in infrequent service or higher fares, either of which makes public transit less appealing. People in suburbs therefore get around mostly by car, resulting in the need for wide roads, which are expensive for cities to build and to maintain.

This passage is an argument that growth in suburban populations sucks the life out of cities, and it gives the following reasons to support this claim: suburbs foster the use of cars, which leads, on the one hand, to a decline in public transit and, on the other hand, to the cities' spending all their money on building big roads.

Note: The response is also an argument. It gives reasons to believe that the passage is an argument. Try to think of all your responses to these exercises as arguments.

1. In areas with cold winters, many types of roses require "hilling" for winter protection. Hilling involves building up soil around the base of the rose. A layer of leaves may also be added.

2. Violence in movies is not evidence of people's declining moral standards, as critics like Michael Medved claim. Ancient myths, medieval biographies of saints, Shakespeare's plays, and nineteenth-century novels like *Dracula* are all full of bloodshed and mayhem. People have always been this way.

3. All dogs need an occasional bath. Dogs with long silky coats, like Afghan hounds, may require bathing on a weekly basis, while sporting breeds like golden retrievers may need only one or two baths a year. The dog's lifestyle can also contribute to the need for bathing.

4. Photo radar is not a good solution for traffic safety problems on our highways. Photo radar does not address the main cause of highway danger, since it only works to reduce the overall speed of traffic, and speed is not the main problem. If speed were the major contributor to highway fatalities, we should expect higher fatalities on the German Autobahn, where there is no speed limit, than on North American roads. But this is not the case. Furthermore, photo radar diverts policing resources from standard highway patrols, since the operator of photo radar can't leave his/her post to pursue other nonspeeding violations.

5. Game agencies ought not to spend time and money on wolf-control programs, which consist of shooting or poisoning wolves at random. In Alberta in 1994, fourteen cattle were killed by wolves; in 1993, twenty-three cattle. By comparison, in 1993, 214 cattle were dead on their arrival at slaughterhouses. The stress of shipping kills a certain number of cattle every year. These dead animals represent a small percentage of the total cattle slaughtered. However, this number still far exceeds the number of deaths attributed to wolves.

6. Bloodhounds are descended from hounds brought to Britain in 1066 during the Norman invasion. They were used in packs to hunt stags. Today bloodhounds are still used for tracking, both in hunting and in law enforcement. Bloodhounds find but do not attack their quarry. In fact they are gentle dogs that make good family companions.

7. Eratosthenes invented a way to find prime numbers without dividing or factoring. Write down the odd numbers after 3, then strike every third

number after 3, every fifth number after 5, every seventh number after 7, and so on. What's left are the prime numbers. This is known as the Sieve of Eratosthenes.

PROPOSITIONS

It will be useful for us to speak of **propositions** sometimes instead of sentences. A proposition is the content or meaning of a sentence. It's important to isolate propositions to discover the structure of an argument, no matter how it's expressed. Conclusions and the evidence that supports them are always propositions.

Propositions can be simple or compound. Let's begin with the simple ones. A simple proposition expresses a single complete thought. To express a *complete* thought, it must contain a subject and a predicate. (The subject is what we're talking about. The predicate is what we're saying about the subject.) To express a *single* complete thought, it must contain only one subject and one predicate. Any proposition must also be able to be true or false. We may not know whether the proposition is true or false; we may have, in practice, no way to determine this. But some notion of what would count to determine the truth of the proposition is required.

> ### REVIEW BOX 1.3
>
> ## Simple propositions
>
> Every simple proposition must
>
> - express a complete thought.
> - express only one complete thought.
> - be able to be either true or false.

Take, for example,

[5] Wolves live in packs.

This sentence expresses the proposition "Wolves live in packs." This proposition contsins one subject, *wolves*, and one predicate, *live in packs*. It can be true or false: we'd established its truth or falsity by investingating the living habits of wolves.

Identifying propositions is not always this easy, however. Consider the following sentence:

■ [6] Wolves live in packs, but polar bears don't.

Here we have a single sentence that contains two simple propositions: "Wolves live in packs" and "Polar bears do not live in packs." There are two separate complete thoughts compounded, or joined together, by the word "but." Usually, when we see a compound proposition containing worlds like "and" or "but" we will separate the two propositions into two separate premises. Similarly, we will want to separate any propositions that are joined by premise or conclusion indicator words like "since," "so," or "because."

However, we should watch out for compound propositions that contain "if" (and related works like "unless") and "or." While we must recognize the simple propositions that make up the compound proposition, we usually do not want to separate the propositions into separate premises. Take for example,

[7] If I don't have my keys, I can't get into my car.

[8] Ahmad will get an A in his critical thinking course or his average will suffer.

We cannot accurately represent the structure of an argument that contains a sentence like [7] or [8] by separating the compound sentences into the simple propositions they contain. That is because the compound propositions do not **assert** that each of their component propositions is true.

When people advance an argument, they assert the propositions that serve as the argument's premises and conclusion. That means that they claim the propositions are true. (Sometimes premises and conclusions are called "assertions" or "claims.") If someone asserts "Wolves live in packs, but polar bears don't," she makes two claims: wolves live in packs, and polar bears do not live in packs. But someone who asserts a sentence like [7] does not assert two independent propositions. Instead, she asserts that there is a logical relationship between these two propositions—that having her keys is required for getting into her car. Similarly, someone who asserts "Ahmad will get an A in his critical thinking course or his average will suffer" does not assert both "Ahmad will get an A in his critical thinking course" and "His average will suffer." Instead, she claims that at least one of these propositions is true.

Let's consider a more complex example.

[9] Photo radar does not address the main cause of highway danger, since it only works to reduce the overall speed of traffic, and speed is not the main problem.

How many simple propositions can we find in this sentence?

[9a] Photo radar does not address the main cause of highway danger. Photo radar only serves to reduce the overall speed of traffic. Speed is not the main problem.

Notice that when we analyze a sentence containing several simple propositions like sentence [9], we distinguish as many components as we can express in full sentences. Each sentence in [9a] can be true or false. The original sentence [9] expresses the logical relationships between three simple statements. Our goal is to identify and separate the simple statements so that we can consider these logical relationships.

EXERCISE 1.2

Identify the simple propositions contained in each of the following sentences.

Example

If the fetus has no legal rights, then a pregnant woman cannot be forced into a substance-abuse program against her will, even if her behavior will result in harm to the child when it is born.
 • The fetus has no legal rights.
 • A pregnant woman cannot be forced into a substance-abuse program against her will.
 • Her behavior will result in harm to the child.
 • It [the child] is born.

1. Humans are limited as far as wisdom is concerned.

2. If people had followed the counsels of God's word instead of relying on their own inadequate abilities, the problems that have plagued human history need never have happened.

3. Since beer is meant to be a full sensory experience, you should be able to see the beer before you taste it.

4. The best way to improve a city's neighborhoods and reduce environmental damage would be to reduce the speed limit for private vehicles to 15 mph within city limits, because reducing the speed limit would decrease automobile use.

5. Some people say that the use of symbols like the "smilie"—":-)"—in e-mail messages makes it unnecessary for people to make their points clear in words alone, and in general reduces flexibility within the language.

6. Women are physically weaker than men, and so are unfit for combat, which requires physical endurance, ability to withstand strain, and stamina.

7. Why on earth did you do that?

8. Society is best served by educated people, so cutting spending on education is a shortsighted solution to economic problems.

9. Sometimes arguments can take place without disagreement—when, for example, someone tries to convince you of something new by giving you reasons to believe it.

10. There can be one premise given in support of a conclusion, or there can be many.

■ EXPLANATIONS

It is sometimes difficult to distinguish an argument from an **explanation**. Explanations can use some of the same indicator words as arguments—"because," "since," "thus," "so," "hence." Consider the following examples.

[10] There are 324 students in this class. I have a registration list.

[11] There are 324 students in this class, because it's a required course in many majors.

Both examples [10] and [11] contain the statement that there are 324 students in this class, and another simple proposition. Example [10] is an argument. The second sentence in example [10] is a reason to believe there are 324 students in this class. Why should you believe that there are 324 students in this class? Because I'm telling you that there are, and I'm in a position to know—I have the list with the official class size. Example [11] is an explanation. It is taken for granted that there are, or that you believe there are, 324 students in the class; the second proposition (which is signaled by the "because") indicates why this should be true. It doesn't give you a reason to believe there are 324 students; rather, it gives you a reason why there are 324 students.

REVIEW BOX   1.4

Arguments and explanations

ARGUMENTS
- give you reasons why you should believe something is true.
- tell you how things are.

EXPLANATIONS
- give you reasons why something is true.
- tell you why things are as they are.

There are several interrelated ways to distinguish arguments from explanations: (1) We can ask whether the passage gives us evidence or causes. (2) We can ask what we're most willing to believe. (3) We can ask whether the passage makes more sense as an argument or as an explanation.

Evidence or Cause?

Like arguments, explanations give reasons, but these reasons do not justify a conclusion. Sometimes explanations tell us why something came to be. They give a *cause*. Example [11] tells us what caused the class to be so large: the fact that the course is required in many majors. Example [10], in contrast, gives evidence that the class contains 324 students.

Sometimes explanations tell us what caused someone to do or believe something by exploring his or her motivations. For example, the following passage tells us what motivated Shawn to choose the course that he did.

> [12] Shawn is an economics major, and a critical thinking course is required for his major. That's why Shawn is taking critical thinking.

Example [12] is not likely an attempt to *convince* us that Shawn is registered for critical thinking. Rather, it offers a reason *why* Shawn took the
class. No conclusion is being drawn. Of course, the same set of reasons
could serve as an argument to register for the critical thinking class.
Shawn may have said to himself:

> [13] I'm an economics major, and critical thinking is a
> requirement. So I'd better register in that class.

Examples [12] and [13] use the same propositions and the same general
line of reasoning, but one is an argument and the other is an explanation.
This shows us again that an argument can be recognized in part by its
purpose. Is it intended to convince us? Although we can't be expected to
read someone else's mind, we can in most cases use context and common
knowledge to tell an argument from an explanation.

Strategies and Conventions

Questions for arguments and explanations

• Does the passage make more sense as an argument or as an
explanation?

• Is it meant to convince me of the truth of something new, or to
explain why something I already know is true?

What am I most willing to believe?

Can you identify the "main point" of a passage? The "main point" is,
loosely speaking, what the passage is about. Examples [12] and [13] are
about Shawn's decision to take critical thinking. Consider the following
passage [14]:

> [14] Why do weight and appearance matter so much to
> people in contemporary society? There are no
> longer many social hierarchies built on one's family,
> money, or education. Yet people still have a desire to

compare themselves to others. Since social status cannot provide a means of measurement, there is a need for new standards—visible ones, like beauty and fitness. [Adapted from Judith Rodin, "Body Mania," *Psychology Today*, vol. 25, no. 1 (January/February 1992), pp. 56–60.]

The main point here is the significance of weight and appearance. When you have identified the main point, ask yourself these questions. Is this main point something new to you? Does the passage give you reasons to believe it is true? If you answer "yes" to these questions, the passage is an argument. Or does the passage assume that you already believe or accept this main point, and give reasons why it's true? If your answer to the latter question is "yes," the passage is an explanation.

If you are less willing to believe the main point than you are to believe the other propositions in the passage, the passage is probably an argument. If you're more willing to believe the main point, it's probably an explanation. Why? As we'll see in Chapter 6, premises must always be more certain (likelier to be believed) than the conclusions they support. Arguments work by leading someone from something he or she already accepts and believes, to something new. If we're more willing to believe the main point of the passage—what would be the conclusion if it were an argument—than we are to believe the rest, the passage ought to be considered an explanation.

Considering example [14], we're probably willing to believe that weight and appearance matter to people—more willing than we are to believe that they are a means of comparing ourselves favorably to others. It's not that we're *un*willing to believe that we measure our appearance against that of others—rather, it's that time spent on grooming and fitness is such a basic part of life that we do not question the importance of our appearance.

What makes more sense?

Another approach to distinguishing arguments from explanations is to ask whether the passage makes a better explanation than it does an argument. Example [12] makes more sense as an explanation, because it does not give us the most straightforward proof or evidence for a conclusion that

Shawn is taking critical thinking. Looking him up on the registration list would be a better proof. Similarly, example [14] is a weak argument, but a plausible explanation. A much more direct argument for the conclusion that weight and appearance matter to people could be based upon the money spent on fashion, weight-loss, and fitness.

REVIEW BOX 1.5

The Principle of Charity

You use the principle of charity when you interpret a passage so that it makes the most sense.

When we interpret a passage so that it makes the most sense, we are using the **principle of charity**. We should interpret the argument in the most compelling way that it can be read, giving the author or speaker the benefit of the doubt. If a passage can be interpreted as either a reasonable explanation or a weak argument, we should consider it an explanation. Our criticisms of an argument are more likely to be compelling if we use the principle of charity. If we criticize the strongest interpretation of a passage, the arguer cannot defend her position by claiming that we have misinterpreted her meaning.

Let's compare two trickier passages, and decide whether they are arguments or explanations.

> [15] Factory farming is a major source of pollution. It concentrates large quantities of manure that would, in traditional methods of farming, be naturally returned to the fields. As a result of this concentration, rivers, lakes, and ground water are contaminated by nitrates. This concentration of manure also means that it decomposes without oxygen, unlike manure that falls in the fields, thereby producing methane.

Example [15] is probably an argument trying to convince us that factory farming is a major source of pollution; the rest of the passage gives us reasons to believe this conclusion. We can imagine circumstances in which example [15] might be used to explain why factory farming is a major source of pollution. For example, someone who already had data linking factory farming and pollution might want to account for those data. But there is no indication in the passage that the link between factory farming and pollution has already been established, and this link is not common knowledge. So the main point is less likely to be believed than the rest of the passage. That does not mean that the main point is less believ*able*; rather, it is not believed yet. Once again, we see that the decision about whether a passage is an argument or an explanation must often be based on the context of the passage. Who is the anticipated audience? What can they be expected to know already?

> [16] The rate of food-borne diseases associated with red meat and poultry has been steadily on the rise in America over the past two decades. Partly because of microwaves, we don't cook our meat as thoroughly as people did in the past. The population is also aging, and there are more people with immune disorders like AIDS. The members of both these groups run a greater risk of incurring a disease from meat.

Example [16], however, is an explanation. The question about what we are most willing to believe probably won't decide the issue, since we may be unaware of the rates of food-borne disease. Instead, we need to use the principle of charity and ask whether the passage makes more sense as an argument or an explanation. Is this a likely argument for the conclusion that food-borne diseases are on the rise? No: that conclusion would be easily proven by comparing the rate of food-borne diseases today with that of ten or twenty years ago, thereby showing that the present rate is higher. Example [16] is, however, plausible as an explanation: given that there are more food-borne diseases than there used to be, changes in food preparation and the population's susceptibility could be part of the cause.

Consider example [17].

> [17] Some people with epilepsy have seizure dogs, whose responsibility is to stand guard over the person in seizure and protect him or her from others, prevent him or her from moving towards danger like traffic or stairs, and in some cases to summon help. Some of the people who have seizure dogs report that the dogs learn to tell when a seizure is approaching, and bark to warn the person. But no one knows how a dog could sense an approaching seizure.

Example [17] is neither an argument nor an explanation. It may provide new information, but it does not offer reasons to believe that information; it lists facts about the jobs that seizure dogs do. These reported duties could serve as a basis for an explanation of why people have or would like to have seizure dogs, but example [17] does not offer that explanation. The last sentence hints at something that we might want explained—how dogs can sense approaching seizures—but says that there is no explanation. Essentially, this passage gives us information, and though there may be reasons that would explain the information, or reasons that would prove it true, the passage is not *about* those reasons.

As you begin to apply what you learn in this book to editorials, letters to the editor, textbooks, articles, advertisements, and conversations, you'll see many passages that are not purely argument, explanation, or neither. Often, a single paragraph can contain aspects of two or even all three. Consider example [18].

> [18] Antilock brakes do not reduce either the frequency or the cost of road crashes that result in insurance claims. The Highway Loss Data Institute (HLDI) compared the frequency of insurance claims for vehicles with and without antilock brakes in twenty-nine northern states in winter, when antilock brakes should make the most difference. They found that there was a reduction neither in claim frequency nor in the average amount of insurance payments for cars with antilock brakes.
>
> This may be because the circumstances under which antilock brakes could reduce crashes are quite rare. Also, many drivers do not know how to use antilock brakes effectively, and most owner's manuals give either no instructions or inadequate ones for using this feature.

Example [18] contains both an argument and an explanation. The first sentence, which tells us that antilock brakes do not reduce the frequency or cost of road crashes, is a conclusion. This conclusion is supported by evidence resulting from the comparative study undertaken by the HLDI, cited in the first paragraph. Once we have been given reason to accept the truth of the conclusion, an explanation of why it should be true is provided. The second paragraph offers two possible reasons: there are few situations in which antilock brakes could reduce accidents, and people may not know how to use them effectively. Example [18] displays quite a common pattern: you are given first a reason to believe that a proposition is true, and then an explanation to account for it.

The next passage exemplifies a different pattern. It begins by explaining a fact of which we're aware, then offers an argument to convince us that the explanation is plausible.

> [19] Pencils are hexagonal in shape because the hexagonal shape of pencils represents a compromise between comfort and cost. A round pencil is more comfortable to use, while a square shape is the most efficient use of resources. The hexagonal pencil is a compromise. Nine hexagonal pencils can be made of the wood it takes to make eight round pencils.

Example [19] explains why pencils are the shape that they are. Most people would probably agree that pencils are hexagonal. First, we've probably been acquainted with hexagonal pencils since elementary school. Second, even if we were not, stating that they are a compromise between comfort and cost would not prove that they are hexagonal. Much more direct evidence could be given by empirical investigation of pencils. The explanation that example [19] gives for the hexagonal shape is that it represents a compromise. It gives us this reason: a round pencil is comfortable and a square pencil is cheap; a hexagon, then, is something in between comfortable and cheap.

Here is a final example.

> [20] Recently demographers decided to investigate patterns of home ownership and retention among people in the United States who bought their houses immediately after World War II. The researchers discovered that a large number of people in their eighties lived in undesirable inner-city neighborhoods. The researchers concluded that people who had raised children in a house maintained a sentimental

attachment to the house and so were unwilling to move despite the neighborhood's decline. Other studies, however, show that a more likely cause of their staying where they are is lack of money. Older people are more likely to be on fixed incomes and cannot afford to move. People in their eighties would have been on fixed incomes for a long time and could not afford to move when the neighborhood began to decline.

Breaking this passage down to its component parts, we see that it contains argument, explanation, and simple description.

[20a] Recently demographers decided to investigate patterns of home ownership and retention among people in the United States who bought their houses immediately after World War II. The researchers discovered that a large number of people in their eighties lived in undesirable inner-city neighborhoods.

These first two sentences are neither argument nor explanation. They give us background needed to follow the rest of the passage. The second sentence contains the main point: that there are a large number of people in their eighties living in bad neighborhoods. An argument in support of this main point could be found in the study done by these demographic researchers. We are not given their argument here, however.

[20b] The researchers concluded that people who had raised children in a house maintained a sentimental attachment to the house and so were unwilling to move despite the neighborhood's decline.

This sentence reports an explanation of the main point: many people in their eighties are motivated by a sentimental attachment to the house in which they have lived for many years.

[20c] Other studies, however, show that a more likely cause of their staying where they are is lack of money.

Sentence [20c] argues that there is a better explanation than that given in sentence [20b]. An argument about the quality or plausibility of an explanation is still an argument. Sentence [20c] tries to convince us that there is a more likely reason that these people have remained in the same house for so long.

> [20d] Older people are more likely to be on fixed incomes and cannot afford to move. People in their eighties have been on fixed incomes for a long time, and could not afford to leave when the neighborhood began to decline.

Finally, example [20d] reports a few details of that alternate explanation.

If we wanted to evaluate this passage as a whole, we'd have to do some research. We'd need to check the studies mentioned, evaluate them using skills we'll learn later, and finally compare them to determine which one provides a more plausible explanation. Before we could begin to evaluate the passage, though, we'd need to examine its structure. Only by understanding its structure could we know what to evaluate and how.

SUMMARY

You should now be able to recognize arguments and to distinguish them from nonarguments by asking whether an attempt is being made to convince you by giving reasons to accept a conclusion. Criteria to help distinguish arguments from explanations include whether the passage makes more sense as an argument or an explanation, and whether the main point is more or less likely to be believed than the rest of the passage. This latter criterion is based on the principle of charity, which we'll see again in Chapter 7.

Attention and practice will help you become proficient at distinguishing argument and explanation from one another. The following exercises will help you develop the habit of distinguishing arguments from other types of discourse. In time no matter what you read or hear, you'll know how all its parts fit together and what role each proposition plays with respect to all the others.

Strategies and Conventions

"I.e." and "e.g."

E.g. means "for example."
I.e. means "that is."

These expressions come from Latin.
E.g. is short for *exemplar gratia*, which means "for example."
I.e. is short for *id est*, which means "that is."

LEMUR Exercise 1.1

EXERCISE 1.3

Determine whether each of the following passages is an argument, an explanation, or neither, and give reasons for your answer. If the passage appears to contain aspects of more than one of these, clarify the roles played by the components of the passage.

Example

Diplomacy should be favored over military action in cases of conflict, since modern war virtually guarantees that civilians will suffer. In a full-scale war, precision weapons may avoid the direct massacre of innocent people only to destroy resources they need for a decent life, as indicated by the 1992 reports from Iraq describing the desperate fate of hospitals, health centers, water purification systems, power supplies, etc.

This passage is an argument. Its conclusion is "Diplomacy should be favored over military action in cases of conflict." The reason given to believe this conclusion is that civilians suffer in war. We're given evidence to believe that innocent victims suffer in the following propositions.

1. Since all drugs potentially affect an athlete's performance, any use of drugs by athletes within forty-eight hours of their scheduled event should be prohibited.

2. Silicone was regarded as ideal for breast implants because it was thought to be chemically inert and thus relatively safe even if it remained in the body for years.

3. Books will never be replaced by computer disks, CD-ROMs, or other technological gizmos, because the information stored in electronic media is not stored in a permanent way. Technological formats rapidly become extinct—for example, 78 rpm records, photographic cylinders, punch cards, reel-to-reel audio tape. . . . There's no reason to believe that today's files will be readable by anything fifty years from now—the file may be in perfect shape, but there may well be no format existing then with which it is compatible. The format of the disk is essential. If the information is to be regularly replicated into more modern formats, the whole collection will have to be duplicated every twenty or thirty years. Books, on the other hand, are relatively long-lasting. Collections of books can be improved and increased over the years rather than copied and replicated. [Adapted from Clifford Stoll, *Silicon Snake Oil* (New York: Doubleday, 1995).]

4. A survey of American patterns in call-waiting use shows that the majority of call-waiting users are clustered in inner cities and suburbs. It stands to reason that the more people in a household, the more need there is for call-waiting. Thus inner-city households, which often contain members of three generations, and suburban households, which contain parents and children, will have the greatest desire for call-waiting.

5. Alcohol is a major problem in society. We should work to prohibit sales of alcohol altogether because of its association with violence and crime. I asked a police officer what the world would be like if there were no alcohol. He immediately answered that he would be out of a job. This just goes to show you how great a factor alcohol is in social problems.

6. While reduced supply and better law enforcement may help, the war on drugs cannot be won without much greater economic opportunity for disadvantaged Americans. This is because the main reason people turn to drugs is that they have no hope for a reasonable life in the American mainstream. And in today's society, a reasonable life requires a good job for all Americans.

7. Rhododendrons must be protected from direct sun in the winter and receive some sunlight in the summer for growth and bud formation. Ideal locations include the northeast side of buildings and fences and beneath large evergreen trees. In more exposed areas, they can be shaded with burlap or wooden slats to protect them from the sun.

8. When you drink alcohol, you feel dizzy. This is partly because alcohol dilutes the fluid in your inner ear. This permits the motion sensors there to move more freely. They send signals to the brain that the head is moving. But since the other senses tell the brain that the body isn't moving, your brain decides that the room must be moving instead.

9. Most anarchist or neo-Nazi gang members come from the lower-middle or lower classes. Their politics, though not entirely without significance, are confused and may be incidental. The main thing they seek is a sense of togetherness, conformity—even among the anarchists—and a kind of order.

10. The odds against two snowflakes being identical are so great as to approach certainty. A snowflake consists of about 10^{18} water molecules. As the snowflake gets larger, molecules attach themselves to it essentially at random. The number of ways that 10^{18} molecules can be arranged into six-sided crystals is astronomical—a great deal larger than the number of snowflakes that have ever fallen on earth.

11. Agricultural technology companies are genetically altering plants to attempt to make them resistant to pests. Corn and potatoes have been implanted with genes from *Bacillus thuringiensis* (Bt) bacteria. This bacterium is toxic to many pests, so that the plants have their own built-in insecticide. However, no one knows whether insects will become immune to Bt in time.

12. Mixing love and pain is not natural. It does not come from within the self. Women are taught masochism through the culture; masochism's causes are external. Masochism is the end result of long training, which makes the denial of autonomy for women seem natural, and makes masochism appear to come from a source within the self.

13. The life expectancy of a crop duster is five years. They fly low, so they sometimes hit buildings and power lines. They have no space to fly out of trouble or to recover from a stall.

14. It doesn't seem plausible that a society in which hard-core pornography is available is better for that reason. But it has been very difficult to draw a line that distinguishes obscenity from material that is sexually explicit but has some aesthetic or other value.

15. Many cows are now injected with bovine growth hormone (BGH) to increase milk production. Since the use of BGH appears to cause health problems for the cows, they are given more antibiotics. This may lead to greater antibiotic resistance among humans who drink the milk from these cows.

EXERCISE 1.4 DISCUSSION AND WRITING ASSIGNMENT

I. Write both an argument and an explanation for the following propositions. You may prefer to use these as a guide to thinking up your own propositions for which you write an argument and an explanation.

1. Dogs make good companion animals.

2. Popular music offers a way for people to identify themselves as members of a certain social group.

3. Not many people are well suited to beekeeping.

4. Censorship limits freedom.

5. Cheating on exams is justified in some cases.

II. As you work through the material in this book, it will be useful for you to apply the skills you're learning to your own writing. Take an essay that you have written for another course. Distinguish your use of argument, explanation, and neither within the essay. You may prefer to trade essays with a friend and work through each other's.

2 Standardizing Arguments

WHEN WE **standardize** an argument, we identify its component propositions and consider how they are related to one another. It is not always easy to see the relations among propositions. Some arguments contain extra words or sentences (for example, "on the other hand" or "we'd certainly all agree that . . .") that don't directly contribute to the argument. Getting rid of these extra elements can help us see more clearly the structure of the argument.

STANDARDIZATION

In Chapter 1, we asked two questions to help us recognize arguments. Is an attempt being made to convince us of something? That's the conclusion. Are we given reasons to believe it? Those are the premises. In standardizing most arguments, it's easiest to identify the conclusion first. Often the conclusion appears in the first or the last sentence

Strategies and Conventions

Identifying premises and conclusions

CONCLUSION: What is the passage trying to convince you of? What does it want you to believe?

PREMISES: What reasons are given to believe the conclusion?

of a passage. This is not a way of deciding that something *is* a conclusion, but it does give you a place to start. You should also look for indicator words. Then ask yourself whether a particular proposition seems to be supported by other propositions in the passage.

We'll learn two methods of representing standardizations. Use the one that works best for you (or the one that your instructor prefers). Let's see how these methods work on example [1].

Strategies and Conventions

Conclusions

In your own writing, always keep your conclusion in mind, and make sure it's clear to your reader. It's not a bad idea to put the conclusion first. Then your reader knows immediately what you're trying to prove and can follow the rest of your argument more easily.

> [1] Single-sex high schools work better than coeducational high schools because adolescents do better when they aren't distracted by the presence of the opposite sex. Also, the developmental needs of adolescent boys and girls are divergent.

Example [1] is an argument. What does it try to convince us of? That single-sex high schools work better than coeducational high schools. This is the conclusion. The other propositions in the passage offer reasons to believe the conclusion.

In the first method of standardization, start by writing the conclusion at the bottom of the page.

> Single-sex high schools work better than coeducational high schools.

The other propositions in example [1] are premises supporting the conclusion; give each of those premises its own line above the conclusion:

> 1. Adolescents do better when they aren't distracted by the presence of the opposite sex.
> 2. The developmental needs of adolescent boys and girls are divergent.
> Single-sex high schools work better than coeducational high schools.

The other method is a diagram and moves in the opposite direction. Here too we start with the conclusion, but we write it at the top of the page. The premises are written under it with arrows connecting the premises to the conclusion they support.

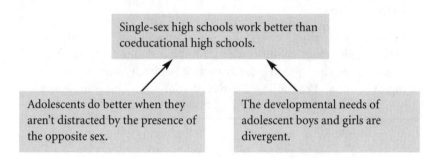

Subarguments

Arguments are not often as easy to standardize as example [1]. Sometimes you will find arguments within arguments. These **subarguments** are used to support one of the premises of the larger argument. The conclusion of a subargument functions as a premise in the larger argument.

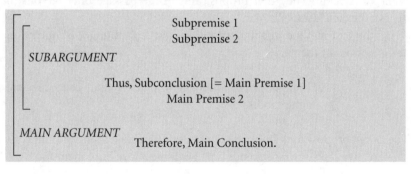

In the schema above, the subargument consists of subpremise 1 and sub-premise 2. Its subconclusion completes the subargument. If the subargument were removed from the larger argument, the subargument would still be an argument with premises and a conclusion of its own. The main argument consists of main premise 1, which is supported by the subargument, main premise 2, and the main conclusion, which the two main premises support. The same proposition that serves as the conclusion of the subargument also serves as a main premise in the main argument. If the subargument in support of main premise 1 were removed from the larger argument, the larger argument would also still be an argument.

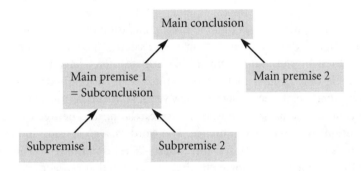

We want to make our arguments as strong as we can. If we support not only the conclusion, but some of the premises as well, we ensure a stronger argument. We can block anticipated objections to a premise by providing evidence for believing that premise. We cannot support every premise—then we'd never finish an argument. But some premises, the ones that we think might be questioned, can be provided with their own supporting premises.

Let's standardize a passage that contains a subargument.

> [2] There is a reason why famous athletes deserve their million-dollar salaries. Their careers are over in just a few short years, so they don't have very long to make their money.

When initially reading through a passage, watch for indicator words—these not only signal the possible presence of an argument, as we learned in Chapter 1, but can help in standardizing that argument. Because premise indicators are different from conclusion indicators, indicator words suggest the role a proposition plays in a passage. In example [2], we recognize the conclusion in the first sentence, but we also see the conclusion indicator *so* in the middle of the second sentence. That's one hint that we have a subargument here—an argument can have only one main conclusion. One of these propositions, then, must be the conclusion of a subargument.

> 1.1 Their careers are over in a few years.
> 1. They don't have very long to make their money.
> Therefore, famous athletes deserve their million-dollar salaries.

This standardization shows that the main conclusion of the passage is that famous athletes deserve their million-dollar salaries. The main conclusion is supported by the main premise that athletes don't have very long to make their money. And that main premise is in turn supported by the assertion that their careers only last a few years. Having determined the main conclusion of the passage, look next at the relationship between the two propositions in the second sentence. The word *so*, a conclusion indicator, indicates that the proposition it introduces, "They don't have very long to make their money," is supported by the proposition that precedes it.

In the numbered method of standardizing, the premises that support the main conclusion are given numbers, as before. The subpremises that support main premise 1 are numbered 1.1, 1.2, 1.3, and so on. (Subpremises supporting a main premise 2 are numbered 2.1, 2.2, etc.) Indenting the subpremise makes it clearer that this is part of a subargument.

In the pictorial method, the arrows point from the supporting proposition to the supported one.

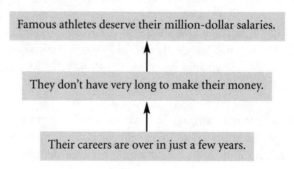

Here's another example.

> [3] The proposed California law requiring the phasing-in of zero-emission vehicles would have had the effect, not of reducing pollution, but of moving it. The power for cars has to come from somewhere, so there would be increased emission from electric plants in midwestern America, the source of California's electrical power.

The proposed California law would have moved, not reduced, pollution.

> The proposed California law would have moved, not reduced, pollution.

↑

> There would be increased emission from electric plants in midwestern America, the source of California's electrical power.

↑

> The power for cars has to come from somewhere.

Remember that the arrows in the pictorial standardization represent a logical relationship between the propositions. You can test your standardization by reading upwards and using the word *therefore* at each arrow. This will reveal whether you've put the propositions in the right order. When learning how to standardize, some people recognize

REVIEW BOX 2.1

Subarguments

If subargument *A* is embedded in argument *B*, the conclusion of subargument *A* is a premise in argument *B*.

that *so* indicates a logical relationship, but get the relationship backwards. It is always a good idea to ask yourself whether your standardization makes sense—whether the proposition that's lower in the diagram really does provide evidence for the one above it.

Here is a much more difficult example.

> [4] If you care about the environment you will wear real fur. The manufacturing process for artificial fur creates chemical reactions that may be dangerous. Artificial fur is not biodegradable or recyclable: it will exist forever, polluting the earth. It cannot be disposed of by burning, because when burned it produces dioxins and other harmful gases. Artificial fur is more harmful to the environment than real fur.

Example [4] is an attempt to convince us that if we care about the environment we will wear real fur. What reason is given to make us believe that? That artificial fur is more harmful to the environment than real fur. Thus the main argument is

> 1. Artificial fur is more harmful than real fur.
> Therefore, wear real fur.

Example [4] also gives reasons to believe the main premise. Why should we believe that artificial fur is more harmful than real fur? Because, first, the manufacturing process itself is dangerous, and, second, because there is no way to get rid of artificial fur once it has been manufactured. Let's ignore the main argument for the moment and represent the subargument. (Remember, the conclusion of a subargument is a premise of the larger argument.)

> 1. The manufacturing process for artificial fur creates dangerous chemical reactions.
> 2. It [artificial fur] will exist forever, polluting the earth.
> Thus, artificial fur is more harmful than real fur.

There is more to the argument. What is the role of the propositions about biodegrading, recycling, and the production of dioxins by burning? These support the proposition that artificial fur will exist forever. So "It will exist forever" is a subconclusion, too, with its own supporting subargument. Thus

> 1. It is not biodegradable or recyclable.
> 2. It cannot be burned.
> It will exist forever.

Finally, we see that premise 2 of the subargument above is supported by the proposition that when artificial fur is burned, it gives off dioxins and other harmful gases. That is reason to believe that it cannot be burned. Notice the word *because* that links these two propositions—it may indicate a premise. So we have one further subargument to represent:

> 1. When burned it gives off dioxins and other harmful gases.
> It cannot be burned.

Now all that remains is to arrange these subarguments within the main argument.

> 1.1. The manufacturing process of artificial fur creates dangerous chemical reactions.
> 1.2.1. It is not biodegradable or recyclable.
> 1.2.2.1. When burned it gives off dioxins and other harmful gases.
> 1.2.2. It cannot be burned.
> 1.2. It will exist forever, polluting the earth.
> 1. Artificial fur is more harmful than real fur.
> Therefore, wear real fur.

There is one main premise, number 1. Main premise 1 has two subpremises that support it directly, numbered 1.1 and 1.2. There is a subargument supporting 1.2, the premises of which are numbered 1.2.1 and 1.2.2. The first two digits tell us that these propositions support subconclusion 1.2. In general, everything except the last digit indicates the conclusion that is supported by the proposition. Subpremise 1.2.2, "It cannot be burned," is supported by the statement that when burned artificial fur gives off harmful gases; hence, subpremise 1.2.2 is also a subconclusion, and the subpremise that supports it is numbered 1.2.2.1.

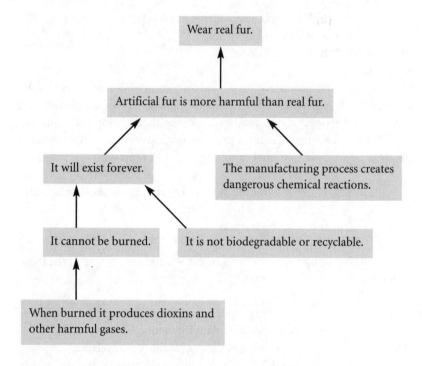

As you can see, more than one layer of subargument is possible. Subarguments are not just found within main arguments. There can be subarguments within subarguments. Any premise—main premise or subpremise—can be supported by its own subargument. Just keep in mind that any time an argument gives a reason to believe one of its premises, a subargument is present.

(By the way, you may be thinking that example [4] is not a very good argument. If so, you're right. We'll have the opportunity to criticize this argument in the exercises for Chapter 6.)

Linked and Convergent Premises

Consider the difference between the following two arguments:

[5] We have to either reduce spending or raise taxes. We can't raise taxes, so we'll have to reduce spending.

[6] We can't raise taxes because people feel they are over-taxed already. The economy will also suffer if people have less disposable income.

How would we standardize these arguments?

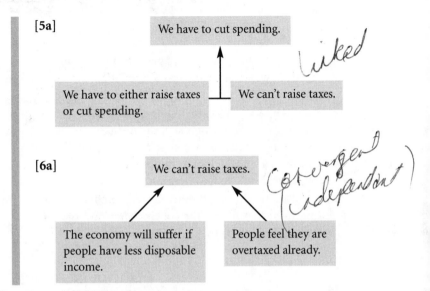

[5a]

We have to cut spending.

linked

We have to either raise taxes or cut spending.

We can't raise taxes.

[6a]

We can't raise taxes.

(convergent (independent))

The economy will suffer if people have less disposable income.

People feel they are overtaxed already.

Both examples [5] and [6] have two main premises that directly support the main conclusion. The ways they do so are different, however. In example [5], neither premise works by itself to support the conclusion. If we said "We either have to raise taxes or cut spending," we could not conclude, from that alone, that we have to cut spending—why would we choose this option instead of raising taxes? Nor could we use "We can't raise taxes" by itself as a premise to support "We have to cut

REVIEW BOX   2.2

Linked and convergent premises

- If two premises are linked, they are interdependent, and work together to support the conclusion.

- If two premises are convergent, they work independently of one another to support the conclusion.

spending"—why would we have to cut spending just because we can't raise taxes? Only the two premises together lead to the conclusion that we have to cut spending. Together the premises say, essentially, that there are only two choices and that one of them wouldn't work; thus we're thrown back on the second choice. The two premises are **linked**—they work together to support the conclusion; one without the other is insufficient.

Compare this with example [6], which gives two reasons to believe the conclusion "We can't raise taxes." For one thing, people feel overtaxed already. For another, less disposable income for individuals (the result of higher taxes) would hurt the economy. Either one of these reasons could be used by itself to support the conclusion. They **converge** to support the conclusion; they don't interact in the way that linked premises do.

Linked premises are *interdependent*: taking away one premise would destroy the argument. Convergent premises are *independent*: each works by itself, though subtracting a premise would, of course, weaken the argument by providing one fewer reason to believe the conclusion. In pictorial standardizations, linked premises are joined by a line, with an arrow pointing from that line to the conclusion. Convergent premises each have an arrow that points to the conclusion.

LEMUR Exercises 2.1 and 2.2

EXERCISE 2.1

Standardize each of the following arguments. In cases where more than one premise directly supports a main conclusion or subconclusion, indicate whether the premises are linked or convergent.

Example

Without proper medical evidence we may never know whether John Kennedy was killed by a single gunman. But the evidence is far from satisfactory. There is controversy about the location and size of the wounds in Kennedy's head. Some experts believe that the X-rays of the head wounds have been faked; some also charge that the X-rays are inconsistent with one another. We may never know whether John Kennedy was killed by a single gunman.

STANDARDIZATION:

> 1. Without proper medical evidence we may never know whether John Kennedy was killed by a single gunman.
>   2.1. There is controversy about the location and size of the wounds in Kennedy's head.
>   2.2. Some experts believe that X-rays of the head wounds have been faked.
>   2.3. Some experts charge that the X-rays are inconsistent with one another.
> 2. The evidence is far from satisfactory.
> Therefore, we may never know whether John Kennedy was killed by a single gunman.

conditions under which [handwritten annotation]

We may never know whether John Kennedy was killed by a single gunman.

Why? we will only know if... [handwritten annotation]

Because [if somehow] linked B we don't have proper evidence (conditions have been met) not [handwritten annotation]

Without proper medical evidence, we may never know whether John Kennedy was killed by a single gunman.

The evidence is far from satisfactory.

Convergent [handwritten annotation]

Some experts believe that the X-rays are inconsistent with one another.

Some experts believe that the X-rays of the head wounds have been faked.

There is controversy about the location and size of the wounds in Kennedy's head.

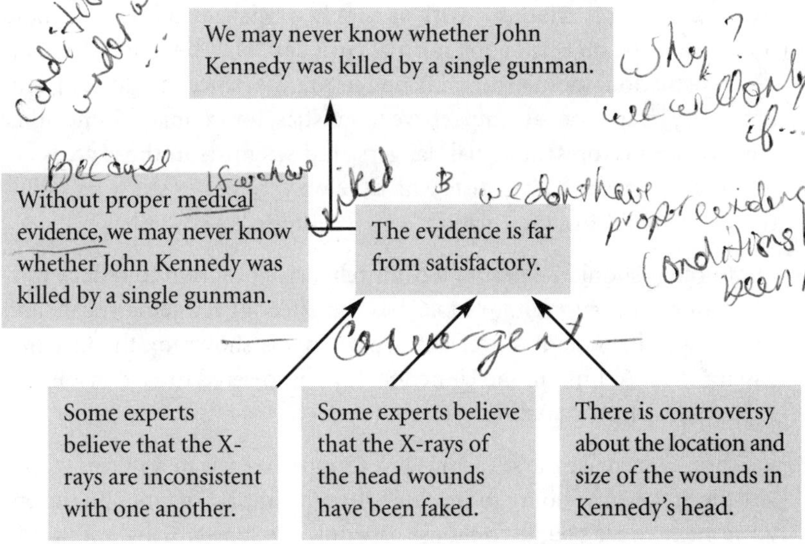

The two premises supporting the main conclusion (1 and 2 in the numbered standardization) are linked: we need to know both that the evidence is unsatisfactory *and* that the evidence may be essential to conclude that we may never know whether Kennedy was killed by one gunman. The three subpremises (numbered 2.1, 2.2, and 2.3) supporting the subconclusion that the evidence is far from satisfactory are convergent: any one of them would, by itself, support the subconclusion.

1. Technology changes so rapidly that vocational training is obsolete. The way to prepare for a career is to develop the ability to adapt and learn, and these abilities are best gained through a wide-ranging humanistic and scientific education.

2. Some current university policies, for example the tendency towards large classes, can be destructive to learning. This is because large classes reduce contact between faculty members and students. This makes students feel resentful. As a result, they may not learn as much as they would in a smaller class.

3. Neither curiosity nor a desire to benefit humanity can be the principle motive of scientists. Curiosity will not hold up as an explanation of motive, because most scientists work on highly specialized things that could not possibly be objects of any normal curiosity. The "benefit of humanity" explanation doesn't work any better. Many sciences couldn't benefit humanity in any way—comparative linguistics, for example. Some other areas of science present actual dangers, and scientists in those areas are just as enthusiastic as scientists who develop vaccines or study air pollution. [Adapted from the Unabomber's Manifesto, §§87–88.]

4. Photo radar should be part of a comprehensive program to reduce traffic fatalities, because photo radar has the effect of reducing speed, and slower speed results in fewer accidents. This is shown by the fact that when the speed limit in the United States was lowered to save gasoline, a reduction in traffic fatalities was a side effect.

5. We should decrease the speed limit to 15 mph for private vehicles within city limits, because doing so would reduce the impact of cities on the environment. Since people could use cars only for shorter trips, and would be forced to use higher-speed public transit for longer trips, the decrease in the speed limit would decrease the number of cars on the road. The result would be lower emissions. Another reason for reducing the speed limit is that it would make the streets safer for children and pedestrians.

█ MISSING PREMISES AND
MISSING CONCLUSIONS

Sometimes propositions required by the argument are not explicitly stated, and must be added when standardizing. An argument can have a missing premise or a missing conclusion.

Both premises and conclusions can take the form of questions. The author asks a *rhetorical* question—a question that anticipates a particular answer.

> [7] Don't animals feel pain and pleasure? Should we torture them needlessly?

Example [7] consists of two questions, but it is an argument. We're clearly expected to answer that of course animals feel pain and pleasure, so of course we shouldn't torture them needlessly. The argument is standardized in example [7a]:

> [7a] Animals feel pain and pleasure. Therefore, we shouldn't torture them needlessly.

Sometimes an argument can have a missing conclusion. (This does not mean that we should add a conclusion every time we encounter a passage that would thereby become an argument.) Missing conclusions are common in advertisements. An advertisement that first shows good-looking people consuming a product, and then unappealing people consuming the competitor's product, is confident that we'll draw the obvious conclusion.

Remember that all advertisements are arguments, and all have the same conclusion: "Buy this thing." Advertisements give you reasons to buy a product—frequently bad reasons. Don't be misled by the fact that many advertisements consist of a single picture. When you see a picture of a handsome cowboy riding a horse across the prairie and consuming a product, the argument expressed by the picture is something like this: This cowboy looks good and enjoys this product. You'd like to look good and enjoy yourself. Therefore, buy this product.

Find an advertisement that consists mostly of a picture or pictures, either from television or a magazine. What premises does the picture suggest? (You know what the main conclusion is: "Buy this product.") Save your advertisement and your standardization—Chapter 7 will give you more than enough ammunition to evaluate most advertising arguments.

Assumptions

Sometimes an argument does not state a premise explicitly, taking it for granted instead. An unstated premise is an **assumption** made by the argument. In many cases, the unstated premise or assumption, though strictly required for the logic of the argument, is obvious, and we do not need to make it explicit. In formal logic, all premises must be explicit, but for our method of analyzing arguments some implicit premises are acceptable.

A villain in an old movie might say this:

> [8] You'd better give me the information, or I'm going to suck all the oxygen out of this room, and then you will die.

Clearly, this argument assumes that you will die without oxygen. Adding "Humans breathe oxygen" to this argument isn't necessary—everyone accepts that already and thus everyone would recognize the strength of this argument in favor of the conclusion "You'd better give me the information."

Sometimes, though, a flaw in the argument lies in a missing premise. That's when it is important to identify that premise. Otherwise we might accept an argument that really isn't very strong, as in example [9].

> [9] Beatrice is a student at McMaster University. Therefore, Beatrice is a careless, irresponsible bum.

We can only regard the given premise as evidence for the conclusion if we assume a relationship between where Beatrice goes to school and her personality. In fact, the missing premise is:

> [9a] Someone who goes to McMaster University is likely to be a careless, irresponsible bum.

This premise is dubious (especially to those attending McMaster). Notice that we state the missing premise as weakly as possible: we do not say *all* McMaster students are careless, irresponsible bums, we say it's *likely*. This is another application of the principle of charity. The stronger a statement is, the easier it is to refute. It is unfair to attribute to an argument a stronger premise than it needs, because in doing so we make the argument easier to refute. That may sound like a plus, but unless we refute the best argument that an author can claim to be making, what we say is *irrelevant*, as we'll see in Chapter 7. Example [9a] is strong enough to draw a connection between Beatrice's school and her personality, and thereby make the conclusion likely to follow, but it is not so strong that we could refute it by one single counterexample.

If a concept mentioned in a conclusion is not mentioned elsewhere in the argument, it is possibly because a premise is missing. If that concept plays an important role, it cannot have come from nowhere; to interpret premises as providing evidence for a conclusion, we must assume that they contain—either implicitly or explicitly—any idea that appears in the conclusion.

> [10] I oppose same-sex adoption, because I think that the welfare of children is more important than satisfying the parental cravings of gay and lesbian couples.

Example [10] also contains a significant missing premise. The conclusion is "Same-sex adoption is a bad thing." Why should we believe it's a bad thing? Because children's welfare is more important than satisfying the desire of gay couples to have children. What's needed is something to connect same-sex adoption with the welfare of children. Clearly, the assumption here is that children's welfare and same-sex adoption cannot go together—that same-sex adoption is a bad thing.

Making explicit the missing premise in example [10] shows that it is a bad argument. The hidden assumption is the same as the conclusion. Assuming that same-sex adoption is bad to prove it is bad is an instance of *begging the question*, a fallacy we'll study more closely in Chapter 6.

Perhaps you have views about same-sex adoption, and you may agree with the conclusion of this argument. It is crucial to realize that there can be bad arguments for propositions we believe true and good arguments for propositions we believe false. When we call an argument bad, we are not saying its conclusion is false; we are saying that the premises do not support it. One purpose of studying critical thinking is to learn to construct good arguments for your views, and, perhaps, to recognize that some of your views need more support. If you are convinced that your views are true, the best practice is to question them and listen carefully to arguments against them. That will help you learn to construct better arguments for your own views, and perhaps to convince others. The danger, of course, is that you may discover your views are wrong—but if you're committed to believing true propositions for the right reasons, you'll recover from such discoveries.

EXERCISE 2.3

Find the missing premise or assumption in each of the following passages. How significant is this assumption?

Example

This government won't be reelected. All they've done is provide tax breaks to business while cutting benefits to the poor.

Missing premise: People will not reelect a government that does not support the poor.

This is a significant missing premise, because it doesn't go without saying that the majority of those who will vote share the arguer's views on the role of government in ensuring social equality.

1. This was a bad course, because the professor wasted time teaching concepts that never appeared on the midterm.

2. Of course Karin got a publishing job when she finished her degree; her uncle is an editor.

3. The United States should not continue to explore space. I think it's appalling that the United States government spends so much on trips into space, when so many people in the United States itself, and elsewhere on Earth, are without food, water, and adequate housing. It will cost $50 billion to go to Mars. Just think what you could do for people if that money were spent here on Earth.

4. There is nothing more important than continuing to explore space. In 200 years no one will care about health-care reforms, but they'll still know what happened in July 1969. [*Note*: in July 1969 people first walked on the moon.]

5. Raising tuition fees means that the university will draw more students from the immediate area and fewer students from farther away, since students from the immediate area can continue to live with their parents while they're in school.

Counterarguments

Often arguments respond to other arguments. These **counterarguments** are common in editorials, political speeches, and some advertisements. Counterarguments do not always state their conclusion explicitly.

> [11] Some people say that women should be prevented from joining the army in a combat role. Women are physically weaker, and so are unfit for combat, which requires physical endurance, ability to withstand strain, and stamina.
>
> But research has shown that women are in many ways stronger than men. Their life expectancy is greater than that of men. Scientists have shown that women respond better to stress. They have a higher threshold of pain. In the past, women have been athletes, racing drivers, pilots,

explorers, and have been active in revolutions—not just as nurses, but as fighters.

In any case, in the kind of war that is fought today, physical strength is not the main requirement.

Example [11] argues against people who say that women should be prevented from joining the army in a combat role. We could state the main conclusion fairly as any of the following: "These people are wrong," "This argument is a bad one," or "Women should *not* be prevented from joining the army in a combat role on the grounds that they are physically weaker." The conclusion is not explicitly stated. Instead, we are given a report of the argument that example [11] opposes—women should not be in combat, because they lack the required physical qualities. The counterargument goes on to address questions of strength, stamina, and what is required in modern war. None of the explicit points made against the reported argument is the conclusion of the counterargument. All these points are premises, offered in support of the conclusion that the cited view is a bad one.

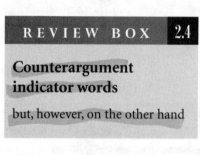

REVIEW BOX 2.4

Counterargument indicator words

but, however, on the other hand

When you are standardizing, don't be misled when the passage begins by stating the opposing view. Generally, the argument that we want to evaluate is the counterargument: does it prove that the opposing view is wrong? Review Box 2.4 supplies a partial list of words that may signal the beginning of a counterargument, as *since* and *thus* signal the conclusion of an argument.

Here is another counterargument:

[12] Many people oppose capital punishment, because they fear that an innocent person may die. But I disagree. If it is used only in cases where proof is certain, then there is no chance that an innocent person will die.

Example [12] argues against people who oppose capital punishment on the grounds that an innocent person will die. If we were to make explicit the conclusion of this counterargument, would we choose something like "Capital punishment should be used"? No. That would run the risk of being unfair to the author of the counterargument. The author has only addressed the issue of an innocent person's death. It's entirely possible that the author would support another argument against capital punishment. Remember, we do not want to choose a conclusion that is too strong for the premises to support, if a weaker conclusion is supportable. The fairest conclusion for this argument would be something like this:

> [12a] People who argue against capital punishment on the grounds that an innocent person may die, have a bad argument.

Example [12] may seem to you like a bad argument. It relies on the provision that the death penalty be used only in cases where proof is certain, but that's a big *if*. The original argument would no doubt support its premise that an innocent person may die with the subpremise that the death penalty is sometimes used in questionable cases. A strong counterargument ought to address this point somehow. But no matter what we think of the quality of the argument presented, we must identify the conclusion before criticizing it.

How shall we standardize counterarguments? It's important to keep in mind that these are *counter*arguments. Thus they have to be evaluated *as responses* to the argument they oppose. For example, if a counterargument does not adequately address the original argument, that's a defect. The best bet, then, is to state the argument, or as much of it as you can reconstruct from the passage, before presenting the counterargument.

> [12b] **Argument:**
>   1.1. Women are physically weaker.
>   1. They are unfit for combat, which requires physical endurance, ability to withstand strain, and stamina.
> Therefore, women should be prevented from joining the army in a combat role.
>
> **Counterargument:**
>   1.1. Women's life expectancy is greater than men's.
>   1.2. Women respond better to stress.

> 1.3. Women have a higher threshold of pain.
>
> 1. Women are in many ways stronger than men. (AGAINST premise 1.1)
> 2. Women have, in the past, been athletes, racing drivers, etc.
> 3. In the kind of war that is fought today, physical strength is not the main requirement.
>
> Therefore, women should be permitted to join the army in a combat role.

ARGUMENT

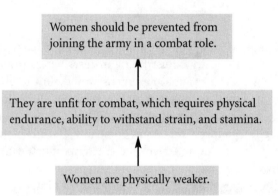

COUNTERARGUMENT

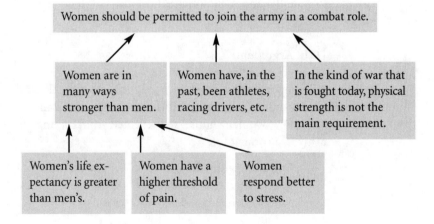

Notice that in example [12b] the conclusion of the counterargument opposes the original argument.

You should make a note of any premise in the counterargument that directly addresses a premise in the original argument. Then evaluate how important that premise is to the original argument. The more important the premise that is countered, the more effective the counterargument can be. In example [12b], we can see that subpremise 1.1 is the foundation of the original argument: the proposition that women are physically weaker is what leads the argument to conclude that women are unfit for combat. So that's an important premise to oppose in a counterargument.

> **LEMUR Exercise 2.3**

EXERCISE 2.4

For the following argument/counterargument passages, standardize the argument to the extent you can. (Some passages do not state the argument fully.) Standardize the counterargument. If any premise in the counterargument appears to address directly any premise in the argument, note this.

Example

People have used the notion of "crack babies," supposedly handicapped for life and fated to be society's burden, to support whatever political platform they favor—liberals, to argue for government-sponsored rehabilitation programs; conservatives, to argue for harsher drug laws. In fact, the crack baby scare was the result of the media's using one small study to create panic, and there is no scientific evidence that babies born to cocaine-addicted mothers are bound to do worse than anyone else.

ARGUMENT:

1. Crack babies will be society's burden.
Therefore, there should be more government programs or there should be harsher drug laws.

COUNTERARGUMENT:

> 1. The media used one small study to create panic.
> 2. There is no scientific evidence that babies born to cocaine-addicted mothers are bound to do worse than anyone else.
> Therefore, the argument based on crack babies is a bad one.

The counterargument addresses the main premise of the argument. If there is no basis for believing that crack babies are bound to do worse than other babies, then no conclusion can be drawn from the circumstances of their birth.

1. People say that if a child watches too much violent TV he/she will grow up to be a violent person. But this can't be true: look at the violence taking place in countries where there is no TV at all.

2. In 1996, Canadian Fisheries Minister Brian Tobin proposed a higher quota on seal hunting as part of an attempt to replenish the depleted cod stock of the Atlantic. Since seals eat cod, said Tobin, reducing the seal population will mean fewer cod are eaten by seals. But although seals do eat cod, which accounts for 3 percent of their diet, seals also eat the cod's other predators. It is possible, then, that reducing the seal population will hinder rather than help the cod's return.

3. *Argument*: CDs retail for far too much. They only cost about $2.50 per unit to manufacture, and they sell for far more than that.
   Counterargument: There is more to the cost of a CD than the materials. The one-time costs of studio recording are huge. Besides, nine out of ten CDs lose money, so they all have to be carried by that tenth. What would you rather have: the choice of ten CDs at a slightly higher price or the choice of one hugely popular CD?

4. Some people believe that synchronous dynamic RAM (SDRAM) will improve the speed of computers, since the memory is always at the same point in the clock cycle. But actual benchmarks of computers running SDRAM show no real improvement over standard EDO RAM. In fact the biggest difference is determined by other questions of configuration of the computer.

5. Government policies should be designed to favor married, child-rearing, heterosexual couples. Some critics argue that the government should not involve itself in sensitive moral issues. But the government regularly takes moral stands on a range of issues—for example, the rights of women and race relations. A position on the need for children to have two committed parents, a mother and a father, would be no different.

Counterconsiderations

Sometimes arguments include **counterconsiderations**. These are propositions that count against the conclusion (later, we'll call these *negatively relevant propositions*). The author of an argument includes them to show that he or she is aware of opposing viewpoints. Sometimes (as in example [13] below) a counterconsideration is accompanied by a brief argument against the opposing view, in which case that part of the argument is treated as any other counterargument. Sometimes (as in example [14]), the counterconsideration is mentioned but not argued against because the force of the argument is thought to outweigh the counterconsideration. (Some words signaling a possible counterconsideration are listed in Review Box 2.5.)

> REVIEW BOX   **2.5**
>
> **Counterconsideration indicator words**
>
> although, it is true that, on the other hand, despite

> **[13]** The government should not cut funding to universities. Although this would mean that government spending would not be decreased as much as possible, the government's responsibility to its citizens is not merely economic: it should also ensure the opportunity for a peaceful and productive life. Besides, the economy will benefit, in the long run, by a more educated workforce, so cutting spending in the university is a shortsighted and short-term solution.

The main conclusion of example [13] is given in the first sentence: the government should not cut funding to universities. The next sentence states a counterconsideration; notice the word *although*. The counterconsideration anticipates the argument that the government *should* cut university funding on the grounds that this would decrease government spending. Example [13] then gives two reasons for rejecting the counterconsideration: that the government is responsible for ensuring quality of life and that making cuts in university funding is not a good long-term strategy to reduce spending.

Example [14] also features a counterconsideration.

> **[14]** If you can possibly manage it, you should buy a house while you are still an undergraduate. It's true that coming up with a down payment is difficult and that a house is a great responsibility. Nevertheless, you can rent to several roommates, whose contribution will help pay off some of the mortgage. Then, once you graduate, you can sell the house and have a big down payment for your next house.

In example [14], the counterconsideration is introduced by *it's true that.* Notice that example [14] does not directly argue against its counterconsideration in the way that example [13] does. Instead, example [14] admits the counterconsideration, but makes several points intended to outweigh it. In this kind of argument, an author attempts to show that there are more reasons to be for something than there are to be against it.

How should we treat counterconsiderations when standardizing? Remember, the whole point of standardizing is to see an argument's structure clearly. Thus, when we see that a passage offers an argument against the counterconsideration, the relationship between the counterconsideration and the premises that directly address it should be made as clear as possible. For example,

> **[13a]** COUNTERCONSIDERATION:
>   Government spending would not be decreased as much as possible.
> 1. The government's responsibility is not merely economic.
>   2.1. The economy will be best served by an educated workforce.
> 2. Cutting spending on education is a short-sighted and short-term solution.
> Therefore, the government should not cut funding to universities.

If, on the other hand, there is no direct argument against the counterconsideration, it is sufficient to list it at the bottom of your standardization. That way, you'll have the "against" side in mind as you evaluate the argument.

Either way, though, it's important to recognize the counterconsideration right away. Otherwise, you may try to place it in the standardization as a supporting premise.

▌ SUMMARY

Though standardization may seem difficult at first, it's a valuable skill to develop. It will help you write better arguments, and it will help you understand other people's arguments. For example, if you know the role of each premise in an argument you want to counter, you will not spend a lot of time arguing against the unimportant ones. Paying attention to indicator words is one way to sort out the roles of propositions in an argument.

LEMUR Exercise 2.4

EXERCISE 2.5

Standardize the following.

1. It's questionable whether photo radar has any effect on reducing traffic fatalities. But the really disturbing part is the loss of freedom that results from it. Freedom is essential for a democracy, but now we can't drive anywhere without the fear of being watched by the government and its secret cameras.

2. Freud and others have held the view that humans are naturally aggressive, but that sports can displace this aggression and give it a less harmful outlet than war. However, one anthropological study showed that aggressive sports didn't replace war. Rather, if a culture had aggressive sports, it also had war. War and aggressive sports went together, so that a culture had either both or neither.

3. Biodiversity is maintained not by protection, but by interference. If the interference does not occur naturally, then it must be manmade. Since the

decrease of large predators means that population control of many species cannot occur naturally, hunting will contribute to the balance of nature.

4. Sex is a means of reproduction for so many species because it has advantages for survival. The DNA of organisms that reproduce by nonsexual means never changes. Thus parasites can rapidly learn the weaknesses of their host organism. But in species that reproduce sexually, DNA varies with each generation, making things more difficult for the parasites.

5. Bruno Frey argues ["Fighting Political Terrorism by Refusing Recognition," *Journal of Public Policy*, vol. 7, (January–March 1987): 179–88] that terrorists act rationally. One of the primary goals of political terrorists is to make the public aware of their cause. Thus authorities should refuse to attribute a particular terrorist act to any group. This would thwart the terrorists' desire to gain public attention. Thereby the terrorists would either reduce such activities or commit more dramatic and riskier acts, which would make them easier to catch.

6. Spontaneous human combustion is a phenomenon in which the human body is completely consumed by fire that starts within the body. Though there have been reports of spontaneous human combustion, it seems to be physiologically impossible. Since the human body is 70 percent water, it is not a thing that burns easily. Some have suggested that those who have suffered spontaneous human combustion had consumed a great deal of alcohol, and that it is the alcohol that burns. But alcohol is metabolized quickly and does not stay alcohol. There is really no explanation at all for how a fire can start internally.

7. Some people have argued that an effort to develop a vaccine for AIDS should not be the main target of AIDS funding. They say that development of a vaccine is simply not practical. For one thing, there are no animals on which preliminary versions of the vaccine could be tested. But since most people with AIDS or H.I.V. believe that they have an irreversible, inevitably fatal disease, they are willing to test vaccinations or any other treatments. In fact many persons with AIDS do anything they can to try new drugs.

8. The Zapruder film of John Kennedy's assassination appears to show that a single gunman could not have had time to fire a second shot between the moment that Kennedy first appeared to be hit and the moment that

Texas governor John Connally, who was riding in the front seat, appeared to be hit. If there was a single gunman, and hence a single bullet that hit both men, we must accept the so-called "magic bullet" theory, according to which one bullet entered Kennedy's back, exited through his throat, then continued on into the front seat, where it caused multiple wounds in Connally. This "magic bullet" was allegedly later found, virtually intact, on Connally's stretcher at the hospital. But it is unlikely that a bullet causing multiple injuries to two people, including smashing bones in Connally, could have survived almost intact. The trajectory that the bullet would have had to take is also implausible. Many bullet fragments were removed from Connally—more than could have come from the magic bullet found on the stretcher. It seems, then, that the failure of the magic bullet theory refutes the lone gunman hypothesis.

9. Some people argue that emoticons—for example "smilies" like :-)— should not be used in e-mail and other Net messages. They say that the use of these symbols makes it unnecessary for people to make their points clear in words alone, and in general reduces flexibility within the language. But interchanges on the Net are more like spoken conversations than like written interchanges. They are more informal and also have the transitory nature of spoken conversation. In spoken language, intonation often conveys a lot of the message of the words. Since intonation is not possible over the Net, emoticons take its place.

10. Is it time to wonder whether increases in AIDS funding are justified? The fact is that resources are scarce. Both money and talent are limited, and funding AIDS takes away funding from other causes. What can account for all the money spent on AIDS? People's perception of AIDS as a world catastrophe. AIDS is only the fifteenth most common cause of death in America. But AIDS activists have convinced people that there will be millions of future deaths unless something is done now.

Although cancer is a far greater health threat, AIDS gets as much funding as cancer does. Heart disease kills even more people than cancer, but its funding is only two-thirds that of AIDS.

It is not just funding: researchers themselves are a scarce commodity, so that many AIDS researchers are most likely to have come from other research areas, primarily cancer.

Some people argue that AIDS research may lead to new discoveries that may be useful in other areas. But in fact, of the five drugs approved in the United States for AIDS treatment, two of them (AZT and alpha interferon) came from cancer research! [Adapted from Michael Fumento, *The Myth of Heterosexual AIDS* (New York: Basic Books, 1990).]

11. "And for those concerned about children growing up in poverty, we should know this: marriage is probably the best antipoverty program of all. Among families headed by married couples today, there is a poverty rate of 5.7 percent. But 33.4 percent of families headed by a single mother are in poverty today. . . .

    "Ultimately, however, marriage is a moral issue that requires cultural consensus, and the use of social sanctions. Bearing babies irresponsibly is, simply, wrong. Failing to support children one has fathered is wrong. We must be unequivocal about this.

    "It doesn't help matters when prime time has Murphy Brown—a character who supposedly epitomizes today's intelligent, highly paid, professional woman—mocking the importance of fathers, by bearing a child alone, and calling it just another 'lifestyle choice.'

    "I know it is not fashionable to talk about moral values, but we need to do it. Even though our cultural leaders in Hollywood, network TV, the national newspapers routinely jeer at them, I think that most of us in this room know that some things are good, and other things are wrong. Now it's time to make the discussion public." [Dan Quayle, "Restoring Basic Values," *Vital Speeches of the Day*, vol. 58, no. 17 (15 June 1992): 517–20.]

Strategies and Conventions

Standardization skills in essay-writing

- We've seen that indicator words help clarify an argument. When you construct arguments, use indicator words to guide your reader through your idea. Make sure you choose the right indicator words.

- We've seen counterarguments—you employ them, for example, when you write an essay opposing another view. Be sure to give an accurate and adequate statement of the view you're opposing.

- We've seen that counterconsiderations are used to anticipate objections. If you include counterconsiderations in your own arguments, you will ultimately strengthen your case.

**EXERCISE 2.6 DISCUSSION AND WRITING
ASSIGNMENT**

1. Find at least one essay you've written for another course and had graded
   and returned. Standardize your essay. Remember to be on the lookout
   for argument/counterargument passages and counterconsiderations.
   Underline or highlight indicator words. You may prefer to work with a
   friend and either trade essays or collaborate in standardizing each.

2. Now here's the painful part: ask yourself whether your essay could have
   been better if you'd organized it differently. If you couldn't find your
   own premises easily, that's a real flaw. Would it have helped if you'd used
   thus and *since* more often or more accurately? Were your counterconsiderations adequately signaled with *although* or *despite*? If not, do you
   think your reader may have wondered what function these propositions
   served?

3. Reorganize your essay to make use of what you've learned in this chapter.

Here's a good way to set up an essay. Start by stating your main conclusion. State the main premises that support the main conclusion. In the following paragraphs, deal with these main premises. Many of them will—or
at least should—have arguments supporting them. State that main premise at the beginning of the paragraph. Then go on to state the subpremises
that support it. If a subpremise has a subargument supporting it, give that
subargument its own paragraph.

Keeping your subpremises, premises, and conclusions in mind and
using them to structure your essay will work whether you're writing an
essay question on a midterm or writing a whole book. The only difference
is the length.

Remember, if your reader thinks your essay is unclear, your essay *is*
unclear.

3 Categorical Logic

CONSIDER THIS ARGUMENT:

> All human beings are mortal.
> Students are human beings.
> Therefore students are mortal.

This argument is of a form known as a **categorical syllogism**, or categorical argument. It is an inference from two categorical premises. Learning how to evaluate categorical syllogisms can help us develop habits of clarity and a grasp of logical relationships. In this chapter, we'll begin with the logic of the statements from which these arguments are constructed—sometimes called **categorical statements**—and then we'll go on to consider the syllogisms themselves. This is a terminology-intensive chapter. I've tried to provide you with numerous charts and review boxes to help you keep the terms straight.

■ CATEGORICAL STATEMENTS

There are four types of categorical statements. Here are examples of each:

 affirmative

[1] All dogs are mammals.
[2] Some plants are carnivores.
[3] No women are fathers.
[4] Some men are not uncles.

affirm — ∨

negative

54

You should notice that these statements have a common form or structure. All contain a **subject term**, which tells us which things the statement is about; a **predicate term**, which characterizes the members of the subject term; a **scope word**, which tells us how many members of the subject term we're talking about (all of them or just some of them); and a **copula**—*is* or *are*—which joins subject to predicate. In example [1], the subject is *dogs* and the predicate is *mammals*. In example [2], the subject is *plants* and the predicate is *carnivores*. In example [3], the subject is *women* and the predicate is *fathers*. In example [4], the subject is *men* and the predicate is *uncles*.

Categorical statements make assertions about interrelations between categories or classes. Examples [1] and [2] are affirmative statements—positive statements that say that all or some of the members of the subject class belong to the predicate class. Example [1] says that everything that belongs to the class *dog* also belongs to the class *mammal*. You will not find anything that is a dog and is not a mammal. Example [2] says that some of the things that belong to the class *plants* also belong to the class *carnivores*, leaving open the possibility that there are some plants that are not carnivores.

Example [1], which tells us that *all* dogs are mammals, is called a **universal affirmation**, because it makes a positive statement about *all* members of the subject class dogs. Example [2], which tells us that *some* plants are carnivores, is a **particular affirmation**; it is about some particular members of the subject class *plants*.

There is a standard short form for referring to types of categorical propositions. Universal affirmative statements like "All dogs are mammals" are called A statements. Particular affirmative statements like "Some plants are carnivores" are called I statements. These short forms are derived from the Latin word for "I affirm," affirmo. You can remember them by thinking of *affirmo*.

Examples [3] and [4] are negative statements. They tell us that all or some members of the subject class do not belong to the class named by the predicate. Negative statements, like affirmative ones, also are either universal or particular. Example [3] is a **universal negation**. It tells us that no women are fathers. That's the same as saying that all women are not fathers. Thus example [4] is universal, since it's about all women, and negative, since it tells us that all women do not belong to the class *fathers*. Example [4], which tells us that *some* men are not uncles, is a **particular**

negation. Like the particular affirmation, it characterizes some members of the subject class. It leaves open the possibility that some men *are* uncles.

The negative statements can also be referred to by short forms. Universal negative statements are *E* statements, and particular negative statements are *O* statements. These short forms come from the Latin word for "I deny," *nego*. Thus *E* and *O* can be remembered by thinking of n*ego*.

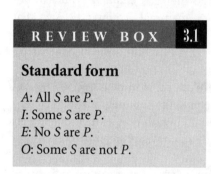

TABLE **1.**	CATEGORICAL STATEMENTS DEFINED	
	Universal	**Particular**
Affirmative	*A*: All *S* are *P*.	*I*: Some *S* are *P*.
Negative	*E*: No *S* are *P*.	*O*: Some *S* are not *P*.

REVIEW BOX **3.1**	## Standard Form
Standard form *A*: All *S* are *P*. *I*: Some *S* are *P*. *E*: No *S* are *P*. *O*: Some *S* are not *P*.	Not all categorical statements appear in the forms "All *S* are *P*," "Some *S* are *P*," and so on. Sometimes we need to "translate" a sentence to determine whether it is an *A*, *I*, *E*, or *O*. Let's look at some examples.

> ▌ **[5]** All of my cousins have curly hair.

It is important to notice that example [5] is not in standard form. In other words, it does not say "All *S* are *P*." Instead, it claims that all *S* have *P*. Therefore we must convert it into standard form. We immediately recognize that *my cousins* is the subject, and that all members of that class pertain. Changing *have* to *are* and *curly hair* to the class *things that have curly hair*, we arrive at

> ▌ **[5a]** All of my cousins are things that have curly hair.

Since example [5] contains the scope word *all*, it must be a universal statement. Since it says all my cousins *are* members of the class *things that have curly hair*, it must be an affirmative statement. Hence we can now see that this is an *A* sentence.

▌ [6] Some trees flower in spring.

Though clearly the subject of this sentence is *trees*, and *some* makes it a particular statement, it is not in standard form. The sentence tells us that some trees *flower*, and we need to change the sentence into one that contains a copula (*is* or *are*), so that it says explicitly that some trees are members of a certain predicate class.

▌ [6a] Some trees are things that flower in spring.

We know that this is a particular rather than a universal statement. It says that some trees do flower in spring, so it's an affirmative statement. Thus it is an *I* statement. Notice, once again, that this statement allows that some trees do not flower in spring.

▌ [7] Nobody with a lot of money goes to jail.

This statement is negative—its scope word is *nobody*, which we convert to *no person*. We add the copula *is* to replace *goes* and state the predicate class as *things that go to jail*. Example [7], in standard form, is

▌ [7a] No person with a lot of money is a thing that goes to jail.

Since *no person* makes a claim about all members of the subject class, this is an *E* statement. Of course, example [7a] sounds awkward—no one would say this in everyday speech.

▌ [8] Some of the students in this class have not been studying.

Here we see the *some . . . not* form that is characteristic of the *O* statement. Again, we need to introduce a copula to replace *have been studying* and clarify the subject and predicate terms.

[8a] Some students in this class are not things that have been studying.

Some of the students in this class may have been studying; the statement claims only that some have not.

What should we do with statements like the following?

[9] Hondas are good cars.

There is no explicit scope word in this statement; still, such a statement would likely be meant to make a claim about *all* Hondas. "Lilacs bloom in spring," "Snakes have no eyelids," and "Good jobs are hard to find" are likewise implicitly universal. Another possibly troublesome example is

[10] The dog was domesticated thousands of years ago.

The dog is clearly not used in example [10] in the same way it's used in

[11] The dog wants to go out.

Example [11] would be used when a particular dog is standing anxiously at the door, whereas example [10] refers to dogs in general. Thus example [10] is an *A* statement—a universal affirmation. Sensitivity to context will help you determine whether a phrase like *the dog* refers to a whole class or a particular member of it.

What about a sentence that *is* about a particular individual? For example,

[12] Mike is not an athlete.

Although example [12] is about one person, it makes no claim about him as an individual member of a larger class. Rather, it makes a claim about all members of the class *Mike*. Of course, there is only one member of this class. Nevertheless, none of the members of the class—consisting of that single member—is an athlete. Because example [12] is about all members of the class, it is universal; because it says that Mike is not an athlete, it is a negation. A universal negation is an *E* statement. Note that the class in question is not *people named Mike*. It's very likely that some people named

Mike are athletes. Rather, the class is *people who are this individual Mike*—and there's only one of those.

Distributed and Undistributed Terms

We need to learn two more technical terms before we complete our discussion of categorical statements. We have to distinguish between what are traditionally called **distributed** and **undistributed** terms. In other words, we have to be able to determine and state explicitly whether we're talking about *all* or *some* of the members of the class named by the subject term and of the class named by the predicate term.

Let's return to our original examples:

> [1] All dogs are mammals.
> [2] Some plants are carnivores.
> [3] No women are fathers.
> [4] Some men are not uncles.

Since determining whether the subject term is distributed or undistributed is easier than determining whether the predicate term is, we'll begin with the subject terms. In example [1]—an *A* sentence, as we know—we're talking about the whole class of dogs. That is, the *A* sentence makes a claim about every dog. If we know that this sentence is true, we know something about every member of the subject class. Thus we can say that the subject term in an *A* sentence is distributed.

In example [2], the subject term is *plants*. Example [2] gives us information about some plants, not all plants. When the subject term tells us about some, but not all, of the members of the class named by the term, we say that the subject term is undistributed.

The same line of reasoning applies to the subject terms in examples [3] and [4]. Does example [3] make a claim about all or

REVIEW BOX 3.2

Distributed and undistributed terms

- A distributed term makes a claim about all members of the class that it names.

- An undistributed term makes a claim about some but not all of the members of the class that it names.

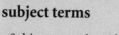

REVIEW BOX 3.3

Distribution of subject terms

- Subject terms in universal statements are distributed.

- Subject terms in particular statements are undistributed.

only some of the members of the class named by its subject term? We've seen that example [3] is a universal negation. Any universal statement tells us about all of the members of the subject class. Thus the subject term in example [3] is distributed. Example [4], as we know, is a particular negation. A particular statement makes a claim about some, but not all, of the members of the subject class. We know from example [4] that some members of the class *men* are not members of the class *uncles.* Thus the subject term in example [4] is undistributed.

Subject terms in universal statements, then, are distributed, and subject terms in particular statements are undistributed.

REVIEW BOX 3.4

Distribution of predicate terms

- Predicate terms in affirmative statements are undistributed.

- Predicate terms in negative statements are distributed.

Predicate terms also name classes. Thus we can also ask whether the sentence makes a claim about the whole class named by the predicate term. As we have seen, an *A* sentence does make a claim about the whole class named by the subject term. It does not, however, make a claim about the whole class named by the predicate term. Why not? The statement "All dogs are mammals" does not indicate whether there are other members of the class *mammals.* Of course, we know that there are many kinds of mammals other than dogs. But if we didn't know, we couldn't learn it from example [1]. All we learn from example [1] is that there is at least one type of mammal—the dog. Some mammals are dogs, but whether or not all mammals are dogs are is left open by the sentence. Thus in example [1], and in any universal affirmation, the predicate term is undistributed.

In a particular affirmative statement, we know that the subject term is undistributed, since it gives us information about some, but not all, members of the subject class. The predicate term similarly gives us information about some, but not all, members of the predicate class. When we know that some plants are carnivores, we do not gain information about whether there is anything other than these plants in the class *carnivores*. In fact we know that many animals are carnivores too. So, like universal affirmative statements, particular affirmations have undistributed predicate classes.

TABLE 2. DISTRIBUTED AND UNDISTRIBUTED TERMS DEFINED		
	Subject term	**Predicate term**
Distributed	A, E	E, O
Undistributed	I, O	A, I

Let's turn now to the negative statements. In an *E* sentence, the predicate term is distributed. Why is that? In order to know that no women are fathers, we must know every single member of the class *fathers*. Only by investigating that whole class can we know that there are no women to be found in it.

In an *O* sentence, the predicate term is also distributed. When we say that some men are not uncles, we say that there are some men—which ones we don't know—who are not in the class *uncles*. That makes a statement about the whole class of uncles, and thus has a distributed predicate class.

TABLE 3. CATEGORICAL STATEMENTS FULLY DEFINED		
	Universal	**Particular**
Affirmative	A: All S are P.	I: Some S are P.
	Subject term distributed	Subject term undistributed
	Predicate term distributed	Predicate term undistrubuted
Negative	E: No S are P.	O: Some S are not P.
	Subject term distributed	Subject term undistributed
	Predicate term distributed	Predicate term distributed

In summary, then, when we're considering whether the subject term is distributed or undistributed, we look at whether the sentence is universal or particular. All universal sentences (*A* and *E*) have distributed subject terms; all particular sentences (*I* and *O*) have undistributed subject terms. To determine whether the predicate term is distributed or undistributed, on the other hand, we look at whether the sentence is affirmative or negative. All negative sentences (*E* and *O*) have distributed predicate terms; all affirmative sentences (*A* and *I*) have undistributed predicate terms. The question of distributed and undistributed terms will be important when we turn to evaluating categorical arguments.

EXERCISE 3.1

For each of the following sentences,

- i.   if the sentence is not in its standard form, state its standard form;
- ii.   identify the subject and the predicate;
- iii.   determine whether the sentence is *A*, *I*, *E*, or *O*;
- iv.   state whether the subject term is distributed or undistributed; and
- v.   state whether the predicate term is distributed or undistributed.

Example

Some animals have fuzzy ears.

STANDARD FORM: Some animals are things that have fuzzy ears.
SUBJECT: *animals*
PREDICATE: *things with fuzzy ears*
This is an *I* sentence.
The subject is undistributed.
The predicate is undistributed.

1. All sports cars are fun to drive.

2. Some dogs are not well trained.

3. Domestic cats can purr.

4. None of my friends can play the saxophone.

5. No fish has fur.

6. Tara plays the violin.

7. Some of my best friends have PhDs.

8. All of my best friends have PhDs.

9. No cat is a reptile.

10. Some students live off campus.

11. The rhododendron is an evergreen.

12. Some cab drivers aren't familiar with this neighborhood.

13. No books should be burned.

14. Some computers are not reliable.

15. Some books are written by professors.

The Square of Opposition

The square of opposition (Diagram 1) shows three different logical relationships that can hold between certain categorical statements. The square of opposition is customarily arranged with the two universal statements in the upper corners, the particular statements in the lower corners, the affirmative statements on the left, and the negative statements on the right.

The logical relationships that we will consider in turn are those between 1) the propositions that are diagonal to one another; 2) the propositions across the top; and 3) the propositions across the bottom.

A: All S are P. ———— Contraries: ———— E: No S is P.
cannot both be true
can both be false

Contradictories:
cannot both be true
cannot both be false

I: Some S are P. ———— Subcontraries: ———— O: Some S are not P.
cannot both be false
can both be true

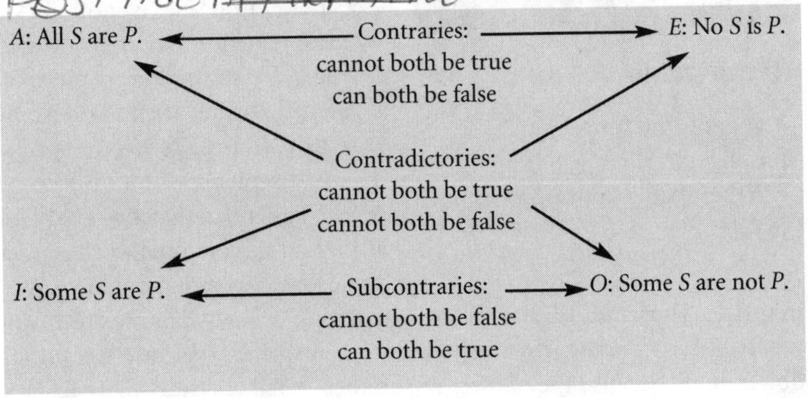

Diagram 1. THE SQUARE OF OPPOSITION

The propositions that are diagonal to one another in the square of opposition are **contradictory**—*A* and *O* contradict each other and *E* and *I* contradict each other.

Let's begin with an *A* sentence: "All of my cousins have curly hair." If you wanted to prove this proposition false, you could do so by finding a **counterexample,** that is, by showing that I have at least one cousin who does *not* have curly hair. If such a cousin exists, then it's false that *all* of my cousins have curly hair.

> ### REVIEW BOX   3.5
>
> #### Counterexamples
>
> Finding a counterexample to a proposition means finding some case that would prove the proposition false.

The *A* statement "All of my cousins have curly hair" is contradicted by the *O* statement "Some of my cousins do not have curly hair." These two statements must have opposite **truth-values.** As we have seen, they cannot both be true. But one of them *must* be true. Either all of my cousins have curly hair, or at least one of them doesn't. There are no possibilities between having curly hair and not having curly hair; similarly, there are no possibilities between all of them and not all of them. (What if I don't actually have any cousins? Then it would seem neither true nor false that all of my cousins have curly hair. This is a traditional philosophical problem for categorical logic. We shall avoid it in what follows by assuming that no subject class of which we speak is empty.)

> ### REVIEW BOX   3.6
>
> #### Truth-value
>
> You know the truth-value of a proposition when you know whether that proposition is true or false.

Similarly, the *I* sentence "Some trees flower in spring" is contradicted by the *E* sentence "No trees flower in spring." If it's false that some trees flower in spring, then it must be true that *no* trees flower in spring. The two sentences cannot both be true. Neither can they both be false. If there are trees in the world, either some flower in spring or none flower in spring. Thus, *I* and *E* statements, like *A* and *O*, have opposite truth-values. It doesn't matter why no trees flower in spring—because trees don't flower at all, because they flower in summer or fall instead—there just are no logical possibilities that fall between these two statements.

A and *E* statements, located at the top of the square of opposition, have a different logical relationship—they are **contraries**. Contrary statements cannot both be true. We can easily see that if "All of my cousins have curly hair" is true, "None of my cousins have curly hair" cannot possibly also be true. Contrary statements can, however, both be false. If some of my cousins have curly hair and some don't, then both the universal statements are false.

I and *O* statements, located at the bottom of the square of opposition, are **subcontraries**. Subcontrary statements cannot both be false. If the *I* statement "Some of my cousins have curly hair" is false, then none of them have curly hair. And if none of my cousins have curly hair, then the *O* statement "Some of my cousins do not have curly hair" is true. This may seem unnatural, but in logic, *all* is taken as implying *some*. Think of it this way: the class *all of my cousins* is made up of Lily, Rose, and Francine. We know that all of them have curly hair. Then certainly we also know that Rose and Francine have curly hair. Rose and Francine are *some of my cousins*. So knowing that all of my cousins have curly hair also enables us to know that some of them have curly hair. It is easy to see, on the other hand, that subcontraries can both be true: it's entirely possible that some cousins have curly hair, while at the same time some do not.

If we know the truth-value of a statement, we can always infer the truth-value of its contradictory and sometimes of its contrary or subcontrary. Let's take this *I* statement as an example:

[13] Some politicians are compassionate.

Let's say that this statement is true. (We certainly hope it is!) Given the truth-value of the original statement, we can determine the truth-values of certain other statements. The contradictory of this statement is the *E* statement

[13a] No politicians are compassionate.

If sentence [13] is true, sentence [13a] is false. Contradictories cannot both be true. Contradictory statements always have opposite truth-values.

Since example [13] is an *I* statement, it has a subcontrary, but not a contrary statement. Its subcontrary is the *O* statement

[13b] Some politicians are not compassionate.

Can we determine the truth-value of sentence [13b] based upon our stipulation that sentence [13] is true? No. Subcontraries can both be true, and cannot both be false. So sentence [13b] might be true. It is not impossible that some politicians are compassionate and some are not. Sentence [13b] might also be false. It is possible that some politicians are compassionate because all of them are—in that case, example [13b] is false. We can definitely say, then, that example [13a] is false, but we do not gain any knowledge at all about [13b].

Here's another example:

[**14**] No Japanese sports cars are fun to drive.

This is an *E* statement—a universal negation. Let's say that [14] has the truth-value false, since the Honda CRX, at least, is a counterexample. The contradictory of this statement is

[**14a**] Some Japanese sports cars are fun to drive.

Sentence [14a] must be true, since contradictory statements have opposing truth-values. Since [14] is a universal statement, it has a contrary and no subcontrary. The contrary statement is

[**14b**] All Japanese sports cars are fun to drive.

Sentence [14b] might be false. It's easy to imagine that of all Japanese sports cars, some are fun to drive and some are not. In that case, both [14] and [14b] are false; contrary statements can both be false, but cannot both be true. But since we assigned the truth-value false to sentence [14], it's still possible that sentence [14b] is true—perhaps [14] is false because *all* Japanese sports cars are fun to drive.

Since it's important to be comfortable with the square of opposition before we go on to inferences, we'll take one more example.

[**15**] Some trees have blue flowers.

Let's say [15] is *false*. Its contradictory is

[**15a**] No trees have blue flowers.

If [15] is false, its contradictory is true, because contradictories always have opposing truth-values. The subcontrary is

[15b] Some trees do not have blue flowers.

Subcontraries can both be true, but cannot both be false. Thus we can determine that [15b] is true. If it's false that some trees have blue flowers, it is true that some trees do not have blue flowers—either because their flowers are some other color, or because they do not have flowers at all.

Why do these relationships matter? If we keep them in mind, we can sometimes disprove certain claims. For example, to disprove any proposition, we can prove its contradictory. We often reason by citing counterexamples. Though it's a less common way of reasoning, we can also disprove a universal proposition by proving its contrary.

One final note about truth-values: in this section, we're *stipulating* truth-values. That means that we're arbitrarily deciding to consider some propositions true and others false. In Chapter 6, we'll consider how we actually determine the likely truth-values of some kinds of propositions. For now, though, we're concerned with relationships among propositions. So don't let your background knowledge interfere. We're not deciding that factual questions of truth are unimportant; it's just that we have to approach these issues one step at a time.

EXERCISE 3.2

For the following sentences,

i.   give the contradictory and the contrary or subcontrary, and
ii. assuming that all the odd-numbered statements are true and all the even-numbered statements are false, state the truth-value of the contradictory and the contrary or subcontrary.

Example

Some animals have fuzzy ears. [Assume this is true.]

CONTRADICTORY: No animals have fuzzy ears.

SUBCONTRARY: Some animals do not have fuzzy ears.
The contradictory is false.
The subcontrary might be true and it might be false.

1. All sports cars are fun to drive.

2. Some dogs are not well trained.

3. Domestic cats can purr.

4. None of my friends can play the saxophone.

5. No fish has fur.

6. Tara plays the violin.

7. Some of my best friends have PhDs.

8. All of my best friends have PhDs.

9. No cat is a reptile.

10. Some students live off campus.

11. The rhododendron is an evergreen.

12. Some cab drivers aren't familiar with this neighborhood.

13. No books should be burned.

14. Some computers are not reliable.

15. Some books are written by professors.

Immediate Inferences

In the previous section, we reasoned about categorical statements. We learned that if a statement is false, for example, its contradictory must be true. There are other inferences we can draw as well. These are called **immediate inferences** because we don't need any information in addition to what the statement already contains to draw the inference. Immediate inferences yield **equivalent** statements. That means that they say the same thing in different ways. Two equivalent statements describe the same fact. There are three immediate inferences that we'll consider: conversion, obversion, and contraposition.

CONVERSION. Conversion is the result of switching the subject and predicate terms in a categorical statement. Conversion can be properly performed only on particular affirmative (*I*) statements and on negative universal (*E*) statements. Take the *E* statement "No women are fathers." If we switch the subject and predicate terms we get "No fathers are women"—another clearly true statement, which contains the same information as the original statement. The *I* statement "Some plants are carnivores" can also be converted. Switching the subject and predicate terms, we get "Some

REVIEW BOX 3.7

Conversion

• Exchange subject and predicate terms.

• Conversion is valid for *E* and *I* statements only.

No *S* are *P* → No *P* are *S*.
No women are fathers → No fathers are women.

Some *S* are *P* → Some *P* are *S*.
Some plants are carnivores → Some carnivores are plants.

carnivores are plants." If the original statement is true, the converted statement is also true.

A and *O* statements, however, cannot be converted. When we switch subject and predicate in the true statement "All dogs are mammals," we get "All mammals are dogs"—a completely different and false statement.

Sometimes it happens, by chance, that both an *A* statement and its converse are true. For example, the statements "All birds have feathers" and "All things with feathers are birds" are both true, but this is not the result of the logic of the statements. We can easily imagine that the world might contain things with feathers that are not birds—fabulous snakes or lizards, such as you may encounter in a fairy tale, could be feathered. If we know that "No women are fathers" is true, we know as well that "No fathers are women" is true. It is logically impossible for an *E* or *I* statement to be true and its converse false. But just knowing that "All birds have feathers" is not enough to know that all feathered things are birds. We have to go into the world to do research to discover that all things with feathers are birds. "No fathers are women" is a *logical* fact, given that no women are fathers. But "All things with feathers are birds" is an *empirical* fact (i.e., known by observation), even given the truth of "All birds have feathers."

We cannot convert *O* statements either. It's true that some people are not students. But it's certainly not true that some students are not people.

EXERCISE 3.3

For the following sentences,

  i. state the converse, and
  ii. state whether it is a permissible conversion.

Example

Some animals have fuzzy ears.
Some things with fuzzy ears are animals.

This is a permissible conversion (an *I* statement).

1. All sports cars are fun to drive.

2. Some dogs are not well trained.

3. Domestic cats can purr.

4. None of my friends can play the saxophone.

5. No fish has fur.

6. Tara plays the violin.

7. Some of my best friends have PhDs.

8. All of my best friends have PhDs.

9. No cat is a reptile.

10. Some students live off campus.

11. The rhododendron is an evergreen.

12. Some cab drivers aren't familiar with this neighborhood.

13. No books should be burned.

14. Some computers are not reliable.

15. Some books are written by professors.

OBVERSION. In **obversion**, we change a statement from affirmative to negative or from negative to affirmative and replace the predicate term with its **complement,** which consists of all the things that do not fall within that class. All classes have complements. For example, the complement of the class of dogs is the class of nondogs—not just cats, iguanas, and other companion animals, but also lawn furniture, supermarkets, and absolutely everything else in the universe that is not a dog. In determining a given class's complement, though, it's important to realize that sometimes a statement restricts the universe, either explicitly or implicitly. If someone tells you "Everyone at the party had a great time," he has explicitly restricted the universe to everyone at the party. If someone tells you "Everyone studied hard for the logic test," she no doubt implicitly means everyone in the logic class—it's unlikely that everyone in the world studied.

Usually, the best way to express the complement of a class is to use the prefix *non-*, though in some cases, a different expression makes more sense—for example, *non-people at the party* is more awkward than *people who weren't at the party*. In a limited number of cases, we can express the complement of a class in a more natural way, by using the prefix *un-* instead of *non-*. That is, we can sometimes regard the complement of *intelligent* as *unintelligent*. Be careful when you

REVIEW BOX   3.8

Complements

The complement of a class is made up of everything that falls outside of that class.

REVIEW BOX   3.9

Obversion

• Change affirmative to negative or negative to affirmative.

• Change the predicate class to its complement.

• Obversion is valid for all statements.

All *S* are *P* → No *S* are non-*P*.
All dogs are mammals → No dogs are nonmammals.

Some *S* are *P* → Some *S* are not non-*P*.
Some plants are carnivores → Some plants are not noncarnivores.

No *S* are *P* → All *S* are non-*P*.
No women are fathers → All women are nonfathers.

Some *S* are not *P* → Some *S* are non-*P*.
Some men are not uncles → Some men are nonuncles.

form complements this way, though. *Unintelligent* is only a complement of *intelligent* if the universe is restricted to the sorts of things that can be said to be either intelligent or unintelligent. Only things with minds can be spoken of this way. Lawn chairs, for example, are not intelligent, but that doesn't mean they're unintelligent—the concept of intelligence simply doesn't apply to them. In an unrestricted universe, then, the best way to form a complement is to use the prefix *non-*.

Obversion can be performed on all four statement types. Examples are provided in Review Box 3.9.

EXERCISE 3.4

Determine the obverse for the following sentences.

Example

Some dogs have fuzzy ears.
Some dogs are not things with nonfuzzy ears.

1. All sports cars are fun to drive.

2. Some dogs are not well trained.

3. Domestic cats can purr.

4. None of my friends can play the saxophone.

5. No fish has fur.

6. Tara plays the violin.

7. Some of my best friends have PhDs.

8. All of my best friends have PhDs.

9. No cat is a reptile.

10. Some students live off campus.

11. The rhododendron is an evergreen.

12. Some cab drivers aren't familiar with this neighborhood.

13. No books should be burned.

14. Some computers are not reliable.

15. Some books are written by professors.

CONTRAPOSITION. **Contraposition** is valid only for *A* and *O* statements. The contrapositive is formed by switching the subject and predicate terms, as in conversion, and exchanging both subject and predicate terms for terms that name their complement classes.

Thus, the *A* statement "All dogs are mammals" becomes "All nonmammals are nondogs." Though this is an awkward way to say it, clearly this statement is true if the original statement is true. Rephrasing it as "Anything that is not a mammal is not a dog" shows that it follows directly from the original *A* statement.

The contrapositive of the *O* statement is even more awkward, and even less likely to be used in ordinary conversation. "Some men are not uncles" becomes "Some nonuncles are not nonmen." Awkward as it is, however, it's true if the original statement is true. To get an intuitive grasp of the plausibility of the *O* contrapositive, let's consider an example that restricts the universe by using more colloquial terms to name the complement classes. Imagine that your sister is complaining about her taste in boyfriends. She says, "Some attractive men are not reliable." But here we can imagine her saying, equivalently and just as plausibly, "Some unreliable men are not unattractive." In the same way, we can imagine that, since it's regrettably true that some intelligent people are not pleasant, someone might actually assert the contrapositive "Some unpleasant people are not unintelligent."

You cannot form contrapositives of *I* and *E* statements. Take the

> ### R E V I E W   B O X   **3.10**
>
> ## Contraposition
>
> • Exchange subject and predicate terms.
>
> • Replace each with its complement.
>
> • Contraposition is valid for *A* and *O* statements.
>
> All *S* are *P* → All non-*P* are non-*S*.
> All dogs are mammals → All nonmammals are nondogs.
>
> Some *S* are not *P* → Some non-*P* are not non-*S*.
> Some men are not uncles → Some nonuncles are not nonmen.

I statement "Some plants are carnivores." We form the contrapositive by exchanging subject and predicate terms and replacing each term with its complement. Thus the complement of the *I* statement is "Some noncarnivores are nonplants." This may be true—cows are neither carnivores nor plants; houses, too, are neither carnivores nor plants. But as in the case of the occasionally true *A* conversion, this is a matter of empirical, not logical, fact. Even if "Some plants are carnivores" is true, its contrapositive need not be. We can imagine a world consistent with the original *I* statement in which absolutely everything, apart from a few plants, is a carnivore. In that case, the contrapositive would not be true. The goal of conversion, obversion, and contraposition is to find a statement that *must* be true if the original statement is true, meaning that we cannot even imagine a science-fiction world in which the inferred statement might be false.

Similarly, the *E* statement "No women are fathers" would have as its contrapositive "No nonfathers are nonwomen." But this isn't true—many nonfathers are nonwomen: they're children or men that don't happen to have children.

EXERCISE 3.5

For the following sentences,

  i.   state the contrapositive, and
  ii. state whether it is a permissible contraposition.

Example

Some animals have fuzzy ears.
Some things with nonfuzzy ears are nonanimals.

This is not a permissible contraposition. It's possible that while some animals have fuzzy ears, all nonanimals have fuzzy ears.

1. All sports cars are fun to drive.

2. Some dogs are not well trained.

3. Domestic cats can purr.

4. None of my friends can play the saxophone.

5. No fish has fur.

6. Tara plays the violin.

7. Some of my best friends have PhDs.

8. All of my best friends have PhDs.

9. No cat is a reptile.

10. Some students live off campus.

11. The rhododendron is an evergreen.

12. Some cab drivers aren't familiar with this neighborhood.

13. No books should be burned.

14. Some computers are not reliable.

15. Some books are written by professors.

TABLE 4. TRANSFORMATIONS OF CATEGORICAL STATEMENTS				
	A	**I**	**E**	**O**
Statement	All S are P	Some S are P	No S are P	Some S are not P
Contradictory	Some S are not P	No S are P	Some S are P	All S are P
Contrary	No S are P	—	All S are P	—
Subcontrary	—	Some S are not P	—	Some S are P
Converse	All P are S BAD	Some P are S	No P are S	Some P are not S BAD
Obverse	No S are non-P	Some S are not non-P	All S are non-P	Some S are non-P
Contrapositive	All non-P are non-S	Some non-P are non-S BAD	All S are non-P BAD	Some S are not non-S

LEMUR Exercise 3.1

The operations that we have performed upon categorical statements may seem unnatural and pointless. If that's how you feel, think of these operations as free-weight exercises for your mind. As dull as it may be to lift weights, the workout is worthwhile if it helps you play your sport better. Similarly, strengthening your logical skills will improve your ability to accept, refute, evaluate, and construct arguments.

▪ CATEGORICAL ARGUMENTS

In this section, we'll learn some new terminology to help us evaluate categorical syllogisms like the one we saw at the beginning of this chapter, and we'll learn the easiest method for evaluating these arguments. All categorical syllogisms contain two main premises, each of which is a categorical statement, and a conclusion, also a categorical statement. Together, these statements contain three terms; each term occurs exactly twice in exactly two of the statements.

Let's repeat the argument we began with:

> a connecting term (MIDDLE)
>
> [16] All human beings are mortal.
> All students are human beings.
> Therefore, all students are mortal. → PREDICATE (MAJOR)
>
> subject (minor)

| REVIEW BOX | 3.11 |

Major, minor, and middle terms

MAJOR: the predicate of the conclusion

MINOR: the subject of the conclusion

MIDDLE: the term that occurs in both premises and not at all in the conclusion

We see that the three terms in this argument are *human beings*, *things that are mortal*, and *students*. *Human beings* occurs twice—once in each premise. *Students* occurs in the second premise and in the conclusion. *Things that are mortal* occurs in the first premise and in the conclusion. These three terms are called the **major** term, the **minor** term, and the **middle** term. The major term is the predicate of the conclusion. In example [16], then, the major term is *things that are mortal*. The minor term is the subject of the conclusion. In example [16], the minor term is *students*. Finally, the middle term is the term that connects the major and minor terms. It appears in both premises, but not in the conclusion. In example [16] the middle term is *human beings*.

Example [16] is made up of *A* statements, but syllogisms can be made up of any of the four statement types, in any combination. Let's look at another example:

> [17] Some clematises have pink flowers.
> All clematises are vines.
> Therefore, some vines have pink flowers.

The conclusion as well as the first premise of this argument are *I* statements. The major term in example [17] is *things with pink flowers*. The minor term is *vines*. The middle term is *clematises*.

Finally,

> [18] Some candidates in this election have been indicted.
> No one who has been indicted is a good candidate.
> Therefore, some candidates in this election are not good candidates.

In example [18] the major term is *good candidates*, the minor term is *candidates*, and the middle term is *things that have been indicted*.

EXERCISE 3.6

For each of the following arguments,

   i.   if necessary, identify premises and conclusion, and
   ii. state major, minor, and middle terms.

Example

Some expensive things are worth having, since some beautiful things are expensive, and all beautiful things are worth having.

> Some beautiful things are expensive.
> All beautiful things are worth having.
> Therefore, some expensive things are worth having.

MAJOR: *things that are worth having*
MINOR: *expensive things*
MIDDLE: *beautiful things*

1. All dog owners love dogs. Some people who love dogs hate cats. Therefore, some dog owners hate cats.

2. Some of my cousins play hockey. Some people who play hockey have broken noses. Therefore, some of my cousins have broken noses.

3. Some tax cuts result in injustice, because some tax cuts result in cuts to social programs, and some cuts to social programs result in injustice.

4. Some kangaroos are highly poisonous, because all kangaroos are indigenous to Australia, and some animals that are indigenous to Australia are highly poisonous.

5. Some people who have traveled to Australia have been attacked by sharks. Jen is traveling to Australia, so she'll be attacked by sharks.

6. Anyone who enters the country must have a visa. Some refugees cannot get a visa. Thus some refugees cannot enter the country.

7. Some in-line skaters are young people. Some young people are irresponsible. Therefore, some in-line skaters are irresponsible.

8. Some concepts in critical thinking are difficult. Some students are required to take a course in critical thinking. Thus some students are required to take a course containing difficult concepts.

9. "Nothing but mortal sin debars people from God's kingdom. But fornication debars people from God's kingdom, as shown by the words of St. Paul [Gal. v. 21]. Thus fornication is a mortal sin." [St. Thomas Aquinas, *Summa Theologica* II-II 154 2.]

10. Suicide results in eternal damnation, like any other act forbidden by God. [*Hint*: missing premises can appear in all kinds of arguments.]

Evaluating Syllogisms

We use three rules to evaluate syllogisms. An argument that breaks any of these rules is a bad one.

1. At least one premise must distribute the middle term.
2. If a term is distributed in the conclusion, it must also be distributed in at least one of the premises.
3. The number of negative claims must be the same in the premises and conclusion.

In order to evaluate the validity of syllogisms, we need to determine whether the terms in a categorical statement are distributed or undistributed, and whether the statement is affirmative or negative.

Let's apply these rules to example [16]:

DISTRIBUTED

UNIVERSAL
AFFIRMATIVE
MAJOR – MORTAL
MINOR – STUDENT
MIDDLE – HUMAN BEINGS

[16] All human beings are mortal.
All students are human beings.
Therefore, all students are mortal.

UNDISTRIBUTED PREDICATE

Example [16] appears intuitively to be a good argument. Both premises are true, and the conclusion seems to be true as well. But does it contravene any of the rules?

RULE 1: At least one premise must distribute the middle term. First we ask, what is the middle term? Remember, the middle term appears in both premises, and not at all in the conclusion. In example [16], that's *human beings*. Is it distributed? Yes: the first premise in example [16] is a universal sentence, and universal sentences have distributed subject terms. That means that the middle term is distributed in at least one premise. So Rule 1 is satisfied.

RULE 2: If a term is distributed in the conclusion, it must also be distributed in at least one of the premises. The conclusion is a universal sentence; that means that its subject term, *students*, is distributed. Is *students* distributed in at least one premise? Yes: the second premise is also a universal statement with the subject *students*. Rule 2, then, is also satisfied.

RULE 3: The number of negative claims must be the same in the premises and conclusion. Since the conclusion is not a negative claim, there should be no negative claims in the premises, and there are not. Rule 3 is satisfied. The argument is valid.

Let's look at another example.

> **[17]** Some clematises have pink flowers.
> All clematises are vines.
> Therefore, some vines have pink flowers.

RULE 1: The middle term in example [17] is *clematises*. This term is distributed in the second premise, since universal statements have distributed subject terms.

RULE 2: The conclusion does not contain any distributed terms. It is not a universal sentence, so the subject term is not distributed, and it is not a negative sentence, so the predicate term is not distributed.

RULE 3: The conclusion is not a negative claim, and neither are any of the premises. Example [17] is also a valid argument.

> **[18]** Some candidates in this election have been indicted.
> No one who has been indicted is a good candidate.
> Therefore, some candidates in this election are not good
>   candidates.

RULE 1: The middle term in example [18] is people who have been indicted. It is distributed in the second premise. The second premise is a universal claim, and in universal claims the subject term is distributed. Rule 1 is satisfied.

RULE 2: Is there any term that is distributed in the conclusion? Yes: *good candidates* is the predicate term in the conclusion; the conclusion is an *O* statement and in *O* statements the predicate term is distributed. That means that *good candidates* must be distributed in at least one premise. It is, in the second premise. Rule 2 is satisfied.

RULE 3:   The conclusion of example [18] is a negative claim. That means that one—and only one—of the premises must also be a negative claim. Only the second premise is negative. Rule 3 is satisfied. So example [18] is a valid argument, too.

> [19] Some students do not study.
> No one who studies fails a test.
> Therefore, some students fail tests.

Certainly it's true that some students fail tests. But never forget that a true conclusion alone doesn't make an argument a good one.

RULE 1:   The middle term is *people who study*. Is it distributed in at least one premise? Yes: the second premise, an *E* statement, has both distributed subject and distributed predicate.

RULE 2:   Is there any term that is distributed in the conclusion? No: the conclusion is an *I* statement, which has neither subject nor predicate distributed.

RULE 3:   The conclusion is an affirmative statement. But both premises are negative statements. This argument contravenes Rule 3 and is therefore a bad argument. An argument with two negative premises is a bad argument. There have to be the same number of negative statements in the premise as in the conclusion. The conclusion is a single statement. Thus no argument with two negative premises can be valid.

Beware of applying Rule 3 too widely. Some premises that *appear* to be negative can be made positive. In particular, the obverse of an *A* or *I* statement contains negation words, although these obverse statements are equivalent to the positive statements.

> [20] Some cloudy days are not rainless.
> Some rainy days are cold and windy.
> Therefore, some cloudy days are cold and windy.

Although the first premise of example [20] contains the word *not*, we must recognize that it can be restated as a particular affirmative statement: "Some cloudy days are rainy days." The restatement also permits us to recognize the middle term.

RULE 1: The middle term is *rainy days*. It is not distributed in any premise. Both premises are *I* statements, and *I* statements do not distribute either the subject or the predicate term. In fact, some cloudy days are cold and windy, but we know this from experience, not because it's been proven to us by this argument. It's easy to imagine that there are days that are cloudy but not rainy, and that these days are always still and hot. We know, then, that this argument is a bad one, because it has already broken a rule. We'll go on to consider the other two rules anyway.

RULE 2: No term is distributed in the conclusion, since the conclusion is also an *I* statement.

RULE 3: There are no negative statements in premises or conclusion.

> [21] Every educated person can do logic.
> No educated person is unemployed.
> Therefore, no unemployed person can do logic.

RULE 1: The middle term is *educated person*. It is distributed in the first premise, which is an *A* statement.

RULE 2: The conclusion distributes both its terms because it is an *E* statement. That means that both *unemployed person* and *person who can do logic* must be distributed somewhere in the premises. Is *unemployed person* distributed? Yes. The second premise is an *E* sentence, so its predicate term is distributed. Is *person who can do logic* distributed in a premise? No. This term is the predicate term of the first premise. The first premise is an *A* sentence, which distributes only its subject term. Thus example [21] is a bad argument because it contravenes Rule 2. Even though we've already rejected example [21], let's consider Rule 3 anyway.

RULE 3: The conclusion is negative. That means that one and only one premise must also be negative. In fact the second premise is negative. So example [21] does satisfy Rule 3.

▨ SUMMARY

In this chapter, we've learned methods to deal with categorical statements and arguments. You'll need to review these methods many times through the exercises in order to understand them. Familiarity with the four standard forms and an ability to translate statements into a standard form are required before you can go any further. The properties of each of the four standard forms—distribution and the square of opposition—are part of this familiarity. To evaluate categorical arguments, you need to remember the three rules, and your familiarity with the statements will enable you to apply the rules.

LEMUR Exercise 3.2

EXERCISE 3.7

Use the three rules of validity to evaluate the following arguments.

Example

Some expensive things are worth having, since some beautiful things are expensive, and all beautiful things are worth having.

> 1. Some beautiful things are expensive.
> 2. All beautiful things are worth having.
> Therefore, some expensive things are worth having.

MAJOR: *things that are worth having*
MINOR: *expensive things*
MIDDLE: *beautiful things*

RULE 1: Is the middle term distributed in at least one premise? Yes: premise 2 is a universal affirmative.

RULE 2: Is any term distributed in the conclusion? No. The conclusion is a particular affirmative, so neither term is distributed.

RULE 3: There are no negative claims anywhere in the argument. Since this argument satisfies the three rules, it's valid.

1. All dog owners love dogs. Some people who love dogs hate cats. Therefore, some dog owners hate cats.

2. Some of my cousins play hockey. Some people who play hockey have broken noses. Therefore, some of my cousins have broken noses.

3. Some tax cuts result in injustice, because some tax cuts result in cuts to social programs, and some cuts to social programs result in injustice.

4. Some kangaroos are highly poisonous, because all kangaroos are indigenous to Australia, and some animals that are indigenous to Australia are highly poisonous.

5. Some people who have traveled to Australia have been attacked by sharks. Jen is traveling to Australia, so she'll be attacked by sharks.

6. Anyone who enters the country must have a visa. Some refugees cannot get a visa. Thus some refugees cannot enter the country.

7. Some in-line skaters are young people. Some young people are irresponsible. Therefore, some in-line skaters are irresponsible.

8. Some concepts in critical thinking are difficult. Some students are required to take a course in critical thinking. Thus some students are required to take a course containing difficult concepts.

9. "Nothing but mortal sin debars people from God's kingdom. But fornication debars people from God's kingdom, as shown by the words of St. Paul [Gal. v. 21]. Thus fornication is a mortal sin." [St. Thomas Aquinas, *Summa Theologica* II-II 154 2.]

10. Suicide results in eternal damnation, like any other act forbidden by God. [*Hint*: missing premises can appear in all kinds of arguments.]

4 Necessary and Sufficient Conditions

IN THIS CHAPTER, we'll consider **conditional statements**. Often we have to state that one thing is a condition for another thing. As we'll see, a condition may be either **necessary** or **sufficient**. Why is it important to know about conditional relationships? First, mixing them up may lead you to accidently make a false assertion. Second, if you want to refute a conditional statement by giving a counterexample, you need to understand exactly what is being asserted. Finally, understanding the logic of conditional statements will help you understand and evaluate arguments that contain them.

We'll start this chapter with a full examination of conditional statements. After we are comfortable with such statements, we'll go on to consider the arguments in which they are used.

▨ CONDITIONAL STATEMENTS

To say that *A* is a sufficient condition for *B* is to say that *A* is *enough* for *B*. You can understand this relationship in terms of causes (if *A* happens, that's enough to cause *B* to happen), of knowledge (if you know *A*, you know enough to know *B*), or of truth (if *A* is true, *B* must also be true). Take, for example,

REVIEW BOX 4.1

Sufficient condition

A is sufficient for *B*:

If *A* is true, then *B* is true.

■ **[1]** Being a poodle is a sufficient condition for being a dog.

This means that if something is a poodle, then it is a dog. To know that something is a poodle is to know it is a dog, rather than a cat, a plant, a rock, or a piece of furniture. If you know that Tanya has a poodle, then you know that Tanya has a dog, because there are no poodles that are not dogs. A poodle is a type of dog, but it is only one type of dog among many. The class of poodles is completely contained in the class of dogs, as

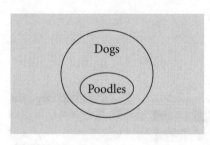

Diagram 1.   BEING A POODLE IS
SUFFICIENT FOR BEING A DOG.

Diagram 1 shows. But the class of dogs extends beyond the class of poodles. In other words, all poodles are dogs, but not all dogs are poodles. To know that something is a dog is certainly not enough to know that it's a poodle—it could be a collie, a golden retriever, or a malamute. So to say that A is a sufficient condition for B is not to say that B is sufficient for A.

To say that X is a necessary condition for Y, on the other hand, is to say that X is required for Y. Y is not true unless X is also true. Whenever Y is true, X is true as well.

■ **[2]** Being human is necessary for attending a university.

REVIEW BOX	4.2

Necessary condition

X is a necessary condition for Y:

If X is not true, Y is not true.

Example [2] means that if something is attending a university, it has to be human. There are no dogs or anteaters or other nonhumans attending any university—there are only humans. If you tell me that Sameer is attending a university, I know Sameer is human, because anything that attends a university *must* be human.

Again, we can represent the state of affairs that example [2] describes. Diagram 2 shows us that being human is a necessary condition for attending a university: it's necessary because the class of university students is completely contained in the class of humans. You would not find any member of the class of university students that is not also a member of the class of humans.

But we cannot say that being a university student is necessary for being human. The class of humans is larger than the class of university students, leaving room for many humans who are not attending universities, such as people who have chosen not to go, children who aren't old enough to go, and people who have already graduated.

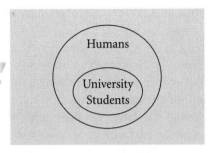

Diagram 2.   BEING HUMAN IS NECESSARY FOR BEING A UNIVERSITY STUDENT.

If we compare Diagram 1 and Diagram 2, we see that they're really the same picture—each represents one class completely enclosed within another class. Diagram 3 represents this schematically. A is completely contained within B. What does Diagram 3 mean in terms of sufficient and necessary conditions? We could interpret it two ways. A, the smaller circle, is playing the role of the *poodle* circle in Diagram 1. A is sufficient for B. And also, B, the larger circle, is playing the role of the *human* circle in Diagram 2. B is

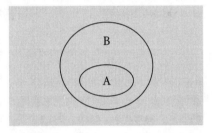

Diagram 3. A IS SUFFICIENT FOR B. B IS NECESSARY FOR A.

necessary for A. Whenever we have information about a sufficient condition, we also have information about a necessary condition. If A is sufficient for B, then B is necessary for A.

We've seen that being a poodle is sufficient for being a dog. Now we can see too that being a dog is necessary for being a poodle. *Dog* is a necessary part of the concept *poodle*. Only dogs are poodles. Similarly, if being human is necessary for attending a university, then attending a university is sufficient for being human. If you know that

REVIEW BOX   4.3

Relationship between necessary and sufficient conditions

A is sufficient for $B = B$ is necessary for A.

something is a university student, you know enough to know that it's human.

Clearly it's important not to confuse necessary and sufficient conditions. It's necessary that university students be human—but being human is not sufficient for attending a university; if it were, to be accepted at a university would mean only having to prove that you are human. You would not have to satisfy any other conditions, such as getting good grades in high school or doing well on entrance exams.

LEMUR Exercise 4.1

All and Only

Sufficient and necessary conditions can appear in many different kinds of sentences. We've seen the term *all* in categorical arguments. *All* is also a word that helps us understand conditional sentences. If we say

     [3] All poodles are dogs,

we say, essentially, that the world is as it is pictured in Diagram 1—the class of poodles is completely contained in the class of dogs. There are no poodles that are not also dogs. *All* signals a sufficient condition.

REVIEW BOX   4.4

All and *only*

- All *A*s are *B*s
  = *A* is sufficient for *B*
  = *B* is necessary for *A*

- Only *X*s are *Y*s
  = *X* is necessary for *Y*
  = *Y* is sufficient for *X*

As we've seen, information about a sufficient condition is also information about a necessary condition. That means that whenever we see a statement about a sufficient condition, we can change it into a statement about a necessary condition. If "All poodles are dogs" tells us that being a poodle is sufficient for being a dog, we know that being a dog is necessary for being a poodle. How would we make this equivalent statement in terms of *only*?

     [3a] Only dogs are poodles.

Examples [3] and [3a] are equivalent. They give us the same information about the world—they just state it differently. Each of these two sentences tells us that the world is as it is pictured in Diagram 1.

If we say

■ [4] Only humans attend a university,

we say that there is nothing that falls in the class of things that attend a university that does not also fall in the class of humans. *Only* signals a necessary condition. Similarly, a statement involving the word *only* is equivalent to a statement involving the word *all*. How could we change example [4] into a statement introduced by the word *all?*

■ [4a] All things that attend a university are human.

It is important to remember that wherever you have a necessary condition, you have a sufficient one, and conversely. This will be crucial when we come to arguments involving necessary and sufficient conditions.

Let's look at some more examples.

■ [5] All rainy days are cloudy days.

Let's start by representing example [5] in Diagram 4. If all rainy days are cloudy days, then there are no rainy days that do not also fall within the class of *cloudy days*. To draw a picture of this, we need to draw the class of rainy days completely contained in the class of cloudy days. Perhaps there are some cloudy days when it doesn't rain—perhaps it snows instead, for example. Example [5] leaves that possibility open.

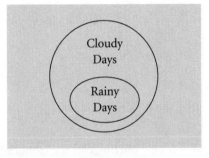

Diagram 4. ALL RAINY DAYS ARE CLOUDY DAYS.

Now what does this mean in terms of necessary and sufficient conditions? The sufficient condition is in the smaller circle.

■ [5a] Being a rainy day is sufficient for being a cloudy day.

We know that we can change a statement about a sufficient condition into an equivalent statement about a necessary condition.

▌ **[5b]** Being a cloudy day is necessary for being a rainy day.

And finally, we can always change a statement introduced by *all* into a statement introduced by *only*:

▌ **[5c]** Only cloudy days are rainy day.

All the statements in examples [5] to [5c] tell us the same thing: it never rains unless there are also clouds. Whenever you see raindrops on the sidewalk, you can look up and see clouds in the sky. Again, it's important not to confuse the two parts of this statement. While clouds are necessary for rain, rain is not necessary for clouds—perhaps there are clouds, but it is snowing.

Here's another example:

▌ **[6]** Only cats purr.

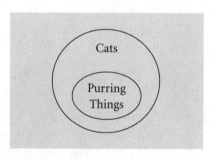

Diagram 5. ONLY CATS PURR.

Example [6] tells us that there is nothing that purrs that is not a cat. The class of purring things does not extend beyond the class of cats. Example [6] does not tell us whether there are some cats that do not purr. So the diagram of example [6] would put the *purring things* circle entirely within the *cat* circle.

It is a necessary condition for something's purring that it be a cat. If you hear purring coming from the next room, you know there is a cat in the next room—because the only things that purr are cats.

▌ **[6a]** Being a cat is necessary for purring.

We know that this can also be stated as

▌ **[6b]** Purring is sufficient for being a cat.

And finally, in a statement using *all*, we can say

    [6c] All purring things are cats.

Once again, to say that all purring things are cats is not to say that all cats purr. Lions are cats, but they don't purr.

Counterexamples

A counterexample to a statement shows that the statement is false. To find a counterexample to a conditional statement, we look for something that falls within the smaller circle but not within the larger circle. If there is such a thing, since it's impossible to draw in our diagram, then that diagram must be an inaccurate representation of the world—i.e., false. So a counterexample to "Only cats purr" would be a purring thing that is not a cat. A counterexample to "All rainy days are cloudy days" would be a rainy day that is not cloudy.

EXERCISE 4.1

For each of the following sentences,

    i.   draw a diagram to represent the relationship between the two concepts;
   ii. state which is sufficient for the other;
  iii. state which is necessary for the other;
   iv. create a sentence using the term that the original did not use (i.e., if it uses *all*, write an equivalent sentence using *only*; if the original uses *only*, state an equivalent sentence using *all*); and
   v. give a counterexample.

Example

    i.   Only roses have thorns.
   ii. Being a rose is necessary for having thorns.
  iii. Having thorns is sufficient for being a rose.

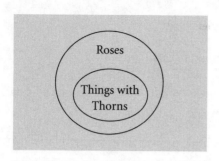

Diagram 6.   ONLY ROSES HAVE THORNS.

iv. All things with thorns are roses.
v. Something that has thorns, but is not a rose—a hawthorn, for example.

1. All basketball players are tall.

2. Only basketball players are tall.

3. Only anteaters have long noses.

4. You may leave an exam only after the first forty-five minutes have passed.

5. Good warriors take their stand on ground where they cannot lose.

6. The only way I can pay my tuition is to find a well-paying part-time job.

7. I only go to the movies on Tuesday nights.

8. Hibiscuses are the only flowers that are bigger than my head.

9. Every person has the right to equal treatment.

10. None but the brave deserve the fair. [*Hint*: can you restate this with *all*?]

If . . . Then

Often conditional statements take the form of *if . . . then* statements. For example,

> [7] If you remember what you study, then you'll get a good grade.

There are two parts to any *if . . . then* statement. In a simple *if . . . then* statement like example [7], the **antecedent** comes immediately after the *if.* The antecedent is the sufficient condition, which in this case is *you remember what you study*. In other words, remembering what you study is enough to get you a grade. The second part of the *if . . . then* statement, called the **consequent**, is the necessary condition. Getting a good grade is a necessary consequence of remembering what you studied. Example [7] does not claim that remembering is the only way to get a good grade. Maybe you don't remember a thing, but you make some lucky guesses. A sufficient condition could by itself result in the consequent— but that condition may be just one of several that could lead to the consequent. (Example [7] is probably not true: if you did not study the right material, remembering it during a test will be of little use. But it is important to understand the meaning of a sentence even when we believe it is false.)

Similarly,

> [8] If Zack doesn't turn off the video game, then he'll be late for school.

Here, the sufficient condition is *Zack doesn't turn off the video game* and the necessary condition is *he'll be late for school*. According to example [8], not turning off the video game would be enough to make Zack late. Of course, he could be late for other reasons—he might turn off the game but then spend too much time making himself a sandwich. Zack's being late for school, then, is a necessary condition of his not turning off the game. But knowing that Zack is late for school is not enough to know that he failed to turn off the video game.

Not every *if . . . then* statement is as straightforward as examples [7] and [8]. Consider the statement

> [9] I'll quit if I don't get a raise.

Here the *if* is in the second half of the sentence, and the word *then* does not appear at all. Nevertheless, this is just another way of saying

> [9a] If I don't get a raise, then I'll quit.

Examples [9] and [9a] both express the same proposition: my not getting a raise is enough to make me quit; my quitting is the necessary result of my not getting a raise. Thus, *if . . . then* constructions do not always contain the word *then*, and sometimes the necessary condition is stated before the sufficient condition.

The skill of translating colloquial statements into statements of necessary and sufficient conditions will, with practice, become completely mechanical. In the case of *all* and *only* statements, drawing a diagram may help. Remember, the small circle represents the sufficient condition and the large circle represents the necessary condition. In the case of *if . . . then* statements, remember that the part following the *if* is the sufficient condition and the part following the *then* is the necessary condition. Even when a sentence is false, the goal is to translate what it says. We're not saying that truth doesn't matter—far from it. But our goal in this chapter is to learn how to evaluate whether conditional arguments are good or bad, and that requires knowing what their premises actually say.

EXERCISE 4.2

For each of the following, state the necessary and sufficient conditions given by the sentence.

Example

If I'm going to grow garlic next summer, I have to plant it this fall.
Growing garlic next summer is sufficient for planting it this fall.
Planting garlic this fall is necessary for growing garlic next summer.

1. If Caesar hesitates, then he will not conquer.

2. If Lisa has a chemistry test tomorrow, she can't go to a party tonight.

3. Only students with a B+ average are eligible for admission to the M.A. program.

4. If your car clicks when it goes around corners, you may have a bad CV joint.

5. I'll call you tonight if I have time.

6. You only read Descartes in philosophy class.

7. I'll take my umbrella if it rains.

8. If it rains, the streets will be wet.

9. If I get a scholarship, I'll buy a new computer.

10. I'll help carry your stuff if you move.

Only If

We've seen that in a sentence like

> [7] If you remember what you study, then you'll get a
>   good grade,

what immediately follows the *if* is the sufficient condition: remembering what you study is sufficient for getting you a good grade. But the word *if* does not always signal a sufficient condition, because sometimes it appears with the word *only*. For example,

> [10] You'll get a good grade only if you remember what
>   you study.

Example [10] says the opposite of example [7]. *Only if* introduces a necessary condition. *Only*, as we know, signals a necessary condition, so when it is joined to *if*, it communicates a necessary relationship. Whereas example [7] says that remembering what you study is enough to get a good grade, example [10] says that while you must remember what you study, there may be other conditions that also have to be fulfilled in order to get a good grade—perhaps studying the right material, showing up for the test on time, and so on. Example [10] more likely is a true statement of the relationship between remembering and getting a good grade than example [7].

Let's consider another example.

> [11] I'll only go home for the weekend if I get my essays
>   written first.

Example [11] is difficult because the *only* and the *if* are separated, but this is a common way to phrase an *only if* statement. Example [11] says that getting my essays written first is necessary for my going home for the weekend. In general, when you see the word *if* in a sentence, look closely to see whether the word *only* appears as well, adjacently or not. This will help you determine whether the condition after the *if* is necessary or sufficient.

EXERCISE 4.3

For each of the following, state the necessary and sufficient conditions.

> ### REVIEW BOX 4.5
>
> ### If and only if
>
> ALL OF THE FOLLOWING MEAN THE SAME THING:
>
> If S then N.
> N, if S.
> S only if N.
> Only S if N.
>
> If you're a student, then you're human.
> You're human if you're a student.
> You're a student only if you're human.
> You're only a student if you're human.
>
> Being a student is sufficient for being human.
> Being human is necessary for being a student.

1. Elvis is still alive only if Jim Morrison is still alive.

2. You should only fight if you know you can win.

3. You can only sell back textbooks that will be used for the course again.

4. I'll go out tonight if I finish studying early enough.

5. You can only pass the course if you pass the final exam.

6. The only way Ted will finish the books for the test tomorrow is if he's a speed reader.

7. I'd only drive to Mexico if I owned a car.

8. Good warriors do not overlook conditions that make an enemy likely to be defeated.

9. I'll believe it if I see it.

10. If you have a faulty ignition, your car won't start.

Negation

There are certain rules for dealing with negations that we have to be familiar with, because negations are a very important factor in necessary–sufficient arguments.

If A then B is equivalent to *If not B then not A.* If A is sufficient for B, then not B is sufficient for not A. Why? Consider this in terms of the following sentence:

▓   [12] If you attend a university, then you're human.

This says that being human is necessary for attending a university, and attending a university is sufficient for being human. If you know that Martin attends a university, you know enough to know that he is human. If you know that Martin is human, you do not know enough to know that he attends a university. Diagram 7 shows the relationship between being human and attending a university.

If we know that Martin is *not* human, that he is instead someone's pet iguana, what else do we know? We know for sure that Martin does not attend a university. Since being human is necessary for attending a university, not being human must be sufficient for not attending a university. To know that something is not human is enough to know that it does not attend a university. Being not human is enough to keep

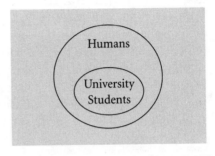

Diagram 7.   Being human/attending a university.

Martin out of any university. Diagram 7 shows that anything outside the class *human* is also outside the class *things that attend a university*.

If *X* is necessary for *Y*, not *X* is sufficient for not *Y*.

Negations work similarly for sufficient conditions. If knowing that Martin attends a university is enough to know that he is human, then knowing that Martin does not attend a university is a necessary part of knowing that he's not human. As we've seen, knowing that Martin does not attend a university is certainly not enough to know that he's not human—many humans do not attend a university. But not attending a university is a necessary condition for not being human.

If *Y* is sufficient for *X*, not *Y* is necessary for not *X*.

Let's return to

▌   [8] If Zack doesn't turn off the video game, then he'll be
      late for school.

Notice that this statement has a negation in it. *Doesn't* is the contraction of *does not*, and *not* is a negation word. Example [8] says that Zack's not turning off the video game is enough to make him late for school. What if Zack does turn off the video game? Is that enough to make him not late for school? No—as we saw, he could turn off the video game and still run late because he makes a sandwich. Turning off the video game is not sufficient for Zack's not being late. But it is necessary. Turning off the video game is one of the things he must do if he's going to make it to school on time. Thus,

> [8a] If Zack is not late for school, he turns off the video game.

Notice that in example [8a] we have turned the sentence around, so to speak—we put the former necessary condition *Zack is late for school* into the sufficient condition place, immediately after the *if*, and added a negation. We have put the former sufficient condition *Zack doesn't turn off the video game* into the necessary condition place, and removed the negation.

Now consider

> [13] If you want a nice pet, don't choose a wolverine.

Wanting a nice pet is sufficient for not choosing a wolverine. Not choosing a wolverine is necessary for wanting a nice pet. If we knew that someone wanted a nice pet, we'd know enough to predict that that person would not choose a wolverine.

What if someone did choose a wolverine? We would know that that person did not want a nice pet. Choosing a wolverine is sufficient for not wanting a nice pet. Not wanting a nice pet is a necessary part of choosing a wolverine.

In the table below, the sentence on the left is equivalent to the sentence on the right.

TABLE 1.	EQUIVALENT NEGATIONS
If A then B = If not B then not A	
If not A then B = If not B then A	
If A then not B = If B then not A	

Unless

Unless is the final word we'll deal with pertaining to statements about necessary and sufficient conditions. To understand *unless*, we must use negation.

> [14] I won't get into law school unless I get good grades.

Example [14] clearly means that I must have good grades to get into law school—that good grades are a necessary condition for my getting into law school. Notice that example [14] is of the form *Not A unless B*. Compare example [14] with this:

> [15] We'll watch *A Better Tomorrow* tonight unless the VCR is broken.

Example [15] has the form *A unless B*—there is no negation. What does example [15] mean? It means that if the VCR is not broken, we'll watch the movie. The VCR's not being broken is sufficient—not necessary—for watching the movie. Example [15] states an intention to watch this movie tonight and gives the single reason we would fail to do so. We could also say that if we do not watch the movie tonight, it could only be because the VCR is broken.

When you see the word *unless*, first check whether there is a negation in the first half of the sentence. If the sentence is of the form *Not A unless B*, then *B* is necessary for *A*. If the sentence is of the form *A unless B*, the judgment of necessary and sufficient conditions is more complicated: *B* is necessary for not *A*. Think of *A unless B* as saying something like this: "*A* is going to happen. The only thing that can stop it is *B* (= *B* is necessary for not *A*). If *B* does not happen, then *A* will happen (= not *B* is sufficient for *A*)."

> ### REVIEW BOX 4.6
>
> ### *Unless*
>
> Not *A* unless *B* = *B* is necessary for *A*.
>
> *A* unless *B* = *B* is necessary for not *A*.

Both Necessary and Sufficient /
Neither Necessary nor Sufficient

If A is both necessary and sufficient for B, the relationship between A and B is very strong. All and only As are Bs. Clearly, if A is both necessary and sufficient for B, then B is also both necessary and sufficient for A. This relationship holds only when you have what is basically a definition. For example,

> [16] Being water is both necessary and sufficient for being H_2O.
> All and only water is H_2O.

Example [16] says that all water has the chemical composition H_2O. And anything with the chemical composition H_2O is water.

Sometimes two things bear neither relationship to one another—for example, *being an uncle* and *having a nephew*. Knowing that Chris has a nephew does not give you enough information to conclude that Chris is an uncle—Chris could be an aunt. Knowing that Chris is an uncle does not give you enough information to conclude that he has a nephew—he could have a niece.

LEMUR Exercise 4.2

EXERCISE 4.4

For each of the following sentences, fill in the blank with either necessary or sufficient.

Example

If Andrew doesn't go to Fortino's, we won't have dinner tonight.
Andrew's going to Fortino's is ____ for our having dinner tonight.

The first thing to notice here is that, whereas it should be clear that Andrew's not going to Fortino's is sufficient for our not having dinner tonight, the second sentence wants to know what the relationship is between Andrew's going to Fortino's—without the *not*—and our having dinner. That means that we have to change the sentence around to get rid of the negations.

The original sentence is equivalent to "If we have dinner tonight, Andrew goes to Fortino's." (You'd probably state this colloquially as, "If we're going to have dinner, Andrew has to go to Fortino's.") We take out the negations, and change the places of the two propositions. Thus Andrew's going to Fortino's is *necessary* for our having dinner tonight.

1. You'll see lots of surfers if you go to Santa Monica beach.

Going to Santa Monica beach is ____ for seeing lots of surfers.

2. All cars with big fins get low gas mileage.

Being a car with big fins is ____ for getting low gas mileage.

3. If I don't have the remote control, I can't change the channel.

Having the remote control is ____ for changing the channel.

4. You can't graduate unless you take all the courses required for your major.

Taking all the courses required for your major is ____ for graduating.

5. Unless there is a blizzard, the midterm is on Thursday.

There being no blizzard is ____ for the midterm's being on Thursday.

6. If I go to the movie, I can't go to the party.

Going to the party is ____ for not going to the movie.

7. You should not fight unless you know you can win.

Knowing you can win is ____ for fighting.

8. I can't get into my car if I don't have my keys.

Having my keys is ____ for getting into my car.

9. I'm not going outside if the temperature doesn't rise.

The temperature's rising is ____ for my going outside.

10. I can't take a trip this summer unless I get a job.

My getting a job is ____ for taking a trip this summer.

11. You can't win if you don't play.

Playing is ____ for winning.

12. Only those who don't move don't die.

Moving is ____ for dying.

13. I can't get rich unless I am ruthless.

Being ruthless is _____ for getting rich.

14. You can't get into law school unless you take the LSAT.

Taking the LSAT is _____ for getting into law school.

15. If you don't have Nintendo, you can't play *Killer Instinct*.

Having Nintendo is _____ for playing *Killer Instinct*.

TABLE 2. EQUIVALENT FORMS OF CONDITIONAL SENTENCES		
A is sufficient for B	Not P is sufficient for Q	X is sufficient for not Y
B is necessary for A	Q is necessary for not P	Not Y is necessary for X
If A then B	If not P then Q	If X then not Y
B if A	Q if not P	Not Y if X
A only if B	Not P only if Q	X only if not Y
Only A if B	Only not P if Q	Only X if not Y
If not B then not A	If not Q then P	If Y then not X
Not A unless B	P unless Q	Not X unless not Y

■ CONDITIONAL ARGUMENTS

Arguments involving necessary and sufficient conditions are common. It's important to be able to recognize necessary and sufficient conditions in whatever form they appear so that these arguments won't mislead you. If you are not fully confident of your ability to determine necessary and sufficient conditions, go over the last section again and do some more exercises. A reliable grasp of conditional sentences is a necessary condition for evaluating conditional arguments.

There are four basic argument forms involving necessary and sufficient conditions. Two are good and two are bad. The good ones and the bad ones look very similar.

Good Arguments

When you were a child, your mother might have said to you,

> [17] If you eat your peas, then you can have a cookie.

If you went ahead and ate the peas, what would you expect? A cookie. Your mother made a conditional statement, that the sufficient condition for your having a cookie was your eating the peas. If the sufficient condition holds, you can affirm the consequent of the sentence.

The argument could be represented this way:

> [18] If you eat your peas, then you can have a cookie.
> You eat your peas.
> Therefore, you can have a cookie.

Notice, first, the *if . . . then* format that's characteristic of a conditional sentence. When we see an *if . . . then* sentence in an argument, our next move should always be to determine whether this is a conditional argument. Your eating your peas is, as we know, sufficient for your having a cookie. We know this means that all you need to do to get the cookie is eat your peas. If the second premise tells us that you eat your peas, we know enough to know that you can have a cookie.

This is known as affirming the sufficient condition. We affirm when we say exactly the same thing. This argument form is traditionally called **modus ponens,** and it is the first of our good conditional argument forms.

Notice that there are two main premises supporting the conclusion and that these premises are linked. Both premises are required to draw the conclusion.

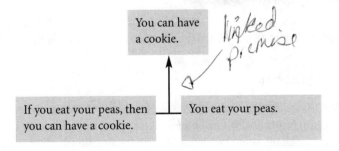

If your roommate asks if you want to come along to a party, and you say

> **[19]** I can only go out tonight if I finish writing this essay soon,

REVIEW BOX   4.7

Good conditional arguments

Affirm the sufficient condition. (*modus ponens*)

Deny the necessary condition. (*modus tollens*)

"Affirm" means "say the same thing."

"Deny" means "say the opposite."

your roommate's next question will likely be something like, "Well, when do you think you'll finish it?" Your assertion was that finishing the essay soon is a necessary condition for going out. If you were to tell your roommate that you won't finish the essay until much later, your roommate knows that he can go ahead without you. *I finish writing this essay soon* is necessary for going out. A necessary condition is one that's required. If that necessary condition does not hold, then the antecedent, *I can go out tonight,* cannot hold either.

The full argument is this:

> **[20]** I can only go out tonight if I finish writing this essay soon.
> I won't finish writing this essay until very late.
> Therefore, I can't go out tonight.

This argument denies the necessary condition, known as ***modus tollens***. We deny when we say the opposite.

Thus there are two good argument forms—affirming the sufficient condition or antecedent, and denying the necessary condition or consequent.

Bad Arguments

Good arguments affirm the sufficient condition or deny the necessary condition. Bad arguments do the opposite. You cannot affirm a necessary condition or deny a sufficient condition. What if your faculty advisor told you,

[21] You can't graduate unless you take your critical thinking requirement.

If you then take critical thinking, are you guaranteed to graduate? Of course not. Example [21] is a statement of a necessary condition. Taking this one course is necessary for graduation, but it's unlikely that this is the only requirement. You have to pass this course, as well as several others.

REVIEW BOX 4.8

Bad conditional arguments

Deny the sufficient condition.

Affirm the necessary condition.

[22] You can't graduate unless you take your critical thinking requirement.
You have taken critical thinking.
Therefore, you can graduate.

Example [22] is a bad argument. It affirms a necessary condition. As we have seen, a necessary condition is one that's required, but it may not be all that's required. You might as well say this:

[23] All poodles are dogs.
Ed has a dog.
Therefore, Ed has a poodle.

Ed may have a dog, but it could be any breed of dog—poodles are not the only dogs, just as a critical thinking course is not the only requirement for graduation.

Strategies and Conventions

Remember,
affirm the sufficient condition,
deny the necessary condition.

Now let's look at the other faulty form of conditional argument, denying the sufficient condition.

> [24] All my roommates are natural science majors.
> Tariq is not my roommate.
> Therefore, Tariq is not a natural science major.

The first premise states that all of my roommates are natural science majors—in other words, knowing that someone is my roommate is sufficient for knowing that person's major. It does not state that every natural science major is my roommate! Example [24] denies a sufficient condition. It's entirely possible that even though Tariq is not one of my roommates, he's a natural science major.

It is important to remember the two good forms and the two bad forms. For a good argument, affirm the sufficient; deny the necessary.

Practice with Conditional Arguments

All conditional arguments have two main premises and a conclusion. One premise states the necessary and sufficient conditions. The other premise affirms or denies one of the conditions. Conditional arguments can include subarguments in support of one of the two standard premises, or the necessary-sufficient argument can be the subargument. Regardless of what role the premises play, however, we approach all conditional arguments in the same way: we first identify the necessary and sufficient condition; then we determine whether the other premise affirms or denies the necessary or the sufficient condition.

> [25] If I win the lottery, then I ought to donate some money to charity. But I haven't won the lottery. So I'm not obliged to donate any money to charity.

REVIEW BOX 4.9
Conditional indicator words
if ... then, if, only if, all, only, unless

The first thing to notice about example [25] is the presence of the word *if*. The fact that example [25] contains an *if* doesn't mean that this is a conditional argument, but it does mean that this is a possibility. The *if* signals the premise that states the necessary and sufficient conditions. This is probably the easiest place to begin with conditional arguments. So,

> **[25a]** If I win the lottery, then I ought to donate some money to charity.
> *I win the lottery* = sufficient; *I ought to donate some money* = necessary.

All conditional premises involve two concepts, which we see stated in example [25a]. Now we know there must be another premise in the argument that affirms or denies either the sufficient or the necessary condition. In example [25], we see that the final sentence begins with the word *so*. Since *so* is a conclusion indicator, the final sentence can't be the premise we're looking for. It must be the second sentence.

> **[25b]** If I win the lottery, then I ought to donate some money to charity.
> I haven't won the lottery.
> Therefore, I'm not obliged to donate any money to charity.

The second premise *denies*, or says the opposite of, *I win the lottery*, which is, as we know, the sufficient condition. Example [25] denies the sufficient condition. As we know, denying the sufficient condition is bad. In this case, we can imagine that, although I haven't won the lottery, I have a great deal of money from earnings, inheritance, or gambling, and I ought to donate some of that to charity. Example [25] is a bad argument.

Here's another example:

> **[26]** Tim is home, because his lights are on, and they wouldn't be on if he weren't home.

First of all, find the necessary-sufficient premise. We see the word *if* near the end.

> **[26a]** The lights wouldn't be on if Tim weren't home.
> *Tim not home* = sufficient; *lights not on* = necessary.

Now we need another premise to affirm or deny either *Tim is not home* or *Tim's lights are not on*. We see both—which is the premise? Remember your indicator words for premises and conclusions. The second proposition says *because his lights are on*, and *because* indicates a premise. So we have

> [26b] The lights wouldn't be on if Tim weren't home.
> The lights are on.
> Tim is home.

The lights are on denies the necessary condition. Remember, *deny* means "say the opposite." If the necessary condition is *the lights are not on*, then we deny this by saying that the lights *are* on. Denying the necessary condition makes for a good argument.

Notice what example [26a] is really saying about Tim and his habits with the lights. Whenever the lights are on, Tim is home. He never forgets to switch them off when he goes out. But sometimes he's home when the lights are not on—perhaps when he's asleep.

There is another way to reconstruct this argument. We know that example [26a] could be stated equivalently as

> [26c] If the lights are on, then Tim is home.

Why? Remember that any sentence of the form *If not B then not A* can also be stated as *If A then B*. Because example [26c] is equivalent to example [26b], we could interpret the argument with example [26c] as the first premise. Then the second premise would affirm the sufficient condition. Any argument that denies a necessary condition could also be said to affirm a sufficient condition, and any argument that affirms a sufficient condition also denies a necessary condition. (The two bad forms are also equivalent to one another.)

Let's try one more argument.

> [27] I'll never go to Cedar Point. I wouldn't go there unless you paid me, because I hate amusement parks. But who would pay me to go to an amusement park?

We know that the first thing to do is to identify the necessary–sufficient premise. Look for the indicator word. In example [27], that's *unless*. So,

> [27a] I wouldn't go there unless you paid me.
> *I go to Cedar Point* = sufficient; *you pay me* = necessary

Where is the second premise, the one that affirms or denies? We have three choices: "I'll never go to Cedar Point," "I hate amusement parks," and the rhetorical question "Who would pay me?" Clearly "I hate amusement parks" is a premise—it starts with *because*. But we're looking for a premise that affirms or denies either the necessary or the sufficient condition. That's why it's important to determine the conditional premise first, because it tells us the two concepts in the conditional argument. In example [27a], we see that *I go to Cedar Point* and *you pay me* are the concepts that could be affirmed or denied. "I hate amusement parks" doesn't address either the necessary or the sufficient condition. In fact, "I hate amusement parks" is a subpremise supporting one of the main premises—it's a reason to believe that the only way you'll get me to go to Cedar Point is to pay me.

The rhetorical question is the second premise. As we know from Chapter 2, this rhetorical question is intended to mean "No one would pay me." In standardized form, the argument would look like this:

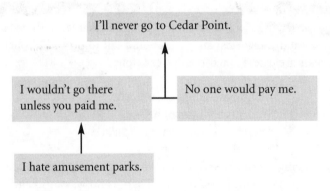

We see two linked main premises, as in any conditional argument, and a subpremise supporting one of those main premises.

> [27b]   1.1. I hate amusement parks.
> 1. I wouldn't go to Cedar Point unless you paid me.
> 2. No one would pay me
> Therefore, I'll never go to Cedar Point.

Does "No one would pay me" affirm or deny the necessary or the sufficient condition? It denies a necessary condition. That makes example [27] a good argument.

You may think that example [27] is a silly argument to spend much time on, but think about the various figures of speech people use that are similar to "I wouldn't do that unless you paid me": "If that's true, I'll eat my hat," or "I'm a monkey's uncle." These figures of speech imply an argument very much like example [27]. There is in each case a premise—usually implicit—that I am not going to eat my hat or that I am not a monkey's uncle. These figures of speech gain meaning from the implicit understanding that denying a necessary condition makes for a good argument.

Valid and Invalid Arguments

We have spoken so far of "bad" conditional arguments. Let's now consider in more detail what "bad" means for these arguments. In Chapters 3 and 4, we have looked at certain kinds of arguments known traditionally as **deductive arguments**. These are arguments in which, if the premises are true, the conclusion *must* be true. As we saw in Chapter 3, there is just no way that a valid categorical argument could fail to prove its conclusion if the premises are true. Remember our example:

> All human beings are mortal.
> Students are human beings.
> Therefore students are mortal.

If human beings really are all mortal, and if students really are human beings, then students must be mortal. There is no way to imagine even a science-fiction world in which the conclusion would not follow. It is sometimes said that deductive arguments are true in all possible worlds. That means that you may imagine flying horses, improbability drives, and time machines, but deductive arguments would still work for these things. Similarly, if it's true that, as in example [26], Tim never goes out and forgets to switch off his lights, then it must follow that Tim is home, given that his lights are on.

So does that mean we have to accept any argument that affirms a sufficient condition or denies a necessary condition? No. We can't fault the argument on its logic. But we can question the *truth* of the premise or premises, and we can question the *relevance* of the premises.

For example,

[28] If aliens had landed in my backyard last night, there would have been a crop circle. But there is no crop circle. Thus aliens must not have landed.

Example [28] is a good argument to the extent that it denies a necessary condition. Does that mean we accept the argument? No, not really. We may accept the truth of the conclusion that aliens did not land in the speaker's backyard, but we probably don't accept it on the basis of this argument. That aliens did not land is our default belief. We'd need a lot of proof to accept that aliens did land. The flaw in this argument is something we'll see in Chapter 6: the conclusion is more likely to be true than the premise is. We'd believe the conclusion anyway, without the argument.

An even more obviously flawed example is this:

[29] If I were an earthworm, I could fly. But I can't fly. So I'm not an earthworm.

Example [29] denies the necessary condition, and to that extent it's a good argument. Furthermore, it's true that I can't fly. But first, no one needs proof that I'm not an earthworm. Second, earthworms cannot fly. The conditional premise is false—it says that being an earthworm is sufficient for flying, but in fact being an earthworm is sufficient for not flying.

So what we're doing in this chapter is determining whether arguments are good or bad solely on the basis of what they affirm or deny. As we learn other reasons why arguments can fail, we'll see how to question the relevance and truth of the premises.

Arguments that affirm a sufficient condition or deny a necessary condition are called **valid** arguments. Arguments that deny a sufficient condition or affirm a necessary condition are called **invalid** arguments. *Valid* and *invalid* are terms that are used to evaluate the logical structure of a deductive argument. A valid argument is not necessarily a good argument in a wider sense, as

---

REVIEW BOX   4.10

Valid arguments

In a valid argument, if the premises are true, the conclusion must be true. However, these arguments can still be unacceptable, because of false or irrelevant premises. Validity is necessary, but not sufficient, for accepting a deductive argument.

examples [28] and [29] show. These arguments are "good" in a logical sense, but ultimately we have to consider more than this when evaluating the argument.

We could say that with conditional and categorical arguments, validity is necessary, but not sufficient, for accepting the argument.

▪ SUMMARY

At this point, you should be able to recognize a conditional statement, determine the conditions given by that statement (in whatever words it appears), and judge whether an argument is good or bad on the grounds of what condition it affirms or denies. You should try to develop the ability to do this quickly and automatically. The best way to learn this material is to practice. Do the exercises, identify your weaknesses, and then do the exercises again.

Though categorical and conditional arguments may seem less useful than other sorts of arguments, there are good reasons to learn about them. The most basic reason is negative: so that you never affirm a necessary condition or deny a sufficient condition. Mistakes like these make your argument worthless and make you look foolish. If someone else makes that sort of error, pointing it out is an easy and unanswerable way to refute the argument. The second reason is that recognizing an argument as a logically acceptable conditional argument prevents you from wasting time trying to criticize what really cannot be criticized. Instead, you'll look for a different sort of problem—the language used, the truth or relevance of the premises, or any of several other issues we'll go on to consider in the following chapters.

LEMUR Exercise 4.3

EXERCISE 4.5

For each of the following arguments,

  i.   standardize the argument;
 ii.   state the necessary and sufficient conditions; and
iii.   judge whether the argument is valid or invalid.

1. If it's not raining I don't need my umbrella. It's not raining, so I don't need my umbrella.

2. If there's someone in the kindergarten class who's allergic to peanuts, then peanut butter sandwiches will be banned. No one is allergic to peanuts. So peanut butter sandwiches will not be banned.

3. If you don't do well on your LSAT, you won't get into law school. Competition for entrance to law school is fierce. So study hard for your LSAT and do well on it, and you will get into law school.

4. If I don't remember to buy lemons, I won't be able to make dinner. Fortunately, I have the lemons right here, so I'll be able to make dinner.

5. The economy will go into decline if taxes are too high. It's obvious that the economy is in decline since people are being laid off and gross domestic product is going down. So taxes must be too high.

6. I have to buy a sports car because life is too short to drive something that corners like a hippopotamus. But that means that I can't go to Paris this summer, because if I buy a sports car I can't afford a trip too. [*Hint*: don't miss the main conclusion indicator!]

7. If the fetus has no legal rights, then a pregnant woman cannot be forced into a substance-abuse program against her will, even if her behavior will result in harm to the child when it is born. The Supreme Court of Canada, in addressing abortion, has ruled that the fetus is not a person, and thus has no legal rights. Therefore, a pregnant woman cannot be forced into a substance-abuse program.

8. There is an advertisement for a hair product that says "If it [the hair] is not strong, it's not beautiful." What do you think is the implicit premise? The implicit subconclusion? (The main conclusion is "Buy this product.") Is it a good argument?

9. The Zapruder film of John Kennedy's assassination appears to show that a single gunman could not have had time to fire a second shot between the moment that Kennedy first appeared to be hit and the moment that Texas governor John Connally, who was riding in the front seat, appeared to be hit. If there was a single gunman, and hence a single bullet that hit both men, we must accept the so-called "magic bullet" theory, according to which one bullet entered Kennedy's back,

exited through his throat, then continued on into the front seat, where it caused multiple wounds in Connally. This "magic bullet" was allegedly later found, virtually intact, on Connally's stretcher at the hospital. But it is unlikely that a bullet causing multiple injuries to two people, including smashing bones in Connally, could have survived almost intact. The trajectory that the bullet would have had to take is also implausible. Many bullet fragments were removed from Connally—more than could have come from the magic bullet found on the stretcher. It seems, then, that the failure of the magic bullet theory refutes the lone gunman hypothesis.

10. In December 1996, Jubal Brown, a student at the Ontario College of Art and Design (OCAD) in Toronto, conceived a performance art project that consisted of vomiting blue, red, and yellow on famous paintings in art museums. He vomited blue and red at the Museum of Modern Art in New York and at the Art Gallery of Ontario in Toronto, but did not complete the project with yellow. There was a demand by the directors of MOMA and AGO that OCAD expel Jubal Brown.

But if OCAD has a responsibility to encourage new thinking in the arts, they should reward, not punish, Mr. Brown's well-planned and successful project, which received wide media coverage. Punishing Mr. Brown would require that OCAD act contrary to its responsibility.

5 Language

OUR PRIMARY TOOL in speaking and writing is language. Language is so essential a part of our arguments that it's easy to regard words as no more than vehicles, and never think about language itself. But it's very important to be aware of the words that we're using in constructing arguments, and also the words that are being used in arguments we're reading or hearing. Words alone can even make an argument a bad one. Sometimes, as we'll see, the choice of words just weakens the argument; the flaws can be fixed. But sometimes, flaws in language can even be the kind of fatal flaws that we saw in fallacies of necessary and sufficient conditions.

We'll begin this chapter with a consideration of some types of definitions. Since definitions can often be important tools, we must learn to distinguish good ones from bad ones. Following that, we'll look at some common fallacies of language use.

▌ DEFINITIONS

It's not just nit-picking to argue over the use of terms. Sometimes you'll hear someone who is engaged in an argument say derisively, "That's just semantics." There's no such thing as "just" semantics, because the meaning of words plays such an important role in arguments.

Imagine that a friend says to you:

115

> If you're a liberal, you can't support the teaching of values in schools, not even values like "It's wrong to steal or to kill people." If you teach this sort of thing to children, you're interfering with their freedom, and as a liberal, you must believe in freedom.

How should you respond? First, you might ask your friend what she means by "liberal" (and ask yourself what you meant when you claimed to be one). You probably agree that individual freedom is important to your concept of liberalism, and that the freedom of the individual to determine himself is the most important consideration in evaluating a political system. Now, however, you must consider what is meant by "freedom of the individual to determine himself." Does it mean absolute, unlimited freedom to do anything whatsoever (within the laws of logic and physics, of course!); or does it mean freedom to pursue personal desires within the limits set by society? If you mean the former, then you should consider whether your friend's conclusion really follows from your position,[1] and ask whether you're willing to accept this conclusion. If it means the latter, then you may criticize your friend's conclusion that liberalism is inconsistent with teaching civic virtues to children.

This example shows how we can use terms without really dwelling on their meanings or their ramifications. Terms like "freedom" and "liberal" do not name simple concepts. Resisting their complexities restricts our understanding of their meanings; since they are important issues, restricting our understanding of them is dangerous and wrong.

You and your friend could have had a more thoughtful—but more cautious—discussion if you had first defined the terms you were using. In doing so, your positions would be clarified. You might find more similarities than differences between your views, and the differences that you did find would be real ones, based on an understanding of one another's meanings and intentions.

---

[1]Note that when we reject a position because of something unacceptable that follows from it, we're performing a good inference of the kind we saw in Chapter 4. We're saying *If* I accept this position, *then* I must accept this conclusion. But I do not accept this conclusion. Therefore, I cannot accept this position, either.

EXERCISE **5.1** DISCUSSION AND WRITING
                  ASSIGNMENT

The concept of *freedom* is central to U.S. political beliefs. What does it mean?

1. Read news reports or listen to political speeches that identify people as liberals or conservatives. What do these terms appear to mean for the people who use them? How do these meanings concern *freedom*? What consequences might these definitions have? How do the meanings differ? How do the consequences differ?

2. Ask your parents how they identified themselves politically during the 1960s and 1970s. Were they "liberal"? Ask what this meant for them. Ask what political position they regarded as opposed to theirs. Compare your parents' position with that of their opponents, in terms of *freedom*. What differences are there in beliefs? In actions? In consequences?

Stipulative Definitions

One sort of definition, the sort we find in a dictionary, is known as a *reportive* definition. It reports how the word is actually used. Dictionaries often list several interrelated meanings even for common words. Everyday language is enormously flexible, and context, familiarity with the speaker, and many other factors help us interpret it. A reportive definition can go wrong only if it fails to report how people actually use the word—for instance, defining "table" as "a small, soft-furred animal."

Although reportive definitions can raise interesting issues, we'll be more concerned here with **stipulative definitions**, which are more likely than reportive definitions to be used in arguments. Stipulative definitions establish or refine meaning for a particular purpose.

We frequently find that authors define the terms that they use. Terms are sometimes used in a slightly different—usually more precise—sense than in everyday language. We defined a term more precisely ourselves at the beginning of this book, when we defined an "argument" as an "attempt to justify a claim." We defined the term that way because the everyday use of "argument" can include quarrels or fights. Since we defined "argument" at the outset, it's not likely that anyone expects a discussion of what objects are acceptable to throw during fights.

A study that we'll see in the exercises for Chapter 9 starts off this way:

> [1] The study aimed to gain information about the distribution and seasonal movement of juvenile (sexually immature, age 0–3) herring in the Southern Gulf of St. Lawrence.

REVIEW BOX 5.1

Stipulative definitions

A stipulative definition establishes or restricts meaning for a particular purpose.

By defining "juvenile" herring as "sexually immature, age 0–3," the authors specify what their study encompasses. Thus the researchers know which herring to collect data on. Moreover, it's likely that many readers have no clear notion of what "juvenile" means for herring; this definition establishes which herring count as juvenile.

When you're writing a paper, there are two great virtues to stipulative definitions. First, they help you delimit your topic. Second, they guide the expectations of your reader so that your arguments receive the consideration you want. Stipulative definitions can also have a role to play in spoken arguments. For example, if you or your friend had defined "liberalism" at the outset of your argument above, you would have had a more productive discussion.

We often find precise, stipulative definitions in legal and government documents. One such example commonly found in college and university catalogs involves the legal definition of "student." In many cases, this definition reads something like the following:

> [2] A student is anyone registered in one or more regular courses.

The meaning assigned to the term "student" is important because only people who fit this definition qualify for financial aid. Without access to financial aid some people could not complete their degree. When understanding a term has ramifications this important, a precise, unambiguous definition is essential.

Evaluating Stipulative Definitions

In order to judge the adequacy of a stipulative definition, we must consider whether it is adequate to its intended purpose. Only relative to that purpose can we assess whether the definition is too broad, too narrow, or, strange as it may sound, both too broad and too narrow. A definition may be regarded as a means to determine which objects belong to the class named by the term, and a good definition will neither include anything that should not be named by that term, nor exclude anything that should be.

Example [2] defines the class of students as people who are registered in one or more regular courses. Clearly, the purpose of this definition is to specify precisely, for legal and financial purposes, who qualifies as a student of the institution that offers the definition. So the adequacy of the definition depends on whether it encompasses all and only the people that the institution wants to regard as students or instead commits the institution to undesirable consequences. We can see how to answer this question more clearly by looking at some inadequate definitions. Consider the following:

> [3] A students is anyone who is engaged in the process of learning.

Definition [3] would probably apply to most humans. Almost any conscious person is constantly learning new things about cars, work, human nature, and many other subjects. According to example [3], even someone who was not registered in any courses at any institution would qualify as a student. Why does this matter? Because according to this definition, almost any human being would be eligible for financial aid. That would be a ridiculous consequence. Since example [3] encompasses people who ought to be excluded from the class *student*, it is too broad.

Next, consider this definition:

> [4] A student is anyone who is registered full-time in a regular course of study.

Definition [4] obviously omits part-time students. Some institutions do not admit part-time students; this definition may be adequate to their purposes. But an institution wishing to admit and allow part-time students to qualify for financial aid would need a more inclusive definition—the definition given above in example [2], for instance.

What about the following example?

> [5] A student is anyone who regards him/herself primarily as a student.

REVIEW BOX 5.2

Definitions and their faults

A definition of a term *t* tells us what things are included in the class named by *t*.

- A definition that is too broad includes in that class things that ought not to be there.
- A definition that is too narrow excludes things that ought to be there.
- A definition that is too broad and too narrow includes some things it should exclude, and excludes some things it should include.

Definition [5] is both too broad and too narrow. First, it may exclude people who should perhaps be included. Someone who takes courses at night while continuing to hold down a job probably regards himself primarily as a teacher, manager, or programmer. Nevertheless, he is also a student. Moreover, example [5] may include people who should be excluded. Someone who has recently graduated and is looking for work may still think of herself as primarily a student.

Let's return briefly to example [1]. The authors provide two conditions that must be satisfied for a herring to be classified as "juvenile." It is likely that neither condition by itself would be adequate. For herring, as for other animals, sexual maturity may begin within a range of ages. So defining "juvenile" as "age 0–3" would probably include some herring that had already reached sexual maturity and were living the lives of adult herring. Similarly, "sexually immature" alone may include some herring that had failed to reach sexual maturity during the standard span. By establishing these two conditions, the authors have precisely stipulated what "juvenile herring" will mean in their study.

In summary, since we stipulate a definition for some purpose, we should consider whether it is adequate to that purpose. To make this judgment, we must consider whether the consequences of a definition are the ones intended. Does it include everything that should be included and exclude everything that should be excluded? And these questions can be answered only relative to its intended purpose.

EXERCISE 5.2

Identify any flaws that you find in the following definitions.

1. Coffee is a drink made from beans that you have in the morning.

2. A dictionary is a book where you look up words.

3. A stereo is what you use to play music.

4. In a study of the effects of maternal smoking, a smoker was defined as someone who reported having at least one puff of one cigarette during the last seven days.

5. The authors of a National Safe Workplace Institute study defined workplace violence as 1) violence against innocent people at a robbery, 2) violence against police and other law enforcement workers, 3) violence against spouses (perpetrated in the workplace because of a restraining order, for example), 4) violence against a past or present employer or coworker, 5) terrorism, for example the World Trade Center bombing. [From H. Bensimon, "Violence in the Workplace," *Training and Development*, vol. 48, no.1 (January 1994); 26–32.]

6. Sexual education is defined (by some) as teaching children the value-neutral "facts of life," including the process of procreation and the prevention of sexually transmitted diseases.

7. Sexual education is defined (by others) as teaching children the moral aspects of sexual relationships.

Operational Definitions

An **operational definition** is one very common and important type of stipulative definition. The following is an operational definition:

[6] The landlord may enter the rented premises when and only when 1) the tenant gives consent at the time of entry or 2) in case of an emergency that may result in damage to property.

Example [6] specifies two cases in which the landlord is permitted to enter a rented premise—it defines "permissible landlord entry." If a landlord were to enter the premises under other conditions, he would be breaking the contract that contains this definition. Notice three aspects of the definition: first, it states what are intended to be necessary and sufficient conditions for entry. The landlord may enter the premises in *all* cases of tenant consent or emergency and *only* in cases of tenant consent or emergency. Second, the definition specifies an *operation* that when performed, will establish whether the landlord was permitted to enter the premises. In this case, it is simple: ask whether the tenant agreed or there was an emergency that might have resulted in property damage. Third, there will ideally be definite *yes* or *no* answers to these questions. There's no gray area. Anyone would arrive at the same answer, and that answer is not open to personal interpretation.

Operational definitions are very important in cases where people must have enough information to determine whether an event or thing fits into a given category. If the issue is legal versus illegal entry, everyone concerned must know what to expect, according to precisely defined conditions, which are not subject to different feelings about personal privacy. Operational definitions are widely used in situations where lawsuits may result if there is misunderstanding.

Operationalization is also important to anyone who wants to measure something. An operational definition starts with a concept that we want to measure and gives a set of measurable criteria that will define the term for the intended purposes. This is especially tricky in fields like sociology, anthropology, or psychology, where what we want to measure is complex human behavior.

Measurement and operational definitions also pertain to the law, for example in the case of drunkenness. Saying colloquially that someone is drunk covers a lot of ground. In legal cases, however, an operational definition for drunkenness is required. Thus the practice is to measure someone's blood alcohol level. If this level is over a certain percentage, the person is legally drunk; if it's under that percentage, he's not. This is what drunkenness means for legal purposes, according to its legal definition. The operation is the blood alcohol test. There can still, of course, be some controversy about what percentage is acceptable. Does the definition omit people who are actually impaired by alcohol? Does it include people who are not impaired? Nevertheless, given the definition, we can obtain a definite *yes* or *no* answer to the question "Is this person drunk?"

A more complicated operational definition of a difficult and important term is IQ testing. Intelligence testing is an operationalization of the term "intelligence." The test is the operation. A multiple-choice test for intelligence determines whether people are intelligent according to the range in which their scores fall. That is what "intelligent" means. If we say that a person is a genius, that means that the person has taken the test and scored over 140. The virtue of this operationalization is that intelligence can be tested and that the testing results in a numerical value. A numerical value is easy to understand and easy to order (in other words, person A is more intelligent than person B if and only if A's score is significantly higher than B's).[2] The fact is that different people within the same society are likely to differ somewhat in gauging someone's intelligence, and the IQ test rules out this "subjective" aspect of ascriptions of intelligence. Once again, different people will arrive at the same answer by following the same procedure.

Criticisms of intelligence testing are often based on the operationalization that is being used. For example, people have said that the tests are culture-biased, because they rely upon background knowledge of Western culture, or because they reward skills more likely to have been learned in Western schools than in those of other cultures. For example, not everyone sees decontextualized geometric forms in the same way. This criticism says that the meaning of "intelligent" given by the IQ test is too narrow—it excludes people with different backgrounds who may be what we'd normally call intelligent.

[2]In this context, "significant" has a technical meaning, which we'll address fully in Chapter 9.

Notice that we're not in a position of having to construct, from the ground up, the meaning of "intelligent." We have an understanding of intelligence that we're attempting to make more precise and measurable. This colloquial understanding can serve as a guide in judging the justice of the proposed definition. Similarly, when we require an operational definition of drunkenness, we do not doubt our ability to judge, in the absence of a Breathalyzer, whether a friend ought to be allowed to drive home from a party. Rather, we need an established legal definition as a standard for making judgments on which everyone would agree. Again, we may disagree on the operationalization that should be used. But given that operational definition, we can all agree on whether it fits a given case.

We might also object that the operationalization of "intelligent" given by the IQ test is too narrow even within one culture. Howard Gardner, a proponent of the theory of multiple intelligences, says that intelligence tests measure only logical–mathematical intelligence. But there are other ways in which we understand people to be intelligent that the tests cannot measure. For example, some people are excellent athletes with an ability to perform physical tasks that the rest of us could not. Some people have musical intelligence that the rest of us envy; other people can understand and fix machines. Some people can intuit the emotions and motivations of others to a great extent. Some or all of these seem to reflect judgments we'd normally make of people's skills and abilities that IQ tests could not measure. Further, we might ask, as Howard Gardner does, whether these other types of intelligence could be operationalized at all.

Finally, we can ask whether IQ tests really measure what we mean to measure. (In Chapter 9, we'll call tests that measure what we mean to measure *valid tests*.) IQ tests measure developed ability, not latent ability. Some people, however, ask whether what we really mean by intelligence isn't what people actually do, but instead what they could do. (How much RAM they have, as it were, rather than how much space is taken up on their hard drives.)

All of this is important because the results of an IQ test may have serious consequences. When they are used in schools, children are often grouped according to their scores. If the IQ test represents a too-narrow definition of "intelligence," then some children may be treated unjustly. Someone with mechanical, musical, or emotional intelligence, rather than logical–mathematical intelligence, may be disadvantaged in school and thereby gain less education and set lower goals. Moreover, someone who has recently arrived in North America may be disadvantaged by a low score resulting from unfamiliarity with the culture.

In general, then, we can ask whether some concepts can even be operationalized, especially if their operational definitions have political or personal force. Though the virtues of operationalization are obvious, we may not be able to obtain numerical values for all important concepts without risking injustice.

EXERCISE 5.3

I. Which of the definitions in Exercise 5.2 are operational definitions? Why?
II. Try to construct an adequate operational definition of each for the following terms. Each is a term that needs a definition for legal purposes.

1. child

2. criminal

3. university

4. vehicle

5. sexual harassment

6. property owner

7. accident

8. tenant

■ FALLACIES OF LANGUAGE

Persuasive Definitions

Stipulative definitions are often good and useful. But one subset of stipulative definitions is common enough, and pernicious enough, to have its own name: **persuasive definition**. A persuasive definition is an attempt to gloss over a too-broad or too-narrow redefinition of a term where that redefinition is used as a premise in an argument. Like a stipulative definition, a persuasive definition restricts meaning for some purpose. But while the stipulative definition is stated by the author as a definition, the persuasive definition is usually smuggled in covertly, as though we all agree. It's important to notice persuasive definitions, because if we do not notice the redefinition of the term, we may not question whether the definition is an adequate one.

An example will be helpful.

> [7] The Internet is a bad thing. It claims to enable widespread communication, free speech, and a worldwide community, but actually it prevents people from real communication, which takes place face to face in a real physical community.

The arguer is trying to convince us that the Internet, rather than enabling communication as it claims to do, in fact prevents communication, and is therefore harmful. But example [7] redefines what we normally mean by the term "communication." It limits communication to whatever takes place face to face in a real physical community, thereby omitting mass media (newspapers, radios, books, magazines) as well as telephones and letters. The definition of "communication" in example [7] is too narrow by far. It's only by defining "communication" this way that the subconclusion—that the Internet does not enable communication—follows.

Words like "authentic," "genuine," "real," "true" suggest the presence of a persuasive definition. In example [7], we see the word "real." Note that these words, like the words that signal the presence of premises and conclusions, are neither necessary nor sufficient for us to conclude that a passage contains a persuasive definition. Not every use of "genuine," for example, occurs in a persuasive definition:

> [8] This is a genuine Hepplewhite table, so I can't afford it.

The use of "genuine" in example [8] means that the table is the real thing, not a reproduction, and that premise can support the conclusion that the speaker can't afford the table.

Here is another argument that does not have any indicator words, but that nevertheless contains a persuasive definition.

[9] Abortion is murdering a helpless baby, so abortion is wrong.

Example [9] contains a persuasive definition of "abortion." Clearly, if abortion really is murdering a helpless baby, then abortion is wrong. Those who believe that abortion is murdering a helpless baby believe that abortion is wrong. The difficulty is that not everyone agrees that abortion is murder. Someone who believes that it is must argue

> **REVIEW BOX   5.4**
>
> ## Persuasive definitions
>
> Persuasive definitions are disguised stipulative definitions, in which the redefinition of the term plays a crucial role in the argument.

for that position, not simply define it. In other words, the premise "Abortion is murdering a helpless baby" must be supported by a subargument. That cannot be presented as a definition, as if it were noncontroversial. If you understand English, then you know that defining "chair" as " a moveable seat for one" is reasonably adequate, and most English-speakers would agree. But there is no widespread agreement among English-speakers about whether abortion is murder, as shown by the controversy that surrounds this issue. So "murder" cannot be the meaning of the word. Nevertheless, speakers on both sides are aware that they are talking about the same thing when they use the word "abortion," so there must be a more neutral definition, on which both sides would agree, and that is the definition that must be used to permit a constructive exchange of views. The arguer in example [9] should define "abortion" in some neutral way, for example "voluntary termination of pregnancy," and then argue that abortion is murder.

Emotional Force in Language

The emotional force of language can be an issue in many contexts, and it's something that has to be closely examined whenever it appears.

Some expressions possess a warranted emotional force, because they name powerful aspects of human experience. These may be negative (for example, murder, illness, or destruction), or positive (for example, love, beauty, or freedom). Any of these expressions can affect our emotions, because of the positive or negative value we attach to the experience. If someone climbs a water tower with an automatic weapon and turns it on passersby, that person has commited a "mass murder." This phrase has emotional connotations because it names a horrible action. We all disapprove of mass murders and feel strongly when we hear about them. But "mass murder," though it has a powerful emotional force, is still the most neutral, customary, standard expression for this action in our language. "Mass murder" is what we call it. This term could be said to have warranted emotional force.

It is, of course, important to be aware of cases in which the subject-matter alone may affect our ability to judge an argument fairly. However, sometimes an author chooses even stronger words with the aim of swaying our emotions. For example, the prosecutor at the mass murderer's trial might speak of "vicious, random slaughter" as part of an attempt to inflame the jury and the media. The defense attorney, on the other hand, who would naturally want to diminish the hostility resulting from people's aversion to the action, might refer to the mass murder as an "incident."

Emotionally charged language is the use of words with *additional* affective force to influence the listener's or reader's emotions. **Euphemism**, on the other hand, is the use of language that deliberately carries *less* emotional force than the subject matter warrants. Neither is necessarily a flaw in an argument, but either can be used to hide flaws. Sometimes they are used to camouflage bad arguments; it is also possible that a perfectly reasonable argument underlies the words the author has chosen. Thus we must recognize words that could be working to either add or subtract emotional force, and "translate" them into neutral or standard terms. Only then can we determine whether they have affected our response to the argument.

Let's begin by considering some arguments that use emotionally charged language.

[10] If some misfit decides to blow his head off, why should I care? Any loser blames society for his problems. If he kills himself it's because he couldn't find a job. If he kills some old lady it's because of the violence on TV. Idiot social workers tell us that if we don't spend more money on social programs more losers will commit suicide, and it's society's fault. You can invent as many stupid handouts as you want, I'm not going to pay for any of it.

This passage obviously contains emotionally charged words that may influence our attitudes—"misfit," "loser," "idiot," "stupid," and "handout," for example. "Misfit" and "loser" suggest that the people so characterized are not valuable members of society, and thus their needs don't have to be considered. "Handout" suggests that any help offered them is not something they are owed. Now let's consider what premises and conclusions underlie this negatively charged language. The conclusion seems to be something along these lines: "I shouldn't have to pay for social programs." What reasons are being given to support this conclusion? That suicide isn't society's fault, and that the author doesn't care about these people.

The author offers no evidence to support his claim that suicide isn't society's fault or responsibility. Instead, he characterizes people who think that suicide *is* society's responsibility as "idiots." Someone reading or hearing this argument may think "I'm not an idiot; I'd better not support the position that suicide is society's fault." But it is unacceptable to attack a position by attacking the people who hold it. (We'll address this fallacy, and others like it, in Chapter 7.) Calling people idiots tells us nothing about why their position is wrong—it just repeats, in very strong language, that these people are wrong. There is also a negative characterization of people who commit suicide—they're losers and misfits. Example [10] is a bad argument, since, shorn of its emotional language, all it really says is

> [10a] I have a low opinion of people who commit suicide. I don't care about them. People who think society is to blame for suicide are wrong. Therefore, members of society, like me, should not have to pay for programs to prevent it.

This argument is unlikely to convince anyone. People who already agree with the arguer will have their beliefs reinforced. They will sympathize with the emotions he expresses. But someone with a detailed theory of the social causes of suicide will simply dismiss this argument. Remember, we argue to convince others and to arrive at a true or acceptable position. Example [10] could help us do neither.

Let's consider another argument.

> [11] The criminal definition of obscenity rests on the "accepted community standard." This is completely

> ridiculous. It means that whatever depraved acts are
> acceptable to AIDS-ridden perverts in Vancouver or
> New York thereby become the standard for decent
> communities. The more this filth appears in decent
> communities, the more inured we become to it, and
> this lowers the moral standard even more.

This passage also contains obvious emotional language. "Depraved,"
"AIDS-ridden perverts," and "filth" carry a negative emotional force. "This
is completely ridiculous" is a strong way of saying "I disagree." Also notice
the positive emotional language in this passage. "Decent communities"
suggests a dichotomy between communities of people with moral standards and immoral communities like Vancouver and New York. Positively
charged language can also influence our attitudes—we might think "I'm a
decent person; I'd better agree." If we translate example [11] into neutral
terms, we end up with

> [11a] The criminal definition of obscenity rests on "accept-
> ed community standards." "Community" should be
> interpreted to mean "local community." Decisions
> should be made locally not nationally. Some com-
> munities have different standards from others. The
> local standard is the one that should be respected.

This argument has more content than example [10]; it is not just an
expression of the author's emotions. But the author of example [11] has
actually weakened his argument by his choice of language. Is anyone who
disagrees with him likely to give his argument a fair hearing? On first
reading, it sounds as vicious as example [10]. Anyone who already agrees
with the author is likely to approve. However, as an attempt to change
people's minds, this argument will probably fail. Instead of insulting citizens of Vancouver and New York (citizens who have an equal stake in their
country's laws, and whose agreement would be required to change obscenity
standards), the author could have concentrated on anticipating and fore-
stalling objections. For example, he could show that some obscenity cases
have brought in standards radically different from those of the local communities, with harmful results. He could also argue that giving local communities the power to make these decisions would not result in injustice.

Here is a final example.

[12] Two doctors have been shot and killed by antiabortion activists. These activists have stalked and harassed abortion clinics' staff and patients, and have sent them death threats. Some staff are forced to wear bullet-proof vests, and they fear for their lives.

These murders show that this intolerable persecution of legal activities cannot be allowed to continue. Any rational person can see that these rabid activists must be stopped before their insane activities escalate.

In example [12], "intolerable," "rabid," and "insane" have a negative emotional force. "Any rational person" has a positive force—again, the arguer hopes you'll say "I'm a rational person; I'd better agree." In neutral terms, this passage says

[12a] Activists against abortion have committed acts that are legally crimes. The victims of those crimes are acting within their legal rights. Therefore, these activists should be stopped.

The use of emotionally charged language in example [12] is more difficult to evaluate. The main premise of the argument is that acting illegally to stop legal activities is wrong. This may not convince an antiabortion activist, but it would frame the debate in a way that could lead to productive discussion. The antiabortion activist may see abortion as a human rights violation, and argue accordingly that acting illegally to stop legal activities is not wrong where these legal activities are immoral. The antiabortion activist may draw an analogy between illegal activities against abortion and illegal activities against other human rights violations. We might ask whether using words like "rabid" and "insane" is likely to permit this discussion to take place. Probably not. If example [12] is part of a larger argument that this discussion must take place soon, these terms might incite people on the arguer's own side to take part in the discussion.

Insulting people who disagree with us is not likely to convince them. The most it can do is inspire fellow feeling in those who already agree. (Sometimes strong emotional language can bully people into agreeing, but forced agreement is not really conviction.) Using positive emotional terms to flatter the reader may have a better effect, but ultimately only the support that the premises give the conclusion determines how convincing our arguments are.

Let's turn now to euphemism. A euphemism is an agreeable or neutral expression that is substituted for one with negative connotations in order to hide or disguise warranted emotional force. Euphemisms used in arguments may obscure the issue, and thus make it difficult to tell whether the premises give good reasons for the conclusion.

Consider a massive layoff. The corporation's spokesperson may say something like this:

> [13] We're making exciting changes in our Capital City plant, to streamline operations. It's just part of our attempt to be more responsible to our shareholders.

Euphemistic statements need not be false. It's easy to imagine that production costs have increased, and that in order to maintain profits, costs have to be cut somewhere. It's possible that the layoff really does streamline operations, and even that the changes are exciting. But the corporation must also be aware that many people will regard the layoff as socially and economically devastating to the Capital City region, so the fact that the layoff has occurred is disguised by the statement. If you read or heard example [13], you would not know that two thousand people had just lost their jobs. Some people believe that large employers have a moral responsibility to their employees and the region in which they are located. Others believe that corporations are not ethical agents, but only economic agents. There are, clearly, arguments to be made on both sides. However, neither of these arguments can be made unless the issues are clear, and euphemism's main function is to guarantee that they are not. By making the changes sound like a purely positive development, then, this statement prevents criticism and the discussion that could follow from it.

We can imagine euphemism and emotionally charged language as two ends of the spectrum. In Table 1, the middle column contains our standard or neutral expression for the activity or event. Some of these standard expressions already have an emotional force because they refer to something negative, but we can imagine, in most cases, an even stronger

REVIEW BOX   5.6

Euphemisms

Euphemisms hide or disguise warranted emotional force, by replacing a term with negative connotations with a term with positive or no connotations.

expression being used. (It's hard to think of something stronger than "genocide.") These are listed in the column at the left. The column at the right contains a euphemism for the term. As you can see, the euphemism can put a positive spin on a negative event—"purification," for example, sounds as though it may be a good thing. Or the euphemism can obscure what the issue is. To say that John's had some problems is to leave many possibilities open.

TABLE 1.   EMOTIONAL FORCE

Emotionally Charged Expression	Standard Expression	Euphemism
vicious random slaughter	mass murder	incident
training people as disposable commodities	laying off workers	right-sizing, rationalizing
John was caught like the lying snake he is.	John was arrested for embezzlement.	John's had some problems lately.
??	genocide	purification, ethnic cleansing
state-sanctioned murder	war	military action

Sometimes euphemisms are used to trick people into agreeing to something that they would ordinarily reject. When you hear or read statements by government spokespersons or PR people, beware. If you don't understand what someone says, ask. If you ask, the worst that can happen is that someone makes you feel foolish. If you don't ask, you may passively assent to things that are wrong.

There are a few exceptions. For example, if John had been arrested for embezzlement and you were speaking to his mother, no one could object to your saying "I'm sorry to hear of John's *trouble*." His mother knows he's under arrest. At your uncle's funeral, you can tell your aunt "I can't believe he's *gone*." Your aunt knows your uncle is dead. Euphemisms are bad if they're being used to gloss over or conceal something to which you might object. But when used in good faith to spare the feelings of someone who understands what is really being discussed, they are a means for being polite and sensitive.

The words we choose can influence our practical decisions by influencing our emotions. In his book *The Rich Get Richer and the Poor Get Prison*,[3] Jeffrey Reiman argues that twice as many Americans die from unsafe or unhealthy workplace conditions as die from murder. He asks why we don't call these workplace-related deaths "murder" too. Your response to this may be that it doesn't matter what we call these workplace-related deaths; what matters is what we do about the conditions that lead to them. But now that we've discussed emotional force in language, ask yourself whether what we call something will actually affect what we do about it. Murder is something about which we feel strongly. Reiman asks us to think of the difference between seeing a headline claiming "25 Die in Mining Disaster" and one that says "Mining Company Murders 25." As he points out, "disaster" is an act of God or the work of impersonal forces beyond our control—something we can regret but not prevent. "Murder," on the other hand, suggests the existence of a murderer, who is responsible for these deaths. If we believe that at least some murders are the result of changeable social forces, it also suggests that these deaths could have been prevented. The words we choose matter.

[3] *The Rich Get Richer and the Poor Get Prison: Biology, Class, and Criminal Justice*, 2nd ed. New York: John Wiley and Sons, 1984.

EXERCISE 5.4 DISCUSSION AND WRITING ASSIGNMENT

1. A proposed expressway has produced controversy. In its favor: residents of a large bedroom community require a means to get to work, since some now commute for over three hours each way. The expressway will also create a large number of jobs in construction.

   Against it: because of the geography of the area, the only possible site for the expressway is through wetlands. The habitat for many animals and plants will be completely destroyed. Also because of the geographical situation, constructing the expressway will be expensive and may add as much as three hundred dollars a year to each resident's local taxes.

   Choose one or the other point of view—either for or against the expressway. Write two or three paragraphs arguing for your position, using emotionally charged language.

   Write a one- or two-paragraph response to this position from the point of view of the other side, using euphemisms.

2. Construct a chart like Table 1 above, listing terms with euphemistic and emotionally charged variations. Try to find some concepts that lack a term for one of the categories. Can this lack tell us anything about our attitudes toward the concept?

Ambiguity and Vagueness

Just as emotionally charged language and euphemism are two sides of the same coin, so are **ambiguity** and **vagueness**. An ambiguous term is one with two or more definite meanings. A vague term is one with no definite meaning.

There are two kinds of ambiguity: syntactic ambiguity and semantic ambiguity. In the case of syntactic ambiguity, an entire sentence can be taken in more than one way. In the case of semantic ambiguity, a word in the sentence can be taken in more than one way.

[14] I love logic more than my boyfriend.

Example [14] is syntactically ambiguous. Does it mean that the speaker loves logic more than her boyfriend loves logic? Or does it mean that she loves logic more than she loves her boyfriend? Either interpretation is possible. Syntactic ambiguity is very often found in newspaper headlines, probably because headline writers must convey a lot of information in just a few words. Example [15] is a headline.

[15] Elderly Often Burn Victims.

> REVIEW BOX 5.7
>
> **Ambiguity**
>
> SYNTACTIC AMBIGUITY: a sentence has more than one definite meaning.
>
> SEMANTIC AMBIGUITY: a word has more than one definite meaning.

This headline is intended to mean that the elderly are often the victims of burns, but could also be interpreted to mean that the elderly often burn their victims. If we read the story that accompanied the headline, the correct interpretation would probably be obvious. Even though the headline's context clarifies its meaning, this example shows us that syntactically ambiguous sentences can be funny when taken in the unintended sense. If we use syntactically ambiguous sentences in our writing, even if their intended meaning is clear in context, our point will often be lost on our reader, who is giggling about some unintended ambiguity.

In the case of semantic ambiguity, the meaning of the sentence is blurred by a particular word.

[16] Sarah gave Cheryl's notes to her sister.

In example [16], the problem is the word "her." If we already knew something about the people named in example [16], for instance that Cheryl has a sister but Sarah does not, the ambiguity would disappear. But many cases of semantic ambiguity do not permit such simple solutions.

Semantic ambiguity can result in bad arguments. The **fallacy of equivocation** occurs when an argument's conclusion depends on semantic ambiguity in the premises. A word is used in more than one sense, and the only reason that the premises appear to support the conclusion is that the two senses are not distinguished. Equivocation is an irreparable flaw in an argument.

This is an example that regularly appears in textbooks to illustrate the fallacy of equivocation:

> [17] 1. Only man is rational.
>   2. No woman is a man.
>   Therefore no woman is rational.

Here is an argument with an obviously false conclusion, but with apparently true premises. What went wrong? In Premise 1, "man" is used to mean "human being." If it were used to mean "male human being," the argument would beg the question, a fallacy we'll see in Chapter 6. In premise 2, "man" is used to mean "male human being." If it were used to mean "human being" the premise would be trivially false. Neither of these senses of "man" is wrong in isolation. But in example [17], these senses are conflated, or confused, resulting in a false conclusion.

Equivocation is sometimes found in advertising. A Gatorade advertisement features a picture of the basketball player Michael Jordan drinking Gatorade, with the slogan "Be like Mike." The argument might be standardized as

> [18] You want to be like Mike. [implicit]
>   If you drink Gatorade, you can be like Mike.
>   Therefore, buy Gatorade.

The equivocation here is in the word "like." It's true that if we drink Gatorade we'll be like Mike—in respect of drinking Gatorade (assuming he actually drinks it). But is that the way that we want to resemble him? Probably not. It's more likely that we want to resemble him in respect of his athletic ability. So the first premise must mean "You want to be an athlete like Mike." But the second premise must mean "You can be a Gatorade drinker like Mike."

> **REVIEW BOX   5.8**
>
> ## The fallacy of equivocation
>
> This fallacy occurs when a word is used in two different senses in an argument. The premises appear to support the conclusion only because these two senses are not distinguished.

In contrast to ambiguous terms, which have more than one definite meaning, vague terms have no definite meaning. What if you tell me your friend is depressed? Do I get a clear idea of his mental state? "Depressed" can have a wide range of meanings. Is your friend a little bit sad, or hospitalized? Is this chronic, or is it because he has three assignments due by Friday? Is it because his girlfriend has broken up with him, or because it's been raining for a week? In conversation, if you tell me your friend is depressed, I can ask questions such as these to narrow down your meaning. But in nonconversational forms of communication, questions aren't an option.

Arguments can be bad due to vague terms, too. Typically, vague terms occur in the premises. If terms that have no definite meaning are used in the premises, the premises cannot offer good reasons to believe the conclusion.

To determine whether a term is vague, we should ask whether the term has a definite meaning that most people would grasp. We can ask if we have clear truth-conditions for using the term. That is, do we have a clear picture of the circumstances in which we'd recognize the vague term as true or as false?

Vague terms are very common in advertising. Here's an example:

> [19] The Psychic Hotline can help you achieve personal growth by reaching into your soul! Psychics are gaining increasing success as personal counselors, advising people on their life choices. Psychics have even diagnosed puzzling medical conditions. Call today: only $3.99 a minute.

Since this is an advertisement, its conclusion is "Buy this product" or more specifically "Call today." Its premises, therefore, must give us reasons to call the Psychic Hotline for $3.99 a minute. But because many of the terms used are vague, the premises do not give us a clear idea of what we will get in return for that $3.99 a minute.

What is "personal growth"? This is a term that would mean many things to many people, depending on their values: it could mean a better job, a happy marriage, a religious experience, or fame. What are the truth-conditions for "reaching into my soul"—will I recognize when someone has reached into my soul? "Life choices" is vague, since I have many different kinds of life choices, some important, others trivial. In any case, why would that make me lay out $3.99 a minute? My friends and family can advise me on my life choices, whatever they are. What are these "puzzling medical conditions"? Is this a life-threatening condition or some strange rash? To whom are they puzzling—to me or to my doctors? We have no clear idea of what will happen on the telephone for $3.99 a minute. And this vagueness weakens the argument, since we are unlikely to spend money unless we know what we will get in return.

A notorious locus for vague terms is in occult or paranormal claims. Fortune-tellers, psychics, and card-readers all say things that are vague enough to be true of almost anyone, depending upon the interpretation put on it. Consider the horoscope in example [20]. Could it be an accurate description of your personality?

> [20] Although you have a serious side, you are fun-loving and enjoy social events. You are pulled between the demands and rewards of your career, and the less tangible rewards of your spiritual and emotional life. While you value material possessions and sensual pleasures, you also desire a deeper peace of mind.

No matter who you are, your personality probably matches this description. Most adults could claim to be torn between their work and their emotional lives, even though what they mean by this claim may vary. Similarly, most people like to have fun, and also have a serious side. But "fun" and "serious" mean different things to different people, and example [20] does not rule out any of those possible meanings. Finally, while most people want material possessions—though the particular possessions differ—they hate to think that's all there is to their lives.

James Randi, the debunker, did an experiment in which he gave a group of people, of different ages and different birth dates, personalized astrological readings similar to example [20]. He asked the subjects if the readings accurately described their personalities; most said they did. Then he revealed that everyone had been given the same "personalized" reading. While astrological or card readings (even vague ones) can perhaps benefit people by giving them the opportunity to reflect upon their lives and personalities, their obvious drawback is that they usually are filled with terms that are vague enough to cover a multitude of interpretations.

A recent trend in business has encouraged the formulation of "mission and vision" statements. These are customarily very vague statements such as:

> [21] We strive for excellence in the production of quality products.

You'll find these mission and vision statements on fast-food wrappers, on company letterhead, and in want ads for large corporations. The problem is that the same statement [20] could serve—and does—for burritos, steel, hazardous waste containers, and anything else that could be called a product. There is nothing wrong with trying to motivate employees and inspire customer loyalty. But a specific statement of quality and production controls would better serve that purpose.

SUMMARY

Be aware of the words used in an argument, whether it's an argument you're reading or hearing, or an argument you're constructing. Does the passage appeal to the emotions, or does it use the most neutral words it can? Is it likely to convince someone who doesn't already agree, or does it insult its opponents? Take a close look at how any argument defines its terms. Do you know what the passage is talking about? Do you have a clear idea of the truth-conditions for the terms?

Some fallacies are fatal flaws in arguments. For example, there's really no cure for equivocation. But if vagueness can be fixed by giving more information, make sure that you do so when you're writing an argument. If you're criticizing an argument, demand clarification where it's needed.

LEMUR Exercise 5.1

EXERCISE 5.5

Point out any flaws in the arguments below and give reasons for your decisions.

1. The right-wing stand on abortion disgusts me. It offends me as a woman. I refuse to let idiotic tyrannical male morons tell me how to run my life.

2. Saturday morning television shows for children glorify violence, introducing the poison of destructive impulses into minds too innocent and unformed to resist their diabolical force. These programs should be abolished.

3. The government shouldn't redefine "spouse" so that gay and lesbian couples are treated the same way as heterosexual couples. Of course, same-sex couples have the right to live together in privacy and this should not be interfered with. But we cannot treat them as families. This would have the effect of publicly endorsing or approving their private affairs. Giving them the status of a family degrades the traditional family and undermines family values. The traditional family is the foundation of our society. It is unfair to the traditional family to treat same-sex couples as if they were families. [Adapted from a letter to the editor, Toronto *Star*, 21 May 1994.]

4. In 1996, there was a strike by the Ontario Public Service Employees Union (OPSEU). OPSEU members had blocked access to the Legislature building. The following is an adapted version of a letter to the editor:

    How dare OPSEU hooligans deny access to the provincial Legislature to anyone. Start facing reality. Just showing up for work is no guarantee of a job anymore. Don't confuse your opinions with my rights. I have the right to go anywhere without being accosted by a bunch of screaming, unruly bozos.

5. I don't think there should be a controversy about whether same-sex adoption is right. "Right" is a relative word that means different things for different people. Who are we to decide what lifestyle is right?

6. How can anyone deny that we ought to take astrology seriously? The stars and the planets affect the earth: planets and stars exert gravitational attraction on us, and radiation from the sun reaches us constantly.

7. Thousands of beautiful unborn babies are being murdered every day at your expense. Your neighbors at Right to Life work ceaselessly to right this wrong, but our deluded and uncaring government has chosen to permit the slaughter of innocents to continue unabated. Won't you please help?

8. Technology is evil, because it makes people lose their jobs, destroys the environment, and pacifies all of us with stupid sitcoms on TV. We should fight against the increased use of technology. We should use typewriters instead of computers, for example.

9. A university president says: I've struck a committee, composed of administration, professors, and students, to ensure that the students here are guaranteed the best student experience they could possibly have.

10. University presidents should be hired from outside academia. A university is really a big company, and obviously it can't be run by someone who's been a professor all his life and has no concept of the real world.

II. The passage below concerns the meaning of the term "traditional family values." What does it suggest is the problem with supporting a "return" to these values?

Why would anyone want to return to "traditional family values"? What does this mean? Father as the breadwinner and mother at home looking after the children? This version of the family is a fairly recent invention. Before the First World War, middle-class women may have stayed at home but they didn't look after their children. A middle-class family employed nannies to do that. The working-class family was not "traditional" either. Women in these families usually took in laundry or hired themselves out to the middle classes to make ends meet. Without servants, washing, cooking, and cleaning in an era of large families and few labor-saving devices took up any remaining time. There would have been little time to spend with the children.

III. The passage below questions the meaning of what term? How is this term operationalized according to economists? How could the term be operationalized to take account of the factors that the author finds important?

In both Canada and the United States, news reports and politicians claim that the economy is "surging." Yet people at many income levels feel less prosperous than they used to; welfare recipients are diverting food money toward rent; food banks are regularly out of food because of a combination of more clients and fewer donors.

Michael Valpy [*Globe and Mail*, 3 October 1996] asked how we measure economic well-being. According to economists' measure of GDP (gross domestic product) growth, the economy is booming. The GDP measures what people consume—it measures money changing hands. But it does not measure environmental damage, the gulf between rich and poor, crime, social stress, numbers of homeless people, the kind of work people do, the decrease in full-time jobs, and so on. The GDP does not measure the quality of life.

6 Accepting Premises

WE'VE ALREADY SEEN EXAMPLES demonstrating the importance of premises in evaluating an argument. In Chapter 4, we saw that two things could go wrong with conditional arguments. They could affirm a consequent or deny an antecedent; these are problems with the argument's structure. Or they could have an acceptable structure but be assailable on the grounds of a false premise. In Chapter 5, we saw that some language could weaken premises: a premise that contains vague words cannot give a good reason to accept the conclusion because its meaning is not determinate.

As we know, premises support a conclusion. If there's something wrong with the premises, then there's no reason to accept the conclusion. We'll begin this chapter by looking at a few criteria that we can use to judge the acceptability of premises. We'll also see that disjunctive premises (premises that contain *or*) ought to be carefully considered whenever they appear. Finally, we'll examine the fallacy of begging the question—an argument flaw in which a premise is unacceptable because it presupposes the conclusion.

■ REASONS TO ACCEPT PREMISES

We have seen that some arguments contain subarguments, which support one of the premises of the main argument. You may remember this example from Chapter 2:

143

[1] If you care about the environment you will wear real fur. The manufacturing process of artificial fur creates chemical reactions which may be dangerous. Artificial fur is not biodegradable or recyclable: it will exist forever, polluting the earth. It cannot be disposed of by burning, because when burned it produces dioxins and other harmful gases. Artificial fur is more harmful to the environment than real fur.

One of the reasons supporting the claim that artificial fur is dangerous is that it will exist forever. The argument provides three subpremises supporting this premise. Together they point out that various normal means of disposal will not work for artificial fur. These subpremises strengthen the argument by making the premise they support more likely to be accepted.

In principle, any premise can be supported by a subargument. But in practice supporting every premise would be impossible. Nevertheless, in many cases, we do in fact ask why we should accept a premise. What we want is an argument in favor of that premise. The arguments that support premises can be evaluated as any argument would be, using the appropriate standards.

In a limited number of cases, these appropriate standards are different. If an argument's premise appeals to common knowledge, testimony, or authority, then the subargument supporting the premise must be evaluated by employing unique criteria. For example, if you're talking to a friend you might say "I know that course is hard, because Rahim told me." Here, you're relying on Rahim's testimony to support your conclusion that the course is hard. That is,

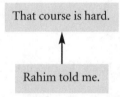

Your premise provides a good reason for accepting your conclusion only if your friend knows who Rahim is, and has some reason to believe that his claims about courses are reliable. The source and reliability of the testimony are considerations in evaluating the argument containing the testimony. Standardized, we see that these reasons to believe Rahim's testimony form a subargument supporting the main premise of the argument.

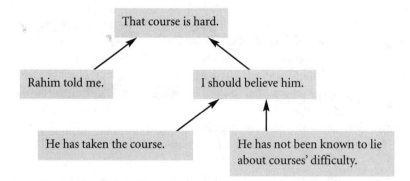

In this section, we'll learn what sorts of subpremises are used to support premises concerning testimony, authority, and common knowledge.

Usually, arguments that appeal to testimony, authority, or common knowledge can be replaced by arguments that do not appeal to one of these distinctive reasons. For example, the conclusion that the course is hard could also be supported this way:

> I know that course is hard because the students' union catalog reports that the grades are well below average, because there are thirty-seven books on the reading list, and because ten essays are required over the course of the term.

Your willingness to accept any premise should in any case depend on how much rides on it. If you're buying a new car, it's best not to rely entirely on your friend's claim that his uncle thinks it's a great car. You'd be as unreasonable to buy a car on that testimony alone as you would be to demand consumer surveys before you try a new candy bar. A car is a major purchase—you must continue making payments on it whether or not it turns out to be the right choice. Besides, your friend's uncle may value different things in cars than you. On the other hand, if you try a candy bar that you dislike, your life won't be altered by your choice.

Common Knowledge

Many claims are acceptable because they're **common knowledge**. For example, most people in our culture would probably accept "Acid rain is harmful to plants," or "Many people are opposed to abortion" without requiring a supporting argument. Other claims may be common knowledge among the members of a subgroup in the culture. For example, "In-line skating is a popular means of transportation" is likely to be common knowledge to urban-dwellers, but perhaps not to people who live outside cities. Claims may also be rejected because they are commonly known to be false—for instance, "Nobody believes in religion any more" or "Education doesn't raise your income expectations."

Let's look at an example of common knowledge used as a premise.

> [2] Since acid rain is harmful to plants, stricter controls on factory emissions should be imposed. If stricter controls are not imposed, many forests will be destroyed.

The conclusion of this argument is that stricter controls should be imposed. The reasons we're given to believe this are that acid rain is harmful to plants, and if it's not stopped, forests will be destroyed. If someone asked the arguer to support the premise that acid rain is harmful, he could respond in one of two ways: he could claim that the truth of this premise is common knowledge; or he could present evidence showing that forests have been destroyed by acid rain.

Here is another argument that uses commonly known propositions as premises:

> [3] It is likely that the issue of abortion will continue to be a potent one in U.S. politics. The fact that many people are opposed to abortion on religious grounds, combined with the lobbying power of large religious groups, means that no candidate can afford to ignore the issue.

In this argument, it's assumed that everyone knows that many people are opposed to abortion on religious grounds. If the arguer were asked to support that premise, she would probably find it difficult to imagine how anyone who reads the newspaper or watches the news could miss this fact; and an appropriate response to "How do you know?" would, again, be "It's common knowledge." Alternatively, though, the arguer could offer an argument based on opinion polls.

Strategies and Conventions

Using common knowledge

• Make sure the audience is likely to accept any unsupported premise in your argument.

• Know what evidence you could offer to support the premise if asked.

Both examples [1] and [2] contain premises that could be supported by two different types of subarguments. One appeals to the notion that the premise is commonly known. The alternative provides specific reasons to support the premise. We cannot avoid the appeal to common knowledge, nor, in many cases, would we benefit from trying to avoid it. In the case of examples [2] and [3], the main point of the argument could be lost if the arguer were sidetracked into a proof of the premise.

However, these arguments assume that the audience members share the knowledge employed. What counts as common knowledge depends on the audience. For example, it would be common knowledge to a group of advanced philosophy students that Descartes thought the mind was a substance; whereas to someone without much philosophy background the meaning, let alone the truth, of this claim might be unclear.

Some shared background is required to engage in argument. We should do all that we can to make our arguments accessible to our audience—especially in cases where some knowledge may not be shared. Remember that our goal in arguing is often to convince those who disagree. Anticipating the points on which we and the members of our audience will differ, as well as those on which we agree, strengthens our argument. We've already seen that we should avoid using value-laden terms when arguing about values. If we cannot agree on neutral definitions, there won't be enough shared meaning to permit us to argue fruitfully. In other words, we need to be sensitive to the values that we share with our audience. Similarly, if an argument relies upon shared knowledge, we ought to make sure that the knowledge really is shared, and, if necessary, provide a subargument to make the claim more plausible. However, we should not provide too much information. This can obscure our main point, or bore the audience so that they tune out before the main point is stated. If we know that we share particular knowledge with our audience, we can skip over subarguments for even fairly complex claims.

Be cautious, though: sometimes people think a proposition is commonly known to be true when it is actually false. It can be worth investigating the bases of widely held claims. For example, Christina Hoff Sommers, in her book *Who Stole Feminism?*,[1] recounts her attempts to trace the source of a widely repeated statistic that she found implausible. She had read in several books, and even in Ann Landers' advice column, that 150,000 girls and women die in the U.S. every year from eating disorders. This is more than three times the number of deaths than annually result from automobile accidents for the total population.

She found this number used as a premise in numerous arguments supporting various conclusions about the status of women. When she traced the source of this number to the American Anorexia and Bulimia Association, she found that the widely repeated claim of 150,000 deaths was simply a mistake. The Association had published information stating that 150,000 to 200,000 girls and women *suffer*, not die, from eating disorders. (Fatalities number from 100 to 400 deaths per year.) Clearly, it is not helpful to anyone suffering from anorexia or bulimia to publicize an inaccurate number that falsely suggests that trying recover from these disorders is almost impossible.

Sometimes a premise that could be supported by an appeal to common knowledge in one place and time could not be similarly supported in another. Women in obstetric hospitals used to frequently suffer and die from an infection called puerperal fever. In 1847, a doctor named Ignaz Semmelweis advanced the hypothesis that this disease was actually spread by doctors and medical students who customarily went directly from cutting up corpses to examining patients without washing their hands. He introduced a hand-washing policy for the staff, and as a result the mortality rate fell dramatically. To us, it's common knowledge that people ought

---

[1]New York: Touchstone, 1995, pp. 11–12.

to wash their hands to prevent the spread of germs. But before Semmelweis showed that hand-washing worked, this was not common knowledge even among medical doctors. It's not that disease works differently now than it did then. Rather it's that the concepts involved were not available to people in Semmelweis' time. When you appeal to common knowledge, you appeal to the best knowledge available to you, relative to the place and time in which you live—and that means that you could turn out to be wrong.

Testimony is someone's communication of his or her personal experience. Since none of us can personally experience everything in the world, testimony is unavoidable. For example, how you could know what your friend had for lunch today? You might know because you were there. Or you could rely on her testimony.

Testimony can be used as a premise in an argument:

> [4] The chair of the English department wants to limit class sizes. He told me that he plans to restrict the popular Shakespeare course to English majors.

Here, the reason for believing that the chair wants to limit class sizes is the account of what the chair said. The arguer has offered testimony about what he or she heard the chair say, and the chair has offered testimony about what he plans to do.

Testimony is unavoidable for two reasons. First, some propositions are difficult or even impossible to establish without it. If your friend had lunch alone in her apartment, there is probably no alternative to her testimony. Second, the difficulty of collecting the evidence may outweigh the value of the resulting knowledge. You probably wouldn't care enough about what your friend ate for lunch to gather alternative evidence, even if it's available.

There are three criteria that we can use to judge whether testimony is acceptable: the claim should be plausible; the speaker should be reliable; and the testimony should be restricted to the speaker's personal experience. Testimony is an acceptable reason for believing a premise only if these three criteria are met.

PLAUSIBILITY.   Is the claim something that could be true? Does it fit with what you know about the world? If your friend tells you she had a cheese sandwich for lunch, that's plausible. If she tells you she shared the sandwich with the ghost of Elvis, that's something else again.

If a claim is bizarre, we do in fact tend to reject the testimony. This is the most rational choice when the testimony is at odds with the experience of a lifetime. Your experience is your primary source of knowledge, and in the absence of an extremely strong reason to doubt it, you'll doubt the testimony instead. In the case of implausible testimony, you make an inference to the best explanation, and conclude that one person is wrong about one thing, rather than that you have been wrong about many things. In the particular case, one person's claim that she saw a ghost must be weighed against your lifetime experience, which includes no ghosts. If you've known people to have been wrong before, but you've never seen a ghost, then the experiential evidence is on the side of disbelieving the other person.

So how, you might wonder, could anyone ever prove something new—for example, that ghosts walk the earth or that there are alien visitors? This sort of proposition would be accepted on the grounds of an argument *containing* testimony, never on the grounds of testimony alone. As a start, we'd need a lot of testimony from a lot of different people. The argument would need to describe the means by which that testimony was collected—from whom, and under what conditions. The argument would also need to show that there is not a more plausible alternative explanation—for example, that several people had been taken in by one or more hoaxes.

Strategies and Conventions

Questions for evaluating testimony

• Is the claim plausible?

• Is the source reliable?

• Is the claim restricted to the speaker's personal experience?

If testimony concerns something about which there is some doubt—if there are differing eyewitness accounts, or if the testimony concerns something implausible—then a regular argument must be produced incorporating, but not limited to, the testimony. For example, we could look for evidence corroborating someone's testimony. However, when several people's testimony is collected, the result is an argument, and we'd believe the proposition in question as the conclusion of that argument, not on the grounds of testimony. Take, for example, a court case concerning a car accident, where three people who were present at the scene all remember something slightly different. People pay attention to different aspects of an event, and sometimes people see what they want or expect to see. In court, the varying witness accounts must be considered and an argument advanced in order to account for the differences and to explain why one account is more apt to be true than another.

RELIABILITY. Is the person giving the testimony reliable? Is there some reason to doubt this person? Has he or she lied to you before, for example? Some people are not unreliable in general, but only about some things. For example, if someone who is red-green color-blind told you he just bought a green sweater, you would have reason to doubt his claim. Testimony would not be adequate in this case—you would need other evidence, such as seeing the sweater yourself. Issues of reliability are obviously too complicated to exhaust in a comprehensive list. Personal knowledge of the speaker might permit you to judge whether he or she is likely to lie, exaggerate, or make mistakes; knowledge of people in general would help determine whether the issue in question is one that people tend to distort, for example their sex lives or their incomes. It is always possible to reject testimony, and to ask instead for other evidence.

Strategies and Conventions

Evaluate an argument even if you agree with its conclusion

Don't forget that there can be bad arguments for true propositions and good arguments for false ones. When we say an argument is bad, we say that the conclusion is not proven by *this* argument—it may be proven by another one.

Remember, what's at issue here is what premises you'll be willing to regard as providing good support for a conclusion. Sometimes, someone's premises are based on his personal experience. You'll want to look for ways in which that account of his personal experience might not be an adequate reason to believe the conclusion. If you're constructing an argument where one of the premises is your own testimony, keep the three criteria in mind. If you think your audience may doubt that one of the criteria is satisfied, provide a subargument to back up your testimony. Prove, for example, that you're reliable on this sort of matter.

RESTRICTED TO PERSONAL EXPERIENCE. Even if a claim seems plausible and the speaker seems reliable, testimony must be based on the speaker's own experience. If a fellow student tells you she enjoys her sociology class, or even if she makes the stronger claim that it's the best course she's ever taken, you should believe her. After all, she's in a better position than anyone else to judge this. But if she tells you that this course is the best the college has to offer, you can accept her claim as testimony only if she has taken every class the college has to offer—an unlikely possibility. (You'd probably also want to ask her what she means by "best class," since the quality of a class could have many facets: lively discussions, a highly organized prof who gives good notes, intrinsically interesting subject matter. . . .)

When you're constructing an argument using your own testimony as a premise, it is easy to be so convinced that a proposition is true that you state it even though it extends beyond your personal experience. This can happen if you and some of your friends have been strongly affected by similar experiences, and on that basis you overgeneralize to say that *everybody* has had or should have had this experience. For example, swimming competitively may be an important part of your life. You're likely then to have friends who also swim competitively, and who value the experience. On that basis, you may find yourself claiming that swimming is the best exercise, or that participating in a competitive sport can help people learn more about themselves. But such claims cannot be supported by your testimony. The strongest claims you could make restricted to your experience are that swimming has been good for you and that you enjoy competition. To make stronger claims, you'd need evidence that is more wide-ranging than the testimony of you and your friends. For example, a representative study of athletes and non-athletes could show the value of competition; data from kinesiology could show the value of swimming as exercise.

Be especially wary of third-hand testimony, in which the speaker recounts not personal experience, but rather that of a more distant person, for example a friend of a friend. Such an account cannot be accepted as the speaker's testimony, and an alternative argument is always required instead. However, since experience is our primary means of acquiring knowledge, the mere suggestion that someone experienced something can lend apparent credibility even to bizarre stories. Take, for example, urban legends, which are a particular type of story relying on third-hand testimony. Sometimes they are true, sometimes they are based on truth, and sometimes they are wholly invented, but in every case they claim a basis in experience. One that you may have heard is told by someone who knew someone—perhaps in another area—who knew someone who tried to dry a wet companion animal in the microwave, with the predictable and horrible result.

Even if you believed the story of the microwaved animal in eighth grade, you probably wouldn't believe it now. But there are adult versions of urban legends, too. One that you may have heard maintains that thieves hide under cars in mall parking lots. When you return to your car, they cut your Achilles tendon with a knife and steal your purchases. This story appears to have no basis in truth, but it is told all over North America. Again, the testimony is third-hand; it may involve, for example, the speaker's aunt's best friend.[2]

Authority

Anyone can give testimony about his or her own experience, but sometimes we need to rely on an **authority**—someone who knows more about a subject than most people. Without expert knowledge, we'd need to drastically reduce the number of arguments that we could accept. We can't possibly know everything; we can't construct an argument for every premise we might have to accept.

Consider Zack, for example. His neurologist tells him

> [5] The seizures are located in the right lobe of your brain. The CAT scan and MRI show no structural damage in that part of the brain. So it's impossible to predict the course of the epilepsy; the seizures could decrease or increase with time.

[2]You can read about many of these stories, and read arguments for and against their truth, in books by Cecil Adams and Jan Harold Brunvand. At the time of this writing you could also go to http://www.urbanlegends.com/. If that's gone, just use a popular search engine and search on *urban legend*.

Zack's basis for accepting the premises and the conclusion that they support, is that the neurologist is an expert on brain disorders, and the technicians who took the CAT scan and MRI are experts on interpreting these tests. The alternative to accepting the argument on the authority of the doctors and technicians is for Zack to become a neurologist himself, thereby gaining the knowledge to evaluate the premises and the strength of the argument supported by them.

However, it's likely that Zack, in his lifetime, will hear many arguments that require expert knowledge to evaluate. If he injures his knee playing football, he may hear arguments from his orthopedic surgeon; if his apartment is robbed and he wants compensation, he may hear arguments from his insurance company and his lawyer. Some of these arguments will need to be evaluated by considering the authority of the person who advances them—no one can gain expertise in all areas: life is too short.

People sometimes say that they won't accept something on authority; they want to know it for themselves. This is reasonable in some cases. If a particular subject is more interesting to you than any other, then naturally you'll want to gain knowledge about it for yourself. You might even make it your career or a primary leisure activity. But there will always be some premises that must be accepted on the basis of someone else's knowledge. The sense of "authority" to which people often object has a connotation of force: it implies someone who can compel you to obey. But this isn't what we mean by "authority." For our purposes, an authority is someone who possesses expert knowledge on a particular subject.

There may be some subjects on which expert knowledge is not possible. How to live a happy life is one example. You could gather advice on this from philosophers, family members, and other people you admire, but ultimately the decision is yours. But don't rule out the possibility of expert knowledge solely on the grounds that a subject is one about which you would prefer to reach your own conclusions. Paying attention to experts is one way of developing knowledge and thus making better decisions. You can disagree with a movie review, but keep in mind that the critic may have attended film school and has probably seen more movies than you will in your entire life. Consequently, it is likely that he knows far more than you do about the history of film and its techniques. So it is pointless to disagree with a movie review by saying "That's just his opinion." The critic's opinion is based on knowledge. If you want to challenge it, you must argue against the points he makes in his review—derivative plot, poor direction, continuity errors, and so on.

Although authority is indispensable, we should not accept it in all cases. Any appeal to authority must satisfy four criteria: (1) the authority must be identified; (2) the authority must be respectable; (3) the matter must be in this authority's field of expertise; (4) the matter must be one on which there is a consensus of experts.

Strategies and Conventions

Criteria for judging acceptability of authority

• The authority must be identified.

• The authority must be respectable.

• The matter must be in this authority's field of expertise.

• The matter must be one on which there is a consensus of experts.

THE AUTHORITY MUST BE IDENTIFIED.   Unless the authority is identified, we cannot judge whether the second and third criteria are satisfied. This is why, when you write a paper, you must cite your sources in your footnotes. Then your readers can judge the acceptability of the authorities on whom you base your argument.

THE AUTHORITY MUST BE RESPECTABLE.   There are standards of expertise in many fields: a degree such as a Ph.D. or an M.D., publication of research, membership in professional organizations, or awards such as Nobel prizes are a few examples. These standards represent judgments made by experts, and they provide us with a means for gauging an authority's work in a field where we are not qualified to make judgments ourselves.

THE MATTER MUST BE IN THIS AUTHORITY'S FIELD OF EXPERTISE.   An authority's credentials in one field do not qualify him or her to give an expert opinion on matters outside of that field. An actor is an expert on acting, not social issues, politics, or some other topic.

So, any claims he makes about issues that are not related to acting must be evaluated just like yours or mine. Someone who wins a Nobel prize in physics cannot be assumed to know about anything but physics; again, his arguments on other subjects have the same status as anyone else's.

THE MATTER MUST BE ONE ON WHICH THERE IS A CONSENSUS OF EXPERTS. An authority can be cited only in support of a claim about which all experts agree. This is why we are counseled to seek a second opinion after being diagnosed with a serious illness. The requirement of consensus means that you can't use authority as the basis for accepting a particular view about a controversial issue in the field. If the authorities possess the same credentials but hold different views, then there is no reason to accept the claims of one rather than another. Instead, you should state that the issue is controversial and give an account of the conflicting views.

Finally, even where all four criteria are satisfied, experts can still prove unreliable. They might, for instance, misinterpret or even falsify data—a university entomologist was quoted as saying, "We can't help but be influenced from time to time by our desire to see certain results happen in the lab."[3] The competitive process of getting research grants, for example, can put pressure on researchers to produce a fascinating result. Someone who has falsified his data cannot be cited as an authority; his arguments must be evaluated. Falsification is not always deliberate, however. Just as witnesses giving testimony may have seen what they expected to see, researchers, too, may see or interpret the results of an experiment or study in a way that is consistent with their expectations. Some features of research design—for example, double-blind studies, which we'll explore in Chapter 9—are intended to reduce the possibility of accidental falsification.

PROVISIONAL ACCEPTANCE.   Sometimes you don't know whether a premise is acceptable. For example, if someone told you that Vancouver has a greater annual rainfall than any city in North America, you probably couldn't accept or reject his claim without doing some research. And since the reference materials required for this research might not be right at your fingertips, your judgment would need to be suspended. In cases such as this, we can accept a premise provisionally; we consider the quality of

---

[3]Susan Benson, Mark Arax, and Rachel Burstein, "A Growing Concern," *Mother Jones* (February 1997): p. 43.

the argument provided that the premise is true. This amounts to saying "If the premise is acceptable, then I accept the conclusion." If it turns out that the argument contains a flaw outside of the questionable premise, the acceptability of the premise no longer matters.

> **LEMUR Exercise 6.1**

EXERCISE 6.1

I. We have considered several different reasons for accepting premises. We may accept a premise because of an appeal to common knowledge, testimony, or authority. In each case, there are specific criteria to satisfy. We may accept a premise because a subargument has been given apart from the conditions for these distinctive reasons. We may only accept a premise provisionally. Determine whether each of these criteria is appropriate for each of the following propositions. State why or why not.

Example

Immigration takes jobs away from citizens.

- This claim is not common knowledge, because it is not a belief that's held by everyone. Even if it were widely believed, the fact that many people have a tendency to xenophobia means that it may be false and should be further investigated.
- This could not possibly be testimony. One person's claim that he or she had lost a job to an immigrant could not provide support for a wide-ranging general claim. If a human resources manager at Company X told us, "I regularly fire people and hire immigrants to replace them," that could still not support this general claim—that would only give us information about Company X under this human resources manager. The process of collecting many workers' or many human resources managers' testimony would create an argument of a type we'll see in Chapter 9.
- A labor studies professor would be the sort of authority we could accept for this claim. We'd have to evaluate his argument unless all the experts agreed.

• We could accept the premise on the basis of an argument. This argument could give us comparative data on unemployment among people born in the country before and after waves of immigration.
• It could be accepted provisionally, if an expert was not available, if there was no consensus, or if we lacked the data to construct the argument.

1. Diesel engines are a significant contributor to acid rain.

2. Laila likes fish and chips.

3. The Goodyear blimp often returns home with bullet holes in it.

4. Cattle get bigger faster than they used to.

5. Bridge infrastructure has been chronically underfunded in North America.

6. Every event has a cause.

7. Siamese cats are beautiful, loyal, and noisy.

8. CDs encode their music with pits and lands.

9. There are 482 students in this class.

10. Wearing sunglasses without UV protection is more dangerous than not wearing sunglasses at all.

II.   For each of the propositions in part I, write an argument using this proposition as a premise. Decide what conclusion could most fairly be drawn from that premise. Provide subarguments to convince your readers that the premise should be accepted.

■ FALLACIES RESULTING FROM BAD PREMISES

If a premise is not acceptable because it fails to satisfy the conditions we've discussed, the argument is not a strong one. There are more factors to consider when looking at premises. First, there's a type of argument that bases its conclusion on a list of options or alternatives offered by a premise. In evaluating this sort of argument, we must make sure that the premise listing the alternatives is acceptable by asking whether all the alternatives have, in fact, been considered. And there's another important criterion for premises that we have mentioned but not fully considered: a premise must be more likely to be believed than the conclusion.

Dichotomy Arguments

[6] You're either rich or you're poor.

[7] Would you like fries, mashed potatoes, or salad?

Sentences like [6] and [7] that contain the word *or* are called **disjunctions**. Disjunctions state a number of options or alternatives, each called a disjunct. There can be any number of disjuncts greater than one in a disjunctive sentence—there are two in sentence [6]; three in sentence [7]. Notice also that each of sentences [6] and [7] implicitly suggest that only one of the disjuncts can be chosen. You can't be both rich and poor in the same sense at the same time. A restaurant would probably offer only one item from the list of fries, mashed potatoes, or salad as part of dinner—if you wanted more than one, you'd have to pay extra.

A **dichotomy argument** uses the implicitly restricted disjunction as a premise; one or more additional premises rule out all but one disjunct. The argument concludes that the remaining disjunct must be true.

For example,

[8] It must have been raining or snowing or sleeting or hailing earlier, because the streets and sidewalks and rooftops are wet. It couldn't be snow or sleet, because it's July. It couldn't be hail, because I would have heard it hitting the porch railing. So it must have rained earlier.

If we standardize this argument, we get

[8a]   1.1. The streets, sidewalks, and rooftops are wet.

1. It must have been raining or snowing or sleeting or hailing.

2.1. It's July.

2. It couldn't be snow or sleet.

3.1. I would have heard hail.
3. It couldn't be hail.
Therefore, it must have rained.

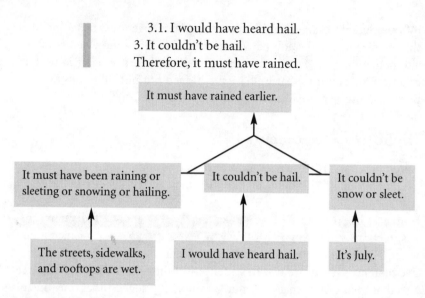

In example [8a], we see disjunctive premise 1, which gives us the alternatives: rain, snow, sleet, hail. Premises 2 and 3 (each supported by a subpremise) rule out snow, sleet, and hail. The only alternative we're left with is rain; so we conclude that it must have rained earlier. Note that in a dichotomy argument the main premises are *linked*; all are necessary to draw the conclusion.

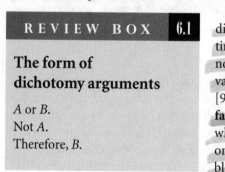

REVIEW BOX   6.1

The form of dichotomy arguments

A or B.
Not A.
Therefore, B.

The potential difficulty with dichotomy arguments is that sometimes the disjunctive premise does not state every option that is relevant to the issue. Take argument [9]. It's an example of the fallacy of **false dichotomy**, which results when the disjunctive premise has omitted at least one relevant plausible alternative.

[9] Despite the shortage of funds, we have to build a new highway to link the suburbs with the city. Congestion on the present roads makes commuting very difficult for people who live in the suburbs and work downtown. We can't allow the economic base of the city to decline, but it's either that or build a new highway.

We should start by identifying the disjunctive premise, since it is the easiest to find and also gives us a framework for standardizing the argument. We notice that there are two alternatives listed: *allow the economic base of the city to decline* and *build a new highway*. A dichotomy argument lists the alternatives and rules out all but one of them. So what alternative is ruled out in this argument? We see that the passage says "We can't allow the economic base of the city to decline." The main conclusion, then, is "We have to build a new highway." The argument standardized is this:

[9a]   1.1. Congestion makes commuting difficult.
1. We either allow the economic base of the city to decline or we build a new highway.
2. We can't allow the economic base of the city to decline.
[Counterconsideration: shortage of funds]
Therefore, we have to build a new highway.

We can see that this argument has the same basic form as all dichotomy arguments. The problem is not in its form but in the acceptability of its disjunctive premise. Are these really the only two choices? If you were at a city council meeting and this argument was advanced, could you suggest another alternative? Yes: public transit could be improved.

> ## REVIEW BOX 6.2
>
> ### Fallacy of false dichotomy
>
> The fallacy of false dichotomy occurs when a disjunctive premise falsely suggests that all possible alternatives relevant to the conclusion have been given.

That would allow people to get to work without adding to congestion and would cost less than building another highway. It may be that this option is not a realistic alternative either. But the argument would still have to establish that it's not; it cannot just omit what seems like a plausible alternative.

We can see the difference between examples [8] and [9]. Example [9] has omitted an alternative that it should have considered. Example [8], however, appears to have exhausted all the plausible reasons that the streets could be wet. There are other conceivable reasons why everything should be wet: for example, an airplane that puts out forest fires could have flown over the neighborhood and dropped its water accidentally—

but that's not very likely. We need only consider plausible alternatives. Similarly, we could say that another alternative for example [9] is that people will decide to ride horses to work. But again, though this is conceivable, it's not very likely, and thus not an alternative that we have to worry about.

It's not unusual for a dichotomy argument to have implicit or missing premises. For example,

> [10] Do you want to get good grades in school, or do you want to work in a low-paying job for the rest of your life?

This is clearly an argument. If your mother said this to you in high school, she clearly meant to argue for the conclusion "You should get good grades." If we were to standardize this argument, it would look something like this:

> [10a] 1. You either get good grades or you work in a low-paying job.
>   2. You wouldn't want a low-paying job. [implicit]
>   Therefore, you should get good grades. [implicit]

But this argument, too, commits a false dichotomy. Its disjunctive premise omits other realistic career plans. Someone could want to become an auto mechanic, for example. Then she does not need good grades so much as she needs experience and skill with cars, and the lack of good grades would not result in a low-paying job.

Finally, a false dichotomy can often appear as an "all or nothing" sort of argument.

> [11] You really don't think every student should be required to take a minimum of six critical thinking courses? I guess you think it's not important that students learn anything about critical thinking.

Our disjuncts may be more difficult to identify here. Example [11] suggests that there are two choices: take six critical thinking courses, or learn nothing at all about critical thinking. In an "all or nothing" argument, the missing alternative should be obvious. There's almost always a great deal of ground between everything and nothing. In example [11], it's clear that students who are required to take just one critical thinking course are still learning something. In fact example [11] leaves out every alternative less than six and greater than zero.

When you are faced with a false dichotomy and you want to claim that some plausible option has been omitted, your claim will be best supported if you suggest what that option is. Remember that you're really making an argument whenever you criticize an argument. Here you're saying this is a bad argument because it has omitted an alternative. Your premise—it has omitted an alternative—will be proven once and for all if you state what exactly has been left out. If you're constructing a dichotomy argument, obviously you should try not to omit any alternatives. That's easier said than done, but talking the issue over with a friend is one way to discover if you've forgotten a plausible alternative.

Begging the Question

Since an argument often works by leading its audience from propositions they already believe (the premises) to a proposition they don't believe yet (the conclusion), the premises should be more likely to be believed than the conclusion. If the premises are more doubtful than the conclusion, they don't provide good support for the conclusion, and the audience is unlikely to be convinced by the argument.

For example, consider argument [12].

> [12] I have seen the ghost of Elvis. Also, when I was picked up by an alien spacecraft last week, the aliens told me that Elvis is dead. Therefore, Elvis is dead.

This is not a very plausible argument, is it? You're probably already willing to believe that Elvis is dead, but far less willing to believe that the speaker is in contact with ghosts and aliens. Example [12] is a bad argument because the premises are less likely to be believed than the conclusion. In fact, the premises would need a detailed argument of their own in order for anyone to believe them.

Begging the question is a species of this flaw in reasoning. Some people lately use the expression "begs the question" colloquially to mean "rais-

Begging the question

Using a proposition *p* as a premise or an assumption in an argument intended to support *p* as a conclusion.

es the question." This is not what it means for us. In an argument that begs the question, the proposition that you want to prove is also used as a premise or as an assumption. Clearly, if the same proposition is used as both premise and conclusion, then the premises can't be more certain than the conclusion. A proposition cannot be more certain than itself. Moreover, if the premise states the same proposition as the conclusion, the argument does not lead the audience from accepted beliefs to something new. We'll look at three loosely demarcated ways in which an argument can beg the question.

The first, easiest kind of question-begging to identify is exemplified in [13]:

> [13] Not everyone can be famous, because it's impossible for all of us to be well-known.

In this example, the premise and conclusion are exactly the same proposition, stated in different words.

> [13a] 1. It's impossible for all of us to be well-known.
> Therefore, not everyone can be famous.

"All of us" means the same as "everyone." "Well-known" means the same as "famous." This is not a good argument—it does not lead us from something we already believe to something new. Would we accept the premise unless we already accepted the conclusion? No. Accepting the premise *is* accepting the conclusion, because they're the same proposition.

> [14] We all have an obligation to help those less fortunate than ourselves. It makes sense that a person who cannot provide for himself has the right to assistance from people with greater resources.

Strategies and Conventions

Identifying question-begging

Ask yourself this question:
Would I accept the premise if I didn't already accept the conclusion?
If you answer "no," the argument begs the question.

Example [14] begs the question in essentially the same way. The only difference in the premise and conclusion of example [14] is that they approach the issue from different directions. The premise speaks of the people who cannot provide for themselves in contrast to those with greater resources, and the conclusion speaks of those less fortunate than ourselves. The premise speaks of rights and the conclusion speaks of obligations. If you don't already accept the conclusion that we have an obligation to help the less fortunate, you will not accept the premise that the less fortunate people have a right to assistance from the more fortunate.

The more complicated the language becomes, the more plausible this sort of question-begging appears. If the premise and conclusion are both stated in long sentences containing long, perhaps unfamiliar, words, it's less likely that you'll notice that they say the same thing.

The next kind of question-begging is made evident only when we standardize the argument. It occurs when there is a subargument that makes sense only because of a missing premise or assumption. However, this missing premise or assumption is the conclusion of the main argument. Remember, if an argument begs the question, then the conclusion appears, somehow, among the premises.

> [15] I can't understand why some people think that God doesn't exist. It says in the Bible that God exists, and you have to believe the Bible because it's the word of God.

We should recognize this passage as a counterargument arguing against people who think that God does not exist. So its conclusion is something like "God exists." The reason given for believing that God exists is that the Bible says God exists. The argument also gives a subargument to support the premise that the Bible is something that you should believe. The sub-premise is that the Bible is the word of God. Example [15] standardized, then, looks like this:

> [15a]   1.1. The Bible is the word of God.
>   1. You have to believe the Bible.
>   2. It says in the Bible that God exists.
>   Therefore, God exists.

What is wrong with this argument? We see the problem when we examine the subargument. The only way that "The Bible is the word of God" could support the claim "You have to believe the Bible" is if we assume the conclusion that God exists. Would I believe the premise that I have to believe the Bible unless I already believed the conclusion that God exists? No. The word of a nonexistent being would not carry much weight. The conclusion is not explicitly stated as a premise. Instead, it is *assumed* by the premises.

Here is another, more complicated, example of an argument in which the conclusion appears as an assumption necessary in a subargument.

> [16] It is well-known that men are more intelligent than women, since their heads are bigger and thus their brain size is larger. Clearly, then, brain size is correlated with intelligence, since the evidence shows that people with larger brains are also more intelligent.

There are two candidates for the main conclusion of example [16]: one is "Men are more intelligent than women" and the other is "Brain size is correlated with intelligence." The second proposition is a better choice for the main conclusion because it is introduced by *then*, indicating that a further conclusion has been drawn.

Given "Brain size is correlated with intelligence" as a main conclusion, what main premise or premises support it? The main conclusion is followed by a clause beginning with *since*, so that clause must contain a main premise. Thus our standardization begins like this:

> [16a] 1. People with bigger brains are more intelligent.
>   Therefore, brain size is correlated with intelligence.

Example [16a] in isolation would not be a question-begging argument. If we could assert that people with the bigger brains are more intelligent, we really would have established that brain size and intelligence go together. For example, we might have collected data on people's intelligence, (and we'd have to operationalize "intelligence" adequately to know what we were looking for). Then we might have waited for these people to die and cut them up to investigate their brain size. By discovering that in general the more intelligent people had bigger brains, we could support the conclusion that brain size and intelligence were correlated.

But example [16] does not establish its main premise by giving details of a study like the one suggested above. Instead, the reason that we're given to believe that the people with the big brains are more intelligent is that men are more intelligent than women. And the reason the argument gives us to believe that men are more intelligent than women is that men's heads are bigger. This is the standardization of the subargument:

> [16b]   1.1. Men's heads are bigger.
> 1. Their brains are larger.
> Therefore, men are more intelligent than women.

Example [16b] does not, taken on its own, beg the question either. It does, however, have a significant missing premise or assumption that is required to draw this conclusion from these premises. That missing premise or assumption must link large brains with intelligence—in fact, the missing premise is the conclusion of the main argument.

The full standardization of example [16] is this:

> [16c] ⌈   1.1.1.1. Men's heads are bigger.
> | 1.1.1. Their brains are larger.
> ⌊ 1.1. Men are more intelligent than women.
> 1. People with larger brains are more intelligent.
> Therefore, brain size is correlated with intelligence.

It is only by assuming the correlation between brain size and intelligence that we can make sense of the subargument (bracketed in example [16c]), which in turn is used to draw the conclusion that there is a correlation between brain size and intelligence.

The third kind of question-begging argument is the most difficult, but it's also the one that you're most likely to see—and perhaps to be fooled by—in your reading. This kind of argument involves a theory or a principle that is being advanced and supported. A counterexample or counterconsideration is raised. The argument refutes the counterexample by appealing to the theory. This qualifies as question-begging because the counterexample is an attempt to refute the theory. Using the theory to refute the counterexample assumes that the theory is true.

> [17] We can prove that the world was created over the course of six days, six thousand years ago. We know this because the Bible tells us the world was created in six days, and because James Ussher, in the seventeenth century, estimated the years that must have elapsed since creation by counting up the generations in the book of Numbers. Some people disagree with this conclusion, because carbon dating and other methods estimate the age of dinosaur bones to be older than six thousand years. This shows us that, despite its wide acceptance, carbon dating must be inaccurate, because it's impossible for anything to be older than six thousand years.

This is an argument for the conclusion that the world was created in six days, six thousand years ago. The premises supporting this conclusion are that the Bible tells us of the six days, and Ussher calculated that creation must have occurred six thousand years ago. Then there is a counterexample, or a proposition that would count against the truth of this conclusion—the fact that there are dinosaur bones that appear to be older than six thousand years. The refutation of this counterexample appeals to the impossibility of anything being older than six thousand years.

> [17a] 1. The Bible tells us the world was created in six days.
> 2. Ussher estimated that creation took place six thousand years ago.
> *Counterexample*: Carbon-dating of dinosaur bones
> *Against counterexample*: It is impossible for anything to be older than six thousand years.

> Thus, carbon-dating is inaccurate.
> Therefore, the world was created in six days, six thousand years ago.

The problem with this argument is that its refutation of the counterexample begs the question. The main argument—premises 1 and 2 and the main conclusion—does not beg the question. The question-begging appears in the argument's refutation of the counterexample. This refutation is part of the argument for the main conclusion. Hence, appealing to the main conclusion in order to refute the counterexample begs the question in a way very similar to assuming the main conclusion in [15] and [16]. In the argument against the counterexample, bracketed in the standardization above, we would only believe the premise "It is impossible for anything to be older than six thousand years" if we already believed the main conclusion that the world is no older than six thousand years. If someone tries to refute a theory, the refutation cannot be answered by appealing to the theory. Naturally, according to the theory the counterexample is mistaken. It is necessary to find grounds independent of the theory that would answer the counterexample. Example [17] would have to argue against carbon-dating on some other grounds.

SUMMARY

Since an argument works by supporting its conclusion with its premises, the conclusion lacks support if the premises are faulty ones. In criticizing an argument, examine the premises carefully. What reasons do we have for believing these premises? Do they appeal to a common belief that is actually false? If a premise is supported by testimony or expert knowledge, are the relevant criteria met? If a premise purports to give alternatives, has it omitted any? Always be sure that the premises do not assume their conclusion.

In constructing an argument, remember that your premises are the foundations of your arguments. Be accurate. If you are reporting someone else's views as an appeal to expert knowledge, get those views right. If you are basing your arguments on personal experience, ask yourself, first, why your readers or hearers ought to believe you—should you provide any account of your reliability? Second, ask yourself whether the experience you're reporting is adequate to draw the conclusion that you're trying to support. If you're constructing a dichotomy argument, be sure that your belief in the conclusion has not led you to omit a plausible alternative. If you don't consider it in your argument, it's likely that your audience will force you to consider it later. Be sure that you're not so convinced of your conclusion that you assume it in a premise.

LEMUR Exercise 6.2

EXERCISE 6.2

Identify any flaws in the following passages.

1. We must conclude that homosexual marriage is unnatural. Marriage is a state-sanctioned union intended for procreation. The state can never sanction an unnatural union like a homosexual marriage.

2. Our labor dispute is going to mediation, but mediation never works, so we'd better prepare for a long strike.

3. Religion is a waste of time and energy that could otherwise be used to improve the world. Every minute of prayer is a minute of unproductive idleness.

Strategies and Conventions

"Criterion" and "criteria"

Criterion is singular.
Criteria is plural.
"His testimony does not satisfy the criterion of plausibility."
"The appeal to authority satisfies all four criteria we've studied."

Similarly, *phenomenon* is singular and *phenomena* is plural.

4. "Animal rights" is nothing but lies and propaganda. Many leading health organizations recommend eating five to seven ounces of lean meat daily. Beef provides essential nutrients like iron. Animal rights terrorists have committed damage amounting to millions of dollars at research facili-

ties. The FBI considers them a terrorist threat. Is it that hard to see who's worse? On the one hand, someone following a diet recommended by health organizations; on the other hand, terrorists.

5. More deaths occurred on the highways in the last five years than on railways in ninety years. There are too many accidents with trucks on the highways. It's time to put the thousands of miles of railways tracks back in service.

6. We have the right to do whatever we have to do to maximize profits for our shareholders. The union must accept our choices: either layoffs or outsourcing.

7. If you care about the environment, you will wear real fur. The manufacturing process of artificial fur creates chemical reactions that may be dangerous. Artificial fur is not biodegradable or recyclable: it will exist forever, polluting the earth. It cannot be disposed of by burning, because when burned it produces dioxins and other harmful gases. Artificial fur is more harmful to the environment than real fur.

8. People argue against abortion on the grounds that it amounts to killing a baby. But they're wrong. The fetus is not the same as a baby. If it were, we wouldn't permit abortion. The reason why abortion is legal is that people recognize that the fetus is not a baby.

9. Our actions are not the result of free choice. They are determined by forces acting on us. The strongest motive that acts on us is the one that determines our actions. For example, the strongest motive is usually self-preservation. Sometimes it might *seem* as though we act on a weaker motive. For example, people race into burning buildings to save others, endangering themselves. But that just shows that we are not very good at determining how strong motives are. In this example, what seemed like the weaker motive must actually have been the stronger one, since it determined someone's actions.

7 Relevance

IT'S A NECESSARY CONDITION for a good argument that the premises be positively relevant to the conclusion. That means that the premises must work towards proving the conclusion. Do you think this goes without saying? In this chapter we'll see many superficially plausible ways in which irrelevant premises are used in arguments and counterarguments.

There are three kinds of **relevance** relations possible between premises and the conclusion they are meant to support: positive relevance, negative relevance, and irrelevance. A **positively relevant** premise works to prove the conclusion. A **negatively relevant** premise works to disprove the conclusion. And an **irrelevant** premise neither proves nor disproves the conclusion.

It is important to be clear about the difference between negative relevance and irrelevance. Negative relevance is still a kind of relevance, it's just that the negatively relevant premise disproves rather than proves the conclusion. We've already seen negatively relevant premises in counterconsiderations. Negative relevance will also have a role to play in the next chapter, when we learn how to attack arguments from analogy. In this chapter, though, we'll concentrate on the difference between relevance and irrelevance. An irrelevant premise has nothing at all to say about the conclusion. But as we'll see, there are many ways to disguise the irrelevance of a premise.

Here is an example of an argument that suffers from irrelevance. When I was an undergraduate, one of my friends said this to me:

172

[1] I can't believe I got only a C-minus on this paper. That professor is so unfair. I worked on this paper and another one the same weekend, and I got a B-plus on the other one and a C-minus on this one. The same weekend! There's no explanation for that.

Here, the fact that my friend worked on two papers on the same weekend is meant as evidence that the C-minus was an unfair grade. But that premise is irrelevant to the conclusion. Grades are based on the quality of a paper—but when it was written proves nothing about whether the paper was a good one. To prove that she received an unfair grade, my friend would need to defend the quality of her paper.

There are many ways in which a premise can be irrelevant to the conclusion. We'll see several named fallacies of relevance in this chapter. But not every argument that contains an irrelevant premise fits one of these categories. In example [1], the premise is simply irrelevant—there is no connection between the premise and the conclusion.

There is no mechanical way to determine if an argument commits a fallacy of relevance. Two arguments may look similar, even though one contains a fallacy of relevance and one does not. We must consider the content of each argument individually, checking to see if its premises really do support its conclusion.

> REVIEW BOX   7.1
>
> **Relevance**
>
> • POSITIVE RELEVANCE: The premise works to prove the conclusion
>
> • NEGATIVE RELEVANCE: The premise works to disprove the conclusion.
>
> • IRRELEVANCE: The premise neither proves nor disproves the conclusion.

FALLACIES THAT OCCUR IN COUNTERARGUMENTS

When you see a counterargument, the first thing you should ask is whether the counterargument really does counter the original argument. That is, does the counterargument respond directly to the original's premises and conclusion? Does it interpret them fairly? Does it identify flaws contained in the original?

Editorials and letters to the editor are a good place to find counterarguments. If you read the editorial page of any newspaper for a week, you're almost guaranteed to see at least one of the fallacies we'll discuss in this section: the straw person fallacy, the *ad hominem* fallacy, and the *tu quoque* fallacy. Notice that the latter two have Latin names. That suggests that people have been making these sorts of mistakes for a long time.

Straw Person Fallacy

The **straw person fallacy** occurs when someone misrepresents an argument while trying to counter it. This fallacy may be committed in any counterargument—for example, a politician's response to another politician's platform, or a letter to the editor. You may commit this fallacy, too. When you write a paper for a course, you are frequently required to state and respond to someone else's argument. If you do not state that argument accurately, you may be committing a Straw Person fallacy.

REVIEW BOX 7.2

Straw person fallacy

This fallacy occurs when someone substitutes another position for the one actually at issue. There are two ways to do this:

1. Misrepresent an opponent's position by substituting a position that is weaker and easier to refute than the position the opponent actually holds

2. Bring in extraneous matters related, but not relevant, to the matter at hand.

The straw person fallacy can be seen as a violation of the Principle of Charity, which requires that we interpret an argument in the most compelling way that it can be read. When you commit a straw person fallacy, you attack a similar but weaker version of the argument. (The fallacy probably derives its name from the fact that a person made of straw, such as a scarecrow, is easier to knock down than a real person.) This may sound like an advantage since attacking a weaker argument is easier. But if you misinterpret your opponent, your own argument is *irrelevant* because you haven't directly addressed the argument at hand.

There are two ways to commit the straw person fallacy. One is to misread the original argument—to pretend that it said something different from what it actually says. The other is to introduce extra material into the debate. This latter method may draw the opponent off track causing him to defend a new position instead of his original argument. It may also undermine his confidence by redirecting the argument to a more complicated set of topics.

This fallacy, like many others is not always committed deliberately. Many people just have a hard time sticking to the point.

Let's look at some examples. First, someone might commit a straw person fallacy by talking about a position that no one actually holds.

> [2] I can't believe these people who want to legalize drugs. They think human life is so trivial that it doesn't even matter if someone kills himself or ruins his health, as long as he gets to do what he wants.

We recognize this as a counterargument. Its conclusion is something like this: "People who want to legalize drugs are wrong." The passage does not explicitly state the argument that it opposes. However, it suggests that the argument for the legalization of drugs contains the premise that people should do whatever they want. It's unlikely that anyone would seriously argue in favor of the legalization of drugs on these grounds. A far stronger argument for legalization of drugs can be made on the grounds of social well-being: illegal drugs give rise to crime; many people die both as a result of drug-related violence and as a result of adulterated drugs, since illegal drugs are not subject to quality control; legalized drugs could be taxed to provide funds for rehabilitation programs, etc. There are many plausible arguments made for the legalization of drugs, and example [2] does not address any of them. The straw person argument has not advanced our understanding of the issue. The person who advanced argument [2] could have used the premise that supporters of legalized drugs trivialize life but he would have needed to show either that more lives would be lost to drugs or more social damage would be done if drugs were legalized than if they remain illegal.

In the following example, the counterargument not only misreads the original argument but does so in a way that invites discussion about topics that are strictly irrelevant to the debate.

[3] **Argument:**

Animals should not be harmed or killed for food or research, because animals are able to feel pain just as humans are.

Counterargument:

You're wrong. Animals aren't very much like humans. Animals cannot use language, cannot reason, and do not have art, religion, or a code of ethics.

The argument in example [3] opposes using animals for food or research, on the grounds that animals feel pain, just like humans. The counterargument, however, does not address the issue of pain at all. Instead, it speaks as if the original argument had claimed that animals are *just like* humans, and it points out respects in which they are not. It is easy to refute the statement that animals are like humans in every way—obviously, there are many respects in which they differ. But the original argument claimed only that animals feel pain like humans, and a relevant counterargument must concentrate on that respect, not introduce others.

The counterargument in example [3] is not a relevant response to the original argument. The person who offered the original argument might be drawn into a discussion about whether animals can use language and reason. He could find himself talking about whether Koko the gorilla actually uses sign language, whether a dog who can find hidden toys is able to reason, or other issues that might cause him to lose his train of thought and which do not advance the argument. In the case of example [3], the arguer making the original claim would be wisest to refuse this tangent altogether. He could say "I don't know about that, but my point was that animals can feel pain. Do you deny that they feel pain?"

Another way to draw people off topic is by making a joke. We do not need to be deadly serious all the time, and sometimes a joke can serve as a good refutation. In some cases, however, humor is used to deflect attention from the real point. For example, in a debate between Bishop Wilberforce and Thomas Huxley about whether evolution was an acceptable theory, the Bishop (who did not accept evolution) asked Huxley whether he was descended from the apes on his mother's side or his father's side. Of course proponents of evolution have never thought that we have apes in our family trees, so the Bishop's response misinterprets the position, and belittles it through humor. This tactic is widely used when arguments and counterarguments are made before an audience—in a political debate or an exchange of letters in the newspaper, for example. Once an audience has laughed at a position, its members are less likely to give it a serious hearing. Acknowledging the joke is a good idea because a common tactic of bullies is to claim that you have no sense of humor. (Of course, if the joke is a racist or sexist one intended to insult you or others, don't laugh. Object.)

Ad Hominem

"*Ad hominem*" is Latin for "against the person," and an ***ad hominem*** **fallacy** is an attempt to refute an argument by attacking the person or people who put it forth. Such attacks are irrelevant because the quality of the argument isn't necessarily related to the character of the arguer. A bad person can have a good argument; a good person can have a bad argument. Consider example [4]:

> [4] People who claim that hunting is wrong because it kills living things are just sentimental wimps who think that feelings are a substitute for facts.

The personality of those who argue against hunting is irrelevant to the issue. Even if they have seen *Bambi* fifteen times, they could still have a good argument. Here, their actual argument is not addressed, though it is mentioned. If you want to refute an argument, you have to present it accurately and respond point by point to its claims, not to the person making them.

Example [4] may have an element of the straw person fallacy as well. The premise reported as part of the antihunting argument—"It's wrong to kill living things"—is extremely strong. Carrots, for example, are living things too. Is it likely that anyone would support an argument against hunting with such a strong statement? Example [4] may not fairly represent an argument that an opponent of hunting might advance.

The sort of counterargument put forth in example [4] is called an **abusive *ad hominem***, since it consists entirely of abuse of the opponent. Notice that an abusive *ad hominem* argument often contains emotionally charged language—if you're insulting someone, you often use strong language to do it.

Another type of *ad hominem* argument, called a **circumstantial *ad hominem***, addresses not the personality but the circumstances of the arguer.

> [5] Did you hear Katie's paper on affirmative action? Big surprise she's in favor of it, when she's a woman who needs a job.

The idea is that Katie's argument doesn't matter because she's advancing it out of self-interest. But whether she will benefit from affirmative action is irrelevant to the quality of her argument. The attempted refutation in example [5] makes it sound as though Katie's argument is bad because the conclusion works to her advantage. But we can—fortunately!—argue cogently for courses of action that will benefit us. Consider, too, that if a middle-aged white male were to make the same argument for affirmative action, it could not be said that he was motivated by self-interest—the argument itself would have to be addressed. Since the same argument could come from different kinds of people, it is the argument, and not the person, that has to be considered.

Let's pause briefly to remind ourselves what we're doing here—there are so many layers of argument that it's easy to get a bit confused. The fallacies we are examining in this section are found in counterarguments. We evaluate a counterargument partly by considering how well it responds to an original argument. In a sense, our evaluation is a counter-counterargument. Another way to look at this is to imagine how the original argument could respond to the counterargument. Since arguments frequently go back and forth, with each person responding to the other, it's important to know what constitutes a good response.

Here's another example of the circumstantial *ad hominem*:

> [6] What's the story on this sudden boom in "green" products? The stores are full of products that claim to be environmentally friendly—detergent, cleaning products, paper products, food. The companies that produce these products know consumers will flock to buy them, because they think they'll be helping the environment. But don't be such a sucker—the manufacturers are just motivated by profit, as usual. They

didn't produce these things to help the environment—they produced them to take advantage of people.

What is example [6] arguing against? It is arguing against the manufacturer's argument, which has the conclusion "Buy this product" and the main premise "It's good for the environment." The conclusion of example [6] is something like "Don't be suckered into buying these products." The reason that the counterargument gives not to buy the products is that the manufacturer introduced them to make a profit. But that shouldn't come as any shock! The point of being a manufacturer is to make a profit. If we were put off by the profit motive, we'd never buy anything. To prove that people are suckers to buy these products, the argument must address the main premise of the original argument directly and show that the products are not better for the environment—that their packaging is just as excessive, that their method of production leads to just as much pollution and waste, or that the use of these cleaning products results in just as much chemical residue introduced into the sewer system. The premises here are simply irrelevant to proving the conclusion. The manufacturers' motives have nothing to do with whether these products are good or bad for the environment, as Katie's motives in example [5] had nothing to do with the quality of her argument for affirmative action.

This is not to say that manufacturers' motivations or desire to make a profit are always irrelevant to buying decisions. If, for example, the desire to make a profit leads to unfair labor practices or to the production of harmful goods because adhering to environmental laws is too costly, that information would be relevant to our decision—especially if we thought that not buying the products could send a message to the manufacturers about their

---

REVIEW BOX 7.3

Ad hominem fallacy

This fallacy occurs when someone attacks the person putting forth the argument, rather than the argument itself.

- An ABUSIVE *AD HOMINEM* attacks the personality of the opponent.

- A CIRCUMSTANTIAL *AD HOMINEM* suggests that something about the opponent's circumstances accounts for the position this person has advanced.

behavior. In that case, though, our objection would still not be to the desire to make a profit; it would be what that profit motive led to.

Here's another example of a circumstantial *ad hominem*:

> [7] Father O'Neill says that abortion is a mortal sin. He says that it is murder, just like killing any person would be, since the fetus has a soul from the moment of conception. But he is a Catholic priest, and priests are required to hold views like his, so I don't think we really have to take him seriously.

Example [7] suggests that the reason or motivation for Father O'Neill's argument is the fact that he is a Catholic priest. But first, the fact that the Catholic church is opposed to abortion need not be why any individual priest holds that view. He could just as easily have been convinced by an argument. Besides, whatever someone's motivation for holding a position might be, it's the argument for that position that needs to be addressed.

You must be cautious in judging whether an argument is an *ad hominem* argument or not. Sometimes the person's character is relevant to assessing what he says.

> [8] I don't believe Justin's claim that he didn't take the money that is missing from our company accounts. He was convicted of embezzlement before we agreed to give him a second chance, and he's lied to me before.

This argument looks like an *ad hominem* attack, but in fact it can more plausibly be seen as questioning Justin's testimony. As we saw in Chapter 6, some people are likely to be unreliable about some things. We would be wise not to take the word of a convicted embezzler and known liar as the only evidence for concluding that he did not take the money. On the other hand, we cannot conclude on the basis of Justin's character that he did take the money; we need evidence from some other source to make any decision. The arguer's character is relevant only when his testimony concerns a matter about which he is unreliable. (For example, we could not refute Justin's argument for affirmative action by saying "Why listen to him? He's an embezzler.")

In general, think carefully about any passage that presents you with information about someone's personality.

There's a certain version of the *ad hominem* attack that is called guilt by association. It does not directly insult the arguer's personality or circumstances, but instead links the arguer's position to one espoused by some undeniably bad person or group.

> [9] I find it a little odd that you'd support euthanasia for the seriously ill. That's one of the policies that Hitler supported.

Adolf Hitler was someone who thought and did bad things. But that doesn't mean you can never agree with anything that he might have believed. For example, you might like the music of Wagner, as Hitler did. Instead of trying to make the original position look suspicious by associating it with Hitler, the counterargument should address the arguer's reasons for supporting euthanasia.

Sometimes an insult is tailored to the arguer. In such instances, the response makes reference to someone that the arguer in particular—though not everyone—would think is bad.

> [10] **Argument:**
> You should come out and support the food bank. You could help box donations or distribute donations. Maybe you'd just like to make a donation. With the welfare cuts, we've got more and more people to feed.
>
> **Counterargument:**
> Sure, that's exactly what the government claims when they support the welfare cuts—put the onus on personal charity. You're buying into their plan.

The first thing to point out here is that it's only an insult to align someone with the current government position if he is not in fact a supporter of that position. In example [10], we'll assume that the counterarguer knows that the arguer is opposed to the government position; then the comparison can function as an *ad hominem* argument. In other words, sometimes the distastefulness of the comparison is relative to the position of the arguer.

The second, trickier, thing to point out is that both examples [9] and [10] could be made into arguments that do not commit fallacies of relevance. Example [9], for example, could be said to imply something like this:

> **[9a]** Euthanasia for the seriously ill entails a general lessening of regard for human life. If euthanasia were permitted, over time killing people off will come to seem standard practice. This could be shown by the fact that Hitler supported euthanasia, and Hitler had a pretty low regard for human life.

Similarly, the counterargument in example [10] might be interpreted as saying

> **[10a]** Part of the idea behind the welfare cuts is that welfare will be replaced by personal charity. By stepping up your commitment to the food bank, you're doing exactly what the government wanted you to do when they made those cuts. You could do more good by refusing to support the food bank and by spending more time protesting the cuts. If the food bank does not take up the slack, all those hungry people will become an increasing social problem, and the government will eventually be forced to help them.

Should we understand the arguments in examples [9] and [10] in the expanded form presented in examples [9a] and [10a]? This is a difficult question. (Example [9a] may commit the fallacy of Slippery Precedent anyway, as we'll learn in the next chapter.) How much does the Principle of Charity require us to add to an argument? Perhaps in these cases we should question the counterarguer to determine whether his reference to Hitler or to the opposite political position is intended to insult the arguer. Given the opportunity, perhaps the counterarguer would elaborate his position along the lines of examples [9a] and [10a]. The enlarged arguments could give rise to productive debate, in a way that the original arguments could not. On the other hand, the principle of charity does not require that we construct a good argument on our opponent's behalf—only that we avoid misinterpreting what he says.

When you suspect an *ad hominem* attack, your best strategy is to give the person who opposes your position an opportunity to explain his remarks in greater detail. This is easy to do when you are speaking to your opponent. In a nonconversational setting you should identify the suspected flaw in his counterargument. You might, for instance, say something like the following: "My opponent has linked my positions with Hitler's. Clearly this is irrelevant. It's possible, however, that he meant to draw a more detailed comparison." Then state (fairly!) what that more detailed comparison is and respond to it. This way you will be certain you've covered all your bases.

Tu Quoque

Another fallacy with a Latin name, *tu quoque* (pronounced "too kwo-kway") means "you too." This fallacy works by accusing the other person of hypocrisy. Hypocrisy is a bad thing, but it is often not relevant to the quality of someone's argument.

> [11] I can't believe you're telling me I should drink less. You drink at least as much as I do. You practically live on a barstool. In fact I've never seen you without a beer in your hand.

Clearly, this is a counterargument to an argument concluding "You drink too much." The problem with this response is that the original arguer's drinking habits have nothing to do with the truth of his claim that the person speaking in example [11] drinks too much. The arguer may even have more insight into drinking *because* of his own problems. He may wish he could cut down, but find that he can't.

The *tu quoque* fallacy also takes place when it is suggested that the counterarguer would, if given the opportunity, act in the way that he is criticizing. For example,

> [12] What's all the fuss about insider trading? Like anybody wouldn't do the same thing if they had a chance to make a million bucks.

> REVIEW BOX 7.4
>
> ***Tu quoque* fallacy**
>
> This fallacy is committed when someone accuses another person of holding a position that contradicts his actions.

Example [12] suggests that the people who argue against insider trading are "just as bad," and that the only reason that they do not actually commit the actions that they criticize is that they haven't had the chance.

There can also be passages that look like *tu quoque* arguments, but aren't. For example, if a trade agreement has been signed by two countries, A and B, and country A accuses country B of imposing overly high tariffs on importations of some product, country B can sometimes cogently respond with "So do you." If country A wants country B to abide by an agreement, then country B is justified in pointing out ways in which country A fails to abide by the same agreement. Here country B is merely insisting that the rules be fairly applied.

There is no general rule for determining whether an *ad hominem* or *tu quoque* fallacy has been committed. Each counterargument must be carefully considered.

The classification of fallacies can be a useful way to learn and recognize flaws in counterarguments, which frequently contain elements of more than one fallacy. Let's look at a few more examples.

First some background: A student in my course habitually forwarded long news items to the course e-mail account. They were not relevant to the course, since they were not arguments and contained no analysis by the student. My assistant sent the student an e-mail asking her to stop forwarding material. He pointed out that the account is always full of messages asking for help, and his time was limited. This was the student's reply:

> [13] Sorry. I thought it would be of interest to anyone who has heard of it. . . . I see why it wouldn't interest you. Please, don't e-mail me again that you have no time to read this—I get enough e-mail from people interested in the world outside these walls to bother reading your stuff.

The student's response is irrelevant to the assistant's original e-mail message. It has elements of a straw person response. The student has misrepresented the assistant's argument: he did not say that he was not interested; he said that the course account has a different purpose, and he has limited time. There is also an *ad hominem* element to the response—the suggestion that the assistant is not interested in the world outside these walls is intended to be insulting. But the student had no way of knowing anything about the assistant's interests, since they were neither featured in nor relevant to his response to the forwarded items. The student also suggested that the assistant was wasting her time by sending her unsolicited e-mail, when in fact the assistant was responding to her messages. (Why would he e-mail her again, unless she persisted in forwarding these items?)

Here is a final example. Commenting on Steve Forbes's chances in the 1996 South Carolina primary, Pat Buchanan said,

> [14] Steve Forbes is mistaken if he thinks he can fool the people of South Carolina.

Mr. Buchanan's statement is a premise in an argument meant to support the conclusion "Steve Forbes won't win this primary." There is no report of Mr. Forbes's arguments or positions—the assumption is that, whatever they are, they are not viable, and he is trying to fool the people in advocating them. There is an abusive *ad hominem* in the suggestion that Mr. Forbes's desire is to "fool" (rather than, say, to convince) the voters.

EXERCISE 7.1

For each of the following exchanges,

i. state the fallacy of relevance committed;
ii. suggest a relevant counterargument; and
iii. state the best response that the original arguer could offer to the counterargument given in the passage.

Example

Argument: I don't support the idea of lowering the blood alcohol level acceptable for driving to half of what it is at present, since this would mean that someone who had taken cough medicine would be over the legal limit.

Counterargument: I can't believe you think there's nothing wrong with drunk driving.

    i. This is a straw person argument, because it misrepresents the position of the original argument. The arguer did not oppose lowering the acceptable blood alcohol level on the grounds that drunk driving is okay; he opposed it on the grounds that someone driving with half the present level would not be drunk at all.

    ii. The counterarguer could have pointed out that many nonprescription drugs, including cough medicines, warn the user not to operate heavy machinery, and asked whether that warning could indicate that someone who has taken cough medicine is impaired.

    iii. The arguer could have responded to the irrelevant counterargument by saying something like this: "Of course I oppose drunk driving. My point was that these people aren't *drunk*. Do you think they're drunk? Why?"

1. *Argument:* Has anyone but me noticed that Woody the Cowboy in the movie *Toy Story* has an empty holster through the entire movie? The Woody doll also has an empty holster and so do the other merchandise figures. What an incredibly subtle and ingenious message!

    Counterargument: Oh, I'm really impressed with your plastic Disney morality. If you tried reading something more than the *TV Guide*, you might figure out that there are "subtle and ingenious" messages in those things called books.

2. The following exchange took place between a graduate student and a visiting speaker at a philosophy lecture.

    Graduate student: Doesn't your argument completely rely on the assumption of natural kinds [a thorny philosophical problem]? Isn't that a bit of a drawback?

    Speaker: Oh, you can hardly expect me to solve *that* problem in an hour, can you? Ha ha ha.

3. *Argument:* Drugs should be legalized, since legalization would probably result in less violent crime among drug dealers, as well as less street crime by drug users. There would be fewer deaths from AIDS and bad drugs as well.

    Counterargument: I can't believe you're not bothered by the idea of fourteen-year-olds addicted to crack.

4. *A student says:* You have to change the time of the tutorial. These tutorials are for us, not for you. They should be scheduled whenever it's convenient for us, not when *you're* free.

5. *Argument:* Children should not be physically disciplined or punished, since it teaches them that the ultimate decision is made by the person who has the most physical force.

   Counterargument: I'd like to know how many children *you've* raised. Anyone who's had children knows that physical punishment is the quickest and most effective way of doing things.

▪ MORE FALLACIES OF RELEVANCE

We're going to look at a few more common fallacies of relevance. The fallacies in the previous section appear exclusively in counterarguments. The fallacies in this section, however, can appear in any kind of argument. They attempt to support a conclusion by using premises that are not strictly relevant.

Irrelevance of all kinds is extemely common in advertisements. For example, many spray products like deodorants and hairspray have a drawing of a globe, the words "ozone friendly," and the claim "No CFCs." This is meant to be a reason to buy the product—it's safe for the environment. But CFCs have been banned as propellants for over a decade. Thus, the boast that a product does not contain them doesn't give us a reason to buy the product—it's true of all products. "No CFCs" does not prove ozone-friendliness either: the replacement propellent, while less harmful, still contributes to low-level ozone pollution.

Fallacious Appeal to Authority

In Chapter 6, we saw that expert knowledge sometimes serves as a reason to accept a premise. An acceptable appeal to expert knowledge must satisfy certain criteria: the authority has to be identified, recognized and respected, working in the field in question, and speaking on a topic about which there is a consensus. An appeal to authority that contravenes one of these conditions is a **fallacious appeal to authority.**

[15] It's ridiculous to believe in God. Stephen Hawking says religion is only superstition.

You cannot support a claim that God does or does not exist by appealing to Stephen Hawking. He is not an expert *in the field*. He is a physicist, not a philosopher or theologian. But also, there is no consensus on the issue of God's existence. So this claim simply cannot be made on the basis of an appeal to authority. We'd have to hear Stephen Hawking's arguments, and evaluate them as we would any other argument.

Advertisements for a fast food chain or for soda featuring famous athletes may make fallacious appeals to authority. Famous athletes have no more expertise than the rest of us in determining what tastes good. There is no consensus, certainly, about what fast food or what soda is best—that's truly a matter of taste. But advertisers assume that because you admire someone's athletic ability, you will trust his taste in food and drink. Authority, however, cannot be transferred from one field to another.

> ## REVIEW BOX　7.5
>
> ### Fallacious appeal to authority
>
> This fallacy is committed when someone supports a claim by appealing to an inappropriate authority—i.e., someone who fails to satisfy one or more of the criteria for authority given in Chapter 6.

The case in which a famous athlete advertises a product like athletic shoes is more difficult. Athletic shoes may be something about which athletes could be said to have some relevant expertise. We could even agree that a famous athlete has probably already worn out more shoes than you'll own in the next ten years. But there are still difficulties standing in the way of accepting the conclusion "Buy these shoes."

You might suggest that one of the difficulties is the fact that the famous athlete is being paid a truckload of money to make an endorsement. After all, you'd be willing to admire a pair of shoes on television for a million dollars and a sponsorship. But this is not the best criticism of the advertisement. If we said this, we'd run the risk of committing a circumstantial *ad hominem* argument. We'd be claiming that something about the athlete's circumstances accounted for his argument: since it's in his financial interests to advertise the shoes, we can dismiss what he says.

A better criticism of the advertisement would be based on the fact that there is no consensus about desirable qualities of athletic shoes, and therefore that this is not an issue in which an appeal to authority is ever properly used. The athlete could play a different sport from the one you do. He could be built in a different way. The comfort of shoes, too, is a matter of personal taste, and just because you like the athlete does not mean you will like his shoes.

Appeal to Tradition

The **appeal to tradition** offers as a premise something like, "We've always done it this way." But we need a cogent argument to believe something, not just a statement that it's always been this way. Maybe the way it's always been is wrong.

> [16] The discussion of the status of same-sex partnerships ignores one thing. Since prehistoric times, the family has always meant a male–female partnership intended for raising children. Who are we just to throw away countless years of family life for the sake of a selfish whim and a shallow desire to follow fashion?

Appeals to tradition are very common these days in arguments about the meaning of *family*. Regarding example [16], even if we accept provisionally the premise that *family* has always meant a male–female partnership intended for raising children, we still have no reason to conclude that this is what *family* should continue to mean. Tradition alone is neither good nor bad and cannot be used as a supporting premise in this way. We could imagine another argument that said

> [17] Throughout history, advanced civilizations have commonly practiced slavery. Who are we to throw away this tradition?

Naturally, we'd be unwilling to accept the argument in example [17]. Even if slavery were economically advantageous, it goes against any basic notion of human rights. The premise that slavery has traditionally been accepted is certainly not a good basis for accepting the conclusion that we ought to practice slavery in our own cultures today.

We might notice that there is also an *ad hominem* element in example [16], when the passage speaks of "selfish whim" and "shallow desire to follow fashion." "Selfish" and "shallow" are bad qualities. Suggesting that people hold a position in order to be fashionable rather than because they have cogent reasons is an insult. Moreover, since proponents of rights for same-sex couples would not give fashion as a reason for their position, we could regard example [16] as a straw person argument as well.

If someone wanted to argue that same-sex partnerships are bad, he would need to present other, relevant premises. For example, he could argue that same-sex couples are harmful to society in some way, that their children are confused or ostracised, or that their relationships are less stable and long-lasting. These premises, if true, would be relevant, but tradition alone is no argument at all.

Again, not everything that looks superficially like an appeal to tradition is one.

> [18] Traditionally, education included Latin and Greek. There is still a need for this, because without it we don't have access to many documents written in Western culture, which could provide guidelines for addressing present crises. Not everything has been translated. So we should return to teaching Latin and Greek in elementary school.

REVIEW BOX	7.6

Appeal to tradition

This fallacy occurs when someone suggests that a belief is true because it has "always" been believed.

Argument [18] contains the word *traditionally*. But *tradition* is not an inherently dirty word. We have to consider its use in the argument. Whereas in examples [16] and [17] tradition was used as the *only* premise supporting the conclusion, example [18] contains other reasons to believe that the tradition it cites is a good one that ought to be continued. The fallacious appeal to tradition says "*X* was traditionally done or believed; therefore continue to do or believe *X*." Example [18], however, says "X was traditionally done; here are some reasons for continuing to do X; therefore, do X."

Appeal to Ignorance

The fallacy of the **appeal to ignorance** can be seen as a case of the conclusion being too strong for the premises.

> [**19a**] There is intelligent life in space, because no one has been able to prove that there isn't.
>
> [**19b**] There is no intelligent life in space, because no one has been able to prove that there is.

In examples [19a] and [19b], we can see that two opposite conclusions are being drawn from premises that essentially say the same thing. That's enough to show us that there must be something wrong. An appeal to ignorance uses *as a premise* a statement that we have no knowledge about the subject at hand. There is nothing wrong with acknowledging that we don't know things. Naturally, there are many issues about which we know very little. But we can't draw a strong conclusion, a statement of fact, from our lack of knowledge. Lack of disproof is not the same as proof.

> **REVIEW BOX   7.7**
>
> ### Appeal to ignorance
>
> This fallacy may be committed when someone argues that since there is no evidence against a position, it is true, or that since there is no evidence for a position, it is false.

The next two examples do not commit an appeal to ignorance, because their conclusion has been weakened by adding "may be" and "may not be."

> [**20a**] There may be intelligent life in space, because no one has been able to prove that there isn't.
>
> [**20b**] There may not be intelligent life in space, because no one has been able to prove that there is.

These weakened arguments are not fallacious but they are not very informative either. From a premise of ignorance, we cannot conclude anything but mere possibility, and many things are possible.

Appeals to ignorance are common in paranormal claims and conspiracy theories. For example,

> [21] TWA Flight 800, which crashed on 17 July 1996, was hit by a United States missile, and the government and the navy have collaborated in a cover-up. There is no explanation for why the plane should have crashed in terms of mechanical failure or pilot error. A pilot from another airline, who is forced to remain anonymous, has stated that the TWA plane was flying in a special warning zone that was activated that night. If there were training exercises that night, and they involved dummy or low-yield missiles, a missile could easily have got out of control and hit the plane.

Notice that the second sentence of example [21] makes an appeal to ignorance. Even though neither mechanical failure nor human error has been identified as the cause of the disaster, they might still turn out to be causes. The absence of one particular explanation is not evidence for any other explanation. An anonymous pilot is not a good source: since he is unidentified, we cannot judge whether he was in a position to know about the warning zone—if there was one. Even if we accepted the claim that a warning zone was activated, that premise would not prove that Flight 800 was hit by a missile, much less that a cover-up followed. All we learn from example [21] is that the warning zone *could* have been activated because of training exercises, and that during such training exercises a missile *could* fly out of control. The fact that there is no evidence against the warning zone/stray missile explanation does not count as evidence in its favor.

Sometimes a conspiracy theory supporter will challenge a doubter to prove that the theory is false. This is called **shifting the burden of proof.** The doubter's inability to prove the theory false is then interpreted as further evidence of its truth. But the burden of proof always rests on the person who advanced the theory. Someone who wants others to accept his position cannot require that the doubters do all the work; a conclusion is not proven true by showing that an opponent cannot prove it false.

Let's look at examples of how the burden of proof can affect the appeal to ignorance. Is the counterclaim in example [22] an appeal to ignorance?

[22] **Claim:**
Each of us has an invisible guardian angel.

Counterclaim:
I don't buy that, unless you can prove that we have these guardian angels.

No. The counterclaim is not an appeal to ignorance even though it says that without proof the guardian-angel claim is unacceptable. We must consider the burden of proof. Remember, the burden of proof rests on the person who makes the original claim. You know that in a court of law, the accused is said to be "innocent until proven guilty." That means that the burden of proof rests on the state, because it is the state is responsible for making the claim that the accused committed the act. You also know that if the state fails to prove its case, the accused is said to be *not guilty*. The fact that the state does not prove its case doesn't show that the accused is *innocent*—only that the state has failed to shoulder the burden of proof.

> ### REVIEW BOX   7.8
>
> ## The burden of proof
>
> The burden of proof belongs to the proponent of an argument. Someone shifts the burden of proof when he or she tries to prove a conclusion true by showing that opponents cannot prove it false.

Without the notion of burden of proof, we'd be forced to accept all sorts of nonsensical claims. There is no proof that the airspace is not full of invisible, immaterial flying horses or that 25 percent of the students in your critical thinking class are not aliens. But we have absolutely no reason to believe these things. In order to judge whether a passage commits an appeal to ignorance, the issue of who bears the burden of proof must be decided.

Let's look at an extremely complicated example.

You are probably aware of the rumor that in July 1947, an alien spacecraft crashed near Roswell, New Mexico. Allegedly, an autopsy performed on one of the alien victims of this crash was filmed. Without a doubt, *something* crashed near Roswell. The army originally announced that it was a "flying disk," then soon after changed their claim stating that the crashed object was a weather balloon.

The *Sceptical Inquirer* magazine published an argument[1] against the theory that the crashed object was an alien craft and proposed instead that it was a terrestrial vehicle—perhaps a Soviet spy vehicle. This argument relies on declassified top-secret and secret Air Force documents dating back to 1948 concerning the source of the reproted unidentified flying objects. Though these documents are not published in their entirety in the magazine, what was published says this:

> [23] There are two reasonable explanations for these objects. They may be domestic, or they may be foreign. We don't know what they are. If they are domestic, we should be able to identify them by comparing the reports of the objects with the objects which were known to have been launched. If they are foreign, they are probably Soviet, and might pose a threat. There are certain Soviet aircraft which are possible candidates. Some UFOs have been said to be very fast, and the Soviets may have developed an unusual energy source to propel them, such as an atomic energy engine.

The *Sceptical Inquirer* article makes this argument:

> [24] There is no mention of alien craft in these declassified documents. The Pentagon would have been the first to know about an alien crash. So if alien craft were a possibility, they would have been mentioned in this document. The fact that they weren't is conclusive proof that the crash near Roswell was a crash of a terrestrial vehicle.

But example [24] makes an appeal to ignorance. It argues that the vehicle was *not* an alien craft because there is no evidence that it was. Moreover, even as an appeal to ignorance example [24] is not compelling. It has not established that the documents mentioned in example [23] are

[1]Philip J. Klass, "That's Entertainment: TV's UFO Cover-up," *Skeptical Inquirer*, vol. 20, no. 6 (November/December 1996): pp. 29–31, 58.

all the relevant documents in the case. It is plausible—if the government really is involved in a massive cover-up of alien visitations—that there are actually two documents: a declassified one which discusses the possibility of terrestrial vehicles; and another still classified document which discusses the possibility of extra-terrestrial vehicles.

Certainly the burden of proof rests on people who believe that aliens *did* crash at Roswell. But they do have evidence for their belief—the original statement by the Army, the alien autopsy film, a statement purported to be by the cameraman who filmed the autopsy, and accounts from people who were there, some of whom remembered picking up weird debris from the crash site and hearing about an autopsy.

Does this mean that we have to accept that an alien craft really did crash? No, certainly not. There are some very weak spots in the evidence. There is no agreement about whether the alien autopsy film—a key piece of evidence—is genuine. The film was "found" by Ray Santilli, a sort of impresario who was looking for Elvis footage. We don't want to make a circumstantial *ad hominem* attack by mentioning the money that Santilli has made from sales of the film. We can doubt him on other grounds, though: he has been shown to have lied about the identity of the cameraman, and when questioned about that, claimed he had done so to protect the cameraman from publicity. Without identification, we must dismiss any testimony purported to come from the cameraman. Santilli also gave some pieces of film to Kodak to authenticate. Kodak determined that the film was 1940s stock, but the film he provided was blank or exposed with a picture of a doorway. Santilli refused to release any film with the alien on it, because the authentication process destroys the film. We do not have proof that the alien autopsy footage dated from the 1940s. The testimony from people who were there was solicited almost fifty years after the event—that's a long time, and people forget. A claim that someone had picked up weird debris could be true no matter what had crashed. "Hearing about an autopsy" is secondhand testimony that must be dismissed.

So in conclusion, the burden of proof still rests on the people who think an alien craft crashed at Roswell. They have provided some evidence, so we can't claim that since there is no evidence there was no alien crash. The evidence they have provided, however, can be questioned using the guidelines we have already studied. We cannot conclusively establish that an alien craft did or did not crash.

EXERCISE 7.2 DISCUSSION AND WRITING ASSIGNMENT

Analyze the following, using the discussion of the Roswell alien crash as a model. What claim, if any, could reasonably be accepted? Remember that you must decide where the burden of proof rests.

1. An instructor accuses a student of cheating on an exam. The student has notes written in a dictionary which was permitted as an aid during the exam. The student claims the dictionary belonged to her roommate, who took the course in a previous semester.

2. After investigations by police and social workers of dozens of children said to have been associated with satanic ritual abuse, people are beginning to believe that the stories of torture and death are not true. Investigations have produced no hard evidence such as bodies or even bloodstains. Fundamentalists, psychotherapists, and social workers have exaggerated the dangers of satanism. The lack of hard evidence has, of course, not proven that there is widespread satanic ritual abuse, but this lack has not disproved it either. There is no basis for the grossly exaggerated claims of the fundamentalists. But there is also no basis for the equally false view at the other extreme. Just because no bodies have been found, we cannot conclude that satanism does not exist. There *is* evil being practiced in the name of satanism.

3. Aircraft, ships, and their crews have inexplicably disappeared from an area in the Atlantic Ocean known as the Bermuda Triangle. Though these disappearances have been investigated, no one has been able to explain the disappearances. So it's possible that beings or forces from another world are kidnapping people, airplanes, and ships from the Bermuda Triangle.

The Gambler's Fallacy

You will agree that if you flip a fair coin, the probability that it will come up heads is 1/2. Now, if you flip a coin fifty times and it comes up heads every time, what is the probability that it will come up heads the fifty-first time you flip it? The probability is still 1/2.

The fact that this seems improbable to many people is the basis of the **gambler's fallacy**. Simply put, the gambler's fallacy is the unsubstantiated idea that your luck is bound to change. If you are in a casino all afternoon playing craps and losing, you might say, "I can't leave now. I've lost so much, I'm bound to win on the next throw." Conversely, you might have a winning streak, and say "I'd better leave now, before my luck changes and I start to lose." Each of these arguments commits the gambler's fallacy.

Previous coin flips and dice rolls have no effect on subsequent coin flips or dice rolls. How could they? The coin does not remember what it did the last time. There is no causal relationship between previous flips and this one. There is no reason, in short, to believe that the coin cannot come up heads once more, no matter how many times it's come up heads already—even when it's a fair coin.

If the probabilities of heads and tails are equal, that means that over the course of time the heads and the tails will be equally distributed. But this means that heads and tails would even out if you flipped that coin forever, not that during any segment of time they're guaranteed to even out. Each throw of the dice or flip of the coin is a random event—that's why they're called games of chance!—and the past behavior of random events is not a guide to the future. That's why this is a fallacy of relevance: the past behavior of the coin or die is irrelevant to predicting its future behavior.

In some cases, perhaps, an unlikely run of events could cause you to ask whether the coin really is a fair one. But though you may ask this, if investigation showed that the coin was not badly weighted or otherwise "loaded," you'd have to accept that the likelihood of heads on the next toss is still 1/2.

There can be arguments that appear to commit the gambler's fallacy but do not.

> [25] We've had four years of supply-side economics and the resulting injustice to the poor. We've seen this government consistently accuse spokespersons for the disenfranchised and for the environment as "special interest groups" while bowing to every pressure exerted by Bay Street, Wall Street, and manufacturing interests. It's obvious from the vocal dissatisfaction of increasingly large segments of the population that the next election will result in a change of government.

> ## REVIEW BOX   7.9
>
> ### The gambler's fallacy
>
> The gambler's fallacy is committed when someone argues that since a random series of events has had a certain run in the past, that run is bound to change.

This argument does, in a sense, argue that everyone's luck will change—the poor's for the better, and the rich's for the worse. But it is not a gambler's fallacy because there is a legitimate causal connection between past government and a prediction about future government. Election outcomes are not random processes, and dissatisfaction with present government really does give some evidence that a change will occur.

In Chapter 9, we'll see how to use the experience of the past as a basis for knowledge about the future. We must remember to ask whether there is any basis in the nature of the events we're considering to believe that past results can affect future ones.

Appeal to the Majority/Appeal to the Select Few

The **appeal to the majority** and the **appeal to the select few** are two sides of the same coin. They are frequently seen in advertising.

The appeal to the majority suggests that a belief is true, or that a product is good, because many people believe it or buy it. Advertisements that state that the product is the "best-selling" one of its kind are guilty of this fallacy. Of course it's possible that everyone buys the product in question because it's the best one you can get for the price. It's also possible that the product is the best-selling one because of the force and extent of its advertisements—we've already discussed how some beliefs can be extremely wide-ranging and yet false. The fact that a product sells very well proves nothing for or against its quality. The appeal to the majority works, as the appeal to tradition does, by suggesting that a very large number of people can't all be wrong—if you disagree, there must be something wrong with you.

An advertisement that shows a lot of good-looking people using the product also commits this fallacy in a slightly different way, by appealing to the audience's desire to be as attractive and happy as the models in the advertisement. The appeal to the majority trades upon a standard human desire to be like everyone else—to be normal, to be part of the group.

In some cases, it's more difficult to judge whether an argument has committed this fallacy. For example,

> [26] A majority of students at this school said in response to a poll that the main problems facing the institution are tuition that is too high, classes that are too large, and cuts to courses that affect the ability to fulfill all requirements for graduation. That shows that this school is in serious trouble unless it starts to respond to these student concerns.

Does example [26] commit an appeal to the majority? We suspect that the school's administration would claim it does—they might say that just because these are concerns for the students, that doesn't mean they're the worst concerns for the school. But if students really are affected by the cuts, if they really believe they are not receiving value for their money, then they'll attend different schools, if they can, and they'll tell other people to apply elsewhere. Then the institution really will be in serious trouble.

REVIEW BOX 7.10

Appeal to the majority
Appeal to the select few

• The appeal to the majority occurs when someone suggests that a proposition is true because "everyone" believes it.

• The appeal to the select few occurs when someone suggests that a proposition is true because not everyone believes it.

The appeal to the select few rests on an opposite, but equally common, human desire to be unique. This fallacy suggests that a belief is true or a product is good because *not* everyone believes it or buys it. You have to be special in some way—not everyone can afford this product, or not everyone has the taste to appreciate it. We might concede that if your primary or only reason for buying the product is to show people how much money you have, and if it's true that few people can afford the product, then the argument offered by the appeal to the select few may be a cogent one. Few people, however, would be likely to accept an argument explicitly based upon these premises—they'd want a good product, not just an expensive one.

■ SUMMARY

There are many named fallacies of relevance; we've considered only a few. But we don't have to know the name of every fallacy to argue well. The important issues are the following. First, *stick to the point.* Don't let others draw you off topic; don't bring in extraneous material yourself. Second, watch out for premises that make you ask, "But what does that have to do with it?" When you're constructing your own arguments, make sure that every premise you have supports your conclusion, either directly as a main premise or indirectly as a subpremise. If you think some side-issue is relevant, make sure that your audience will, too, by providing subarguments where necessary. When you're constructing an argument that criticizes someone, be fair to your opponent; make sure you criticize the argument that the opponent actually puts forth.

If you've ever been in a seminar with another student whose comments made you think, "*What* is he talking about?" now you might have a better idea of how to respond to him. If you're active in student government or other politics, and you've spent long hours in meetings where it seemed that everything under the sun was being addressed, now perhaps you have a way of bringing the meeting back to order. If you and your brother have constant battles every time you go home for the holidays, in which you both bring up events dating back to the time you put a crayon in his soup—well, good luck, but remember that sticking to the point even with your brother will help you develop a relationship you can both live with for the next fifty years.

> **LEMUR Exercise 7.1**

EXERCISE 7.3

Evaluate the following arguments. State any fallacies they contain and give reasons for your decision. Remember, some arguments can contain more than one fallacy.

1. An advertisement says: Wholesale warehouses are a whole new retailing phenomenon. People come to them to save money, and they do! Our "no frills," low-cost warehouse concept is what saves you money. Most of our stores don't even have offices!

2. Why should we be forced by political correctness to say "Season's Greetings" instead of "Merry Christmas" to all these immigrants and refugees who come to our country, do not believe in our culture, and try to change our ways?

3. The stereotypical notion that all male ballet dancers are homosexual is simply false, especially today. The increase of athleticism in today's choreography means that male dancers must be very muscular. The physical demands of ballet are probably more challenging even than those of hockey or football.

4. *A university administrator says:* We can't give Professor Antonelli tenure. Sure, she teaches 1,500 students a year, and her classes will keep getting bigger now that we've been forced to accept a larger number of students to increase revenue from tuition. I won't deny she's popular with the students, but since we were founded over a hundred years ago, we've always been a research institution, not a teaching school. Besides, anybody can teach, really—it's research that takes innovation.

5. Sara: Confrontational unions should be replaced by workers' councils. If they were, workers could work together to make the most of both the company and the employees. Unions are aggressive and confrontational, and that's not productive.

   Dan: These workers' councils were tried in Italy under the fascists. Without unions, workers lost their right to strike. As a result, workers were exploited. Unions protect workers from arbitrary treatment and from unsafe working conditions.

   Sara: I'd just like to remind you that my parents' families lived in Italy under the fascists. I hardly need you to tell me what tyranny is like.

6. *From a letter to the editor of a men's fashion magazine, complaining about a photo of a naked woman's torso:* I'm just sick of seeing the garbage in your magazine in these times. If men spent as much time and effort on important things as they spend pursuing women's breasts, they could probably do something about war, famine, poverty, and disease.

7. It's pretty hard for me to believe that the singer Madonna could be afraid of a stalker when she's brave enough to wear some of the clothes she does.

8. The National Rifle Association, or NRA, a United States organization supporting gun ownership, said in an advertisement that naturally the FBI was recommending mandatory licensing of all handgun owners: they had just spent $47 million on a new computer system.

9. Why all this fuss about cloning a sheep? Because everyone's afraid that the technology might be extended to create human clones someday? That shows how ignorant and fearful even educated people are about scientific matters. For one thing, there are already "natural" clones—they're called identical twins. For another, people don't seem to see this isn't a mad scientist's Frankenstein experiment: human clones would be born and grow up; they'd be human individuals in every legal sense.

10. *A biology professor responds to an editorial in a student newspaper on animal experimentation:* I cannot understand how you could have published a "feature" so full of misinformation. Let me correct just one ridiculous claim: that we can help end animals' "suffering" in medical experiments by making donations to various animal rights organizations. It's lucky for these organizations that people as naive and credulous as the author of this article are ignorant of the fact that these donations go to paying salaries of the executive members, to fund-raising, and to illegal terrorist activities directed at the professional laboratories that carry on life-saving medical research.

EXERCISE 7.4 DISCUSSION AND WRITING ASSIGNMENT

What is the difference—if any—between the (a) and (b) arguments in each of the following sets? You might want to argue that one commits a certain fallacy and the other does not. You might want to argue they both commit the same fallacy. You might want to argue that they commit different fallacies. You might want to argue that both arguments are good ones.

1. (a) Over half of students polled stated that they would support Tara Green for student union president. That means it's likely she'll win.

   (b) Over half of students polled stated that they thought the recently introduced first-year critical thinking requirement was a bad idea. That shows the students don't need critical thinking courses.

2. (a) Spring training in baseball is a bad idea. Face it, any player only has a certain number of slides before he breaks his wrist and a certain number of catches before he gets beaned. Why push it?
(b) You're pushing your luck if you train your pitcher too hard. After a certain number of pitches, his arm's just going to go.

3. (a) What do you mean, it's my turn to take out the garbage? I notice you never take it out when it's your turn, either.
(b) You'd better believe I'd use this gun if I had to, and I'd shoot to kill. If some junkie breaks into my house, he's not going to hesitate to do me harm if he has to.

4. (a) There was nothing wrong with dropping the bomb on Hiroshima and Nagasaki. If they'd had the bomb, they would have dropped it on us.
(b) There was nothing wrong with dropping the bomb on Hiroshima and Nagasaki. The Pacific war could have been won by invasion, but that would have resulted in the loss of 10,000 Allied soldiers' lives.

8

Arguments
from Analogy

ARGUMENTS FROM ANALOGY are a common and interesting form of argument. They draw a conclusion about one thing by comparing it with another thing. The basic form of an argument from analogy that we'll see in this chapter will also help us make sense of, and criticize, inductive and causal arguments in the next two chapters.

Before we learn the methods for addressing arguments from analogy, let's look at several places where arguments from analogy are found in everyday reasoning.

The underlying principle of arguments from analogy is that similar cases should be treated similarly, or can be expected to behave similarly. This is something we all expect, perhaps without always realizing it. But imagine that a student, Angelo, went to his professor, and said he missed the midterm test because he was sick and had a doctor's note to prove it. The professor tells Angelo that he can take a makeup test. Then another student, Eric, goes to the same professor, says that he was sick for the midterm, and also has a doctor's note to prove it. The professor tells Eric that he will have to forfeit a grade for the midterm. Eric would complain, and rightly so, because the professor has not been fair. The two cases are similar in all the ways that matter—both students were sick, both missed the same test, and both had doctor's notes. But the professor has not treated the students similarly, and that is inconsistent and unjust.

We see the same sort of reasoning when someone buys a Honda because he found his three previous Hondas reliable. The cars are all similar, because they're all Hondas, so the buyer can conclude that his new Honda will be reliable too.

The argument from analogy appeals to a principle that could be stated this way: "These two cases are similar. So if you are going to say that p holds of the one case, you have to say that p holds of the other case too."

In law, sometimes one case is seen as setting a precedent for another case. A lawyer with a case before the court researches previous cases that are similar in relevant ways. Then the lawyer can argue by analogy: since these cases are similar, they should be treated similarly—the court should reach the same decision in this case as in the previous one.

An argument from analogy is also involved when something needs to be classified. We can argue about the category to which something belongs, and that will sometimes determine how it ought to be treated. For example, a city government might try to block a certain art exhibition because some consider it pornographic. The court case would consist largely of arguments about the classification of the work—is it art, or is it pornography? Does the work have more in common with art or with pornography?

It may have something in common with each. Then the court must consider which similarities are more decisive. Does the work portray naked people? That can't be decisive, because it has that in common with pornography and with art. Does the work portray people in an exploitative manner? That's a more decisive similarity.

Arguments from analogy not only help decide how something should be treated; they also help predict how something will behave. For example, in constructing a new baseball stadium, it's important to design a stadium that will allow for home runs, because home runs are one of the exciting aspects of baseball that people pay to see. On the other hand, people don't want to see a game in which every hit is a home run; that would be dull. Part of the excitement stems from the fact that home runs are uncommon but not unheard of. So it's important that wind currents likely to be found in the proposed stadium be neither too helpful nor too harmful to the batter. How can this be determined before the stadium is built? Sometimes a scale model of the stadium is built. That's one analogy—the scale model is similar to the real stadium. Then water is made to flow through the model stadium. That's a second analogy: water behaves similarly to wind, so the water currents will be good predictors of the wind currents.

Now that we've seen some examples, we'll learn how to standardize and evaluate any argument that is based on analogy, including all the types we've seen so far. Our ability to learn from experience is based on analogies, as we'll see in Chapters 9 and 10, so this chapter will also provide a basis for the skills we'll learn later.

▌ ANALOGIES

Let's begin with a silly argument that has an obviously false conclusion. It will permit us to identify the components of the argument from analogy easily and to introduce the means by which we criticize these arguments.

> [1] Calculators are similar to people, because both calculators and people can do arithmetic. People enjoy music. Therefore calculators can enjoy music too.

Like all arguments from analogy, example [1] compares two things. In this case, it's calculators and people. All arguments from analogy are based on similarities that are known to hold between the two things being compared. Sometimes these similarities are stated explicitly; sometimes they are implicit. In example [1], the similarity is that both things do arithmetic. On the basis of that similarity, the argument claims that they must be similar in another respect as well. Let's standardize example [1]:

> [1a]   1.1. Both people and calculators can do arithmetic.
>   1.   Calculators are similar to people.
>   2.   People enjoy music.
>   Therefore, calculators enjoy music too.

There are four new terms that we use to understand the structure of arguments from analogy. The **primary subject** is the subject of the conclusion, the thing that the conclusion gives us new information about. In the case of example [1], that's clearly *calculators*. The **analogue** is what the primary subject is being compared with, in example [1], *people*. The **similarities** are the respects in which primary subject and analogue can be compared: in example [1], *able to do arithmetic*. Finally, the **target property** is what is said about the primary subject in the conclusion—the property that's being stated to hold of the primary subject. It's also affirmed of the analogue in premise 2. In example [1], that's *enjoy music*. Example

[1b] gives us a summary of these four components from example [1]—we'll use initials for the names of the components.

> [1b] PS: calculators
> A: people
> S: able to do arithmetic
> TP: enjoy music

This argument is clearly a bad one. We know that calculators do not enjoy music. The premises in example [1] are true: calculators and people do share the ability to do arithmetic, so they are similar in that respect. But in any argument from analogy, the PS and A are just *similar*—they are not the *same*. This means that whatever similarities there may be, there must also be differences. We then have to ask whether the differences are more relevant to the conclusion than the similarities are. In other words, are there negatively relevant differences that stand in the way, or count against the truth, of the conclusion?

Consider the differences between calculators and people. Although

REVIEW BOX 8.1

Components of an argument from analogy

PRIMARY SUBJECT: the subject of the conclusion

ANALOGUE: what the primary subject is being compared to

SIMILARITIES: the similarities that hold between the primary subject and analogue prior to the conclusion

TARGET PROPERTY: what is said about the primary subject in the conclusion and about the analogue in the premise

there are an indefinite number of them, not all of them matter. For example, calculators are smaller than people; you're allowed to take a calculator into your exams but you're not allowed to take a person; calculators are sold in stores, etc. None of these has any direct relevance to the question of enjoying music. We need to find a difference that would account for why people can enjoy music and calculators cannot. The fact that calculators do not have ears means that they cannot even perceive music, much less enjoy it. But even if calculators were provided with the input, would they enjoy music? No. What does it mean to enjoy music? A person has an emotional, sensual, aesthetic response to the music. Part of what allows people to enjoy music,

REVIEW BOX 8.2

Form of an argument from analogy

1.1. PS and A share S.
1. PS and A are similar.
2. A has TP.
Therefore, PS has TP.

then, is their possession of characteristics that calculators lack—imagination, sensation, and emotion.

When we criticize an argument from analogy in this way, we're accepting the premise that the primary subject and the analogue are similar. But we conclude that these similarities are not enough to support the conclusion.

Here is another example.

> [2] Health care for old people is a waste of money. When a car needs too much work, like a new transmission or extensive body work or a new engine, you scrap the car. The same for people.

The main conclusion of this argument is that health care for old people is a waste of money, or that old people should be "scrapped" instead of "repaired." This conclusion is supported by an analogy.

> [2a] **Conclusion:** Old people should be scrapped.
> PS: old people
> A: old cars
> S: worn out with age; need to be repaired
> TP: scrapped

Alternatively, we could state the components this way:

> [2b] **Conclusion:** Health care for old people is a waste of money.
> PS: old people
> A: old cars
> S: worn out with age; need to be repaired
> TP: waste of money.

Whether we interpret the argument as presented in example [2a] or as in example [2b], the point is the same: old people who have many health problems are like old cars. Considering cost and benefit leads you to decide that the car is not worth fixing. A similar cost–benefit consideration should lead you to believe that the old person is not worth fixing either.

There is something we should notice here, before we go on to criticize the argument. Both the similarities and the target property are shared between the analogue and the primary subject. Thus they must be stated in such a way that the terms can apply to both. This is obvious for the similarities—we've stated them in examples [2a] and [2b] as worn-out *parts*. The only parts that the argument mentions are engines and transmissions; old people have neither. But it's clear that the intended similarity is worn-out parts, whatever parts are relevant.

Beware of two problems that could arise when you state the target property. First, like the similarities, the target property must also be stated in a way that can apply to both analogue and primary subject. This may cause us to decide that example [2b] is, after all, the better statement of the argument's components. We may think that speaking of *scrapping* old people carries an emotional force that would prejudice hearers against the argument. And, as we shall see, the argument can be criticized decisively without being unjust in our statement of it. Second, the target property is a *property*, not a proposition—a part of a sentence, not the full sentence. It would be a serious mistake to state the target property as either *Old people should be scrapped* or as *Old cars should be scrapped*. *Scrapped* has to apply to both.

Strategies and Conventions

Criticizing an argument from analogy

- Ask whether there are differences between the primary subject and the analogue that are negatively relevant to the conclusion.

- State explicitly how the differences are directly relevant to the conclusion.

Let's consider what relevant differences could stand in the way of drawing the conclusion. You are likely to say that people are alive, and cars are not. Although that's true and relevant, it is the basis for our criticism, and not yet the criticism itself. Why would something's being alive make a difference to scrapping it? Is it relevant that the old car is useless when its parts are worn out? A car is meant to provide transportation, and it cannot fulfill this function unless it has a working engine. The old person, however, still has a role to play—he or she has knowledge gained from experience, even with worn-out parts. Moreover, no matter how much you love your car, it's not the same as the way you love your grandmother. The car is replaceable, while people are individuals, and a new one cannot just be substituted for the old one. This is one difference that stands in the way of the conclusion. But a consideration of the old person's social role still doesn't exhaust the differences—we'd tend to think that even a useless old person couldn't be scrapped. A further difference is that the car has no reason for being other than its use to you. Is that true of the person? No. The person also enjoys his or her life. If you send your car to the scrapyard, your car has no feelings about it. But the person would certainly object.

It's important to see that although example [2] is a bad argument, and it's obvious why in a general sense, a forceful criticism of the argument must spell out the differences in detail and make them relevant to the conclusion. People tend to find arguments from analogy very compelling. The strength of these arguments lies partly in the concrete examples they offer. So to convince people an argument from analogy is a bad one, you'll have to make your criticism just as concrete.

Bear in mind that in the two examples that we have seen, we are not objecting to the truth of the premises. People and calculators, and old cars and old people, really are similar. They just aren't similar enough to outweigh the differences. Sometimes, though, the problem with an argument from analogy can lie in the fact that the primary subject and analogue don't share any strong similarities to begin with.

Here's a little background to example [3]: Mike Harris was premier of Ontario in 1996. Harris cut funding for programs that particularly affected women and children, such as welfare, including welfare to single mothers, and the day-care subsidy program, which had for many years made it feasible for many women with children to work at jobs that would not have supported a child in day care. Harris had been accused of enforcing his fiscal policies on the people least able to fight back and most likely to become a social problem in coming years. The following criticism of Harris's cuts appeared in a letter to the editor:

[3] First we had O. J. Simpson telling us he was 100 percent innocent. Now we have Mike Harris saying, "To suggest our motive is not to help women or children is 100 percent wrong." Does anyone actually believe this stuff?

As we can see, there is a rhetorical question serving as the conclusion of this argument. The conclusion is something like "Harris is lying" or "Don't believe Harris." If we remember that, although O. J. Simpson was acquitted, there was some controversy about his acquittal, we see that there is an implicit suggestion that O. J. Simpson, too, was lying. We could partially standardize the argument like this:

[3a] 1. Mike Harris and O. J. Simpson are similar.
2. O. J. Simpson was lying.
Therefore, Harris is lying too.

We can identify the PS, A, and TP now:

[3b] PS: Mike Harris
A: O. J. Simpson
TP: lying.

We have not yet stated the similarities between O. J. Simpson and Mike Harris that permit us to draw this conclusion. If we look at the argument, we see that the similarity between these two men that the argument suggests is that each used the expression "100 percent." But that certainly isn't a similarity that is significant or relevant enough to draw a comparison between the two. Many people use this expression. Moreover, we cannot claim that using the expression "100 percent" is in any way relevant to lying. If I say that I'm 100 percent certain that bloodhounds have long ears, I'm not saying anything false—bloodhounds do have long ears.

This shows us another way in which arguments from analogy can go wrong. The similarity between PS and A can be inadequate to support any argument from analogy, making premise 1 unacceptable. Since the similarity is the basis for the entire argument, if the similarity is lacking, the argument must be a bad one.

Sometimes arguments from analogy equivocate. Consider this example:

[4] Several years ago, three whales were trapped in ice when the water froze quickly. The whales would have died without help. The former USSR and the United States cooperated to free the whales using ice-breakers. People only want what these whales did—freedom. People are trapped by war and poverty as the whales were trapped by ice. If these two powerful nations could put aside their differences to work together and free these whales, why couldn't they do that for all humanity?

The conclusion of this argument is that people could be freed if powerful nations worked in cooperation. This conclusion is drawn by an analogy between people and whales. So the primary subject is *people*, the analogue is *whales*, and the target property is *could be freed by nations working in cooperation*. What similarities are there between people and whales? There are many similarities, but we have to choose the ones that are relevant to this argument. For example, people and whales are both mammals, but does this matter? No. If there had been three giant iguanas trapped in the ice, the same analogy could have been drawn. The relevant similarity on the basis of which the argument is constructed is that both people and whales are trapped—one by poverty and war, the other by ice.

Before we continue with an evaluation of this argument, let's ensure that we have the four components of the argument straight. Again, keep in mind that the target property has to be stated in such a way that it can be understood to apply to both the analogue and the primary subject.

[4a] PS: people
A: whales
TP: could be freed by nations working in cooperation
S: trapped

The standardization of this argument, then, is

[4b]   1.1. The whales and people are both trapped.
1. The whales and people are similar.
2. The whales were freed by nations working in cooperation.
Therefore, people could be freed by people working in cooperation.

If you prefer the pictorial means of standardizing, all your standardized arguments from analogy should be this shape:

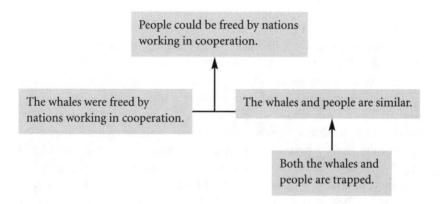

There are two linked main premises directly supporting the main conclusion. One states that the analogue has the target property, and the other states that the analogue and primary subject are similar. The latter premise is supported by a subpremise that spells out the similarities.

The subpremise that spells out the similarities is where we find the weakness in this argument. What does "trapped" mean for the whales and for people? Something very different. The whales were physically trapped in ice. People, on the other hand, are metaphorically trapped by social or economic situations. There is nothing wrong, in itself, with a target property or a set of similarities that is used slightly differently in the two premises. For example, when we spoke of the similarities between the old cars and the old people, we said that they both had worn-out parts. In the car, the parts are engines or transmissions; in the person, they're hearts or livers. But these "parts," whatever they are, are similar: they allow the car or the person to function; they're also necessary, replaceable, and expensive to replace. So we have no problem accepting that there are similarities at least superficially acceptable as support for the conclusion that it's not economically feasible to replace them.

In the whale argument, though, the different meanings of "trapped" stand in the way of the conclusion. It was easy for the USSR and the

United States to cooperate in freeing the trapped whales, because that consisted only of bringing out their ice-breakers. But "freeing" people from war and poverty would require complicated socioeconomic changes. There is a world of difference between cooperating in managing a couple of ice-breakers and cooperating in changing social and political systems in order to end war and poverty. Even if the two countries could agree on what changes would be necessary, implementing them would also be much more difficult than implementing a decision to free whales.

In a sense, then, we could say that the whale argument *equivocates*. Equivocation in an argument from analogy is somewhat more complicated than it is in a non-analogy argument. We can expect that in many cases, words will be used in a slightly different sense in an argument from analogy without directly harming the argument. What we need to consider is the difference in sense in the context of the conclusion. The different meanings of "trapped" lead to different meanings of "free." Thus there is no reason to believe that cooperating in freeing the whales is evidence that cooperation is possible for radical social change.

So far, we have seen arguments in which the main conclusion is directly supported by an argument from analogy. But analogies can also appear as subarguments within the main argument. For example,

> [5] We cannot continue to accept as entertainment the unspeakable acts of violence that we see in movies like *Child's Play 3*. There are several cases in which movies like this cause children who watch them to imitate the acts of violence that they see. It is common sense that constant exposure to scenes like those in the movies have an effect. Television advertisers spend billions of dollars a year. That shows that they know that advertising will influence the people who see.

The conclusion here is clearly the first sentence. But we should also notice that the last sentence of the passage discusses television advertisements. The passage is about violent movies, so what is the sentence about television advertisements doing here? It provides a comparison. Example [5] contains an analogy.

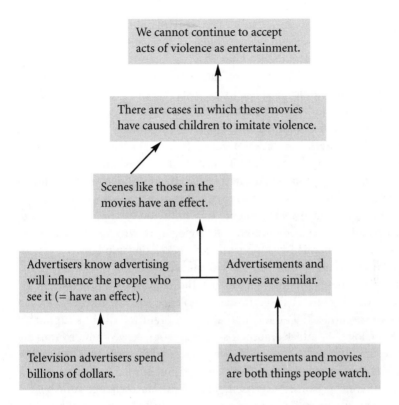

Let's consider, first, the analogy in the subargument. It says that we should believe that violent movies have an effect, because advertisements, which are also things that people watch, have an effect. We know that advertisements have an effect because otherwise advertisers would not spend so much money on them. Notice that the similarities between movies and advertisements are not explicitly stated in the argument; presumably, the similarities are that both movies and advertisements are things on video that people watch.

[5a] PS: violent movies
     A: television advertisement
     TP: have an effect
     S: video things that people watch

The main conclusion is that violent movies are not acceptable entertainment. What reasons are given to believe this, and what role does the
analogy have? The argument states that there are cases in which these
movies have caused children to imitate acts of violence. This is a causal
inference, which would be subject to the standards for good causal arguments that we'll address in Chapter 10. This premise could be supported
by stating the cases in which this imitation took place and by satisfying
several other criteria for causal arguments. It seems that the analogy is
meant to show that the causal premise satisfies at least one of these criteria. The analogy is probably meant to refute the possible counterargument
that children who watch violent movies already have a propensity to violence, and this propensity to violence caused them both to perform acts of
violence and to have been drawn to the violent movies in the first place.
The analogy is intended to support the *causal* relationship between watching the movies and committing the violent acts.

Thus the main premise supporting the conclusion is that there are
cases in which children have imitated violence seen in movies. We can
attack the argument by attacking that causal premise, which is supported
by the analogy. We attack arguments from analogy, as we know, by looking
for relevant differences between the analogue and the primary subject.

What differences are there? First, movies and advertisements are created for different reasons. Advertisements are meant to change your behavior—to cause you to buy the advertised product. Movies, on the other
hand, are meant to entertain, and not necessarily to serve as a model for
behavior. Why would that matter? First, techniques of persuasion present
in advertisements are likely to be absent in movies. An advertisement for
peanut butter, for example, will do everything it can to make the peanut
butter look luscious and irresistible. The result for the viewer is likely to be
a desire to seek out the peanut butter that's in the advertisement. A violent
movie of the *Child's Play* sort will make the acts of violence disgusting or
frightening—a large part of the thrill of watching a horror movie is the
fear, suspense, and disgust that the viewer feels. So the viewer of the violent movie is more likely to form the desire to avoid violence. Second,
advertisements are seen frequently—sometimes three or four times in a
half-hour. Movies are usually seen once or twice. Repetition is likely to
strengthen the advertisements' message. Third, the advertisement wants
you to buy something—a normal activity that everyone performs several
times a day. Even if the movie did try to influence you to commit a violent

act, there are moral prohibitions to overcome: violence is not a normal everyday activity.

In short, there are enough relevant differences between advertisements and violent movies for you to question the value of the analogy and to decide that the conclusion that violent movies are unacceptable entertainment is not adequately supported by this argument.

Here's a slightly different kind of argument from analogy, in which similarities were used to classify something.

> [6] During the 1970s and 1980s, the United States federal government sponsored a successful program to breed the endangered red wolf in captivity and then reintroduce it into the wild. But a 1989 study analyzing mitochondrial DNA from red wolves failed to uncover any consistent genetic differences between the red wolf and coyote/gray wolf hybrids. Some people concluded that the red wolf is not a species of wolf, but is rather a "wild mutt," and that the United States ought to scale down or abandon its program to rescue the red wolf.

Because of the similarities between the DNA of red wolves and coyote/gray wolf hybrids, the argument concludes that they ought to be treated similarly; thus the red wolf does not merit a rescue program. Clearly, the primary subject is the red wolf and the analogue is the gray wolf/coyote hybrid. They are similar in genetic make-up. The target property is found in the unstated premise that hybrids ought not to be rescued. Thus red wolves ought not to be rescued.

Although this is an argument that attempts to classify something, we can criticize it in the same way that we criticize any argument from analogy—by weighing the similarities and differences between the analogue and primary subject. At the time, people who disagreed with the conclusion that red wolves ought not to be rescued pointed to a difficulty in evaluating the similarities. The classification of red wolves as hybrids may be questioned. There is no consensus on whether DNA testing is an adequate criterion for species-membership. The science of such testing was quite new in 1989, and perhaps not yet refined enough to be the last word. Even the researchers who originally made the discovery pointed out that they may have missed a unique red wolf genotype, and that more research was needed. Moreover, there was no agreement amongst the experts about how the results were to be interpreted. It may be consistent with these findings to regard the red wolf as a subspecies of the gray wolf. In habits and appearance the red wolf is very like a wolf and unlike a coyote. For example, the red wolf can kill large moose, and its skull is characteristically wolflike. Finally, there is reason to question the truth of the (implicit) premise that hybrids ought not to be preserved. Living things are constantly evolving, and over time hybridization may lead to the creation of new species. Failing to protect mixed-gene animals, then, may interrupt an important natural process.

FALLACIES OF ANALOGY

In this section we'll look at three fallacies. The first one is similar both to the "all or nothing" version of the false dichotomy, which we saw in Chapter 6, and to the *tu quoque* fallacy, which we saw in Chapter 7. The second is a fallacy that can occur if you are not cautious in evaluating whether one thing really sets a precedent for another thing. The third is perhaps not strictly a fallacy of analogy, but it is similar enough to the second to be included in this chapter.

Fallacy of Two Wrongs

You've heard the expression "Two wrongs don't make a right." There is a type of fallacy that seems to rely on some underlying assumption that two wrongs *do* make a right. The following example appeared in a letter to the editor.

> [7] Canada is the only country where immigrants come and receive all the benefits that citizens get, like housing and health care. They should be properly grateful. But instead they have the nerve to expect us to change things for them. I very much doubt that if I was to go to their country they would make any changes for me. It's not fair to change our country for them. Soon there will be nothing left that is ours.

The main idea of this passage could be baldly stated this way:

> [7a] Other countries would treat me badly if I were an immigrant.
> Thus Canada should treat immigrants badly too.

The idea, as in arguments from analogy in general, is that similar cases should be treated similarly. There is a similarity between the author's immigrating to another country, and other people's immigrating to Canada. Since the author (believes he) would be treated badly in other countries, Canada, to be consistent, should treat its immigrants badly too.

The problem is that consistency does not seem to demand that bad treatment be standardized. We remember that sometimes the false dichotomy appears to suggest that if we can't do everything, we ought to do nothing. But, we pointed out, you have to start somewhere. The case of the **two wrongs fallacy** is somewhat similar. The fact that one bad action is permitted does not mean that we are bound by consistency to commit similar bad actions.

Slippery Precedent

Sometimes an argument will say "This action may be all right on its own. But if it were permitted it would set a precedent for other things, and those other things are unacceptable. So the first action cannot be permitted either." This type of argument sometimes commits the fallacy of **slippery precedent**.

It's easy to imagine that if you asked a professor for an extension, she might say this to you:

> [8a] I can't give you an extension on your paper just because you have a lot of assignments due in your other courses and some extra time would let you do a better job on this one. Every student I have is

> overworked at this time of year, and anyone could benefit from some extra time. So if I gave it to you, I'd have to give it to everyone, and then I wouldn't be able to get the grading done in time to meet my own deadline.

The professor is pointing out that granting you an extension would set a harmful precedent. In this case, you'd have to accept the professor's argument. You asked for an extension on the grounds that you have too much work. To be consistent, then, the professor really would have to give an extension to anyone else who had the same grounds—and that would, as the professor pointed out, be almost everyone.

But compare example [8a] to example [8b]:

> **[8b]** I can't possibly give you an extension on that paper. I'm sorry that you fell out of that second-story window and broke both your arms, but if I give you a two-week extension, the next thing I know I'll have every student in the class wanting an extension. If I give it to you, I'll have to give it to everyone, and I won't get the papers graded in time to meet my own deadline.

REVIEW BOX 8.4

Fallacy of slippery precedent

This fallacy may occur when someone argues that although an action may be acceptable on its own, it will set a precedent for further, unacceptable actions.

If you were the student in example [8b], you could accuse your professor of committing the fallacy of slippery precedent. Example [8b] is a bad argument. As in any argument involving an analogy, we look for relevant differences. There is a big difference between a student with two broken arms and every other student. There is no reason to believe that granting an extra two weeks to a student with broken arms would set a precedent for other students. If any other student complained about the extra time given to the broken-armed student, the professor could point to the broken arms as the relevant feature that merited an extension in the one case and did not set a precedent for the other cases.

Although the arguments look similar, one is acceptable and one is not. Whenever an argument claims that a precedent will be set, you have to examine the cases to see if that precedent really will be set. You determine that by asking if there are relevant differences between the case that's being claimed as a precedent and the other cases for which it would set a precedent.

Strategies and Conventions

Evaluating arguments from precedent

Ask whether the precedent will in fact be set. Are there relevant differences that would undermine the notion that the one action will set the precedent for the others?

Slippery Assimilation

The fallacy of **slippery assimilation** occurs when someone claims that since a definite line cannot be drawn, no line can ever be drawn at all. A traditional example of this is the bald man. We'd all agree that a man with no hairs on his head is bald. If he had one hair on his head, we'd still call him bald. If he had two hairs, or even two hundred hairs, we'd still call him bald: humans customarily have many thousand hairs. So clearly, no one hair makes the difference between bald and not-bald. Thus, we can conclude, all men are bald.

What went wrong here? This argument ignores the fact that, while any one hair may not make a difference, the cumulative effect of many hairs does make a difference. There are some people whom we'd definitely call bald. And there are some people whom we'd definitely call hairy. Perhaps there is a gray area, where we wouldn't all agree on whether to call the person bald or not. But just because there is some gray area, doesn't mean that it's all a gray area. Certainly we cannot come up with an operational definition for "bald." That doesn't mean that we can't use the term.

There was a television advertisement some years ago, which you may remember, that was guilty of this fallacy. The advertisement was for a men's hair dye, and it featured Rocket Richard. The idea of the advertisement was that this dye worked gradually, so that there was no point at which the hair suddenly and dramatically changed color. The advertisement, in fact, had Rocket Richard say, "The change was so gradual, no one even noticed." But the fact is that although no one may notice the difference in hair color between Monday and Tuesday, or between Tuesday and Wednesday, eventually, after a couple of weeks, someone will think, "His hair used to be gray. Now it's black. He must have dyed it."

The fallacy of slippery assimilation also leads to a dangerous argument that you hear from time to time:

> [9] There's no good reason for anyone to vote. The chance that one person's vote will determine the outcome of an election is less than the chance that he'll be struck by lightning. The odds of making a difference are too small to determine anyone's behavior.

REVIEW BOX 8.5

Fallacy of slippery assimilation

This fallacy occurs when someone ignores the fact that many insignificant differences can add up to a significant one.

The idea is that since your vote is not likely to be the significant determining vote, there's no point in voting. But while an individual vote, like an individual hair, is unlikely to make any difference by itself, the cumulative effect of all those votes does make a difference. What if everyone bought into example [9]? There would be no cumulative effect, and no one would be elected.

SUMMARY

In this chapter we have introduced the idea that some arguments rely on the comparison of two or more things to draw a conclusion about one of them. We'll build on this idea in the two following chapters. It's important to leave this chapter with the ability to identify the components of the argument from analogy: analogue, primary subject, target property, and similarities. Although we'll rename those elements in the next chapter, their roles are similar. It's also important to keep in mind, both in the following chapters and whenever you hear an analogy drawn, that there is one question to ask—are there relevant differences that undermine this comparison? That's the same question you should ask when faced with an argument that claims that a precedent will be set.

LEMUR Exercise 8.1

EXERCISE 8.1

For each of the following arguments,
  I. If it is an argument from analogy,
   i.   state the primary subject, analogue, target property, and similarities; and

   ii. evaluate the argument,

  OR

  II. If it commits one of the fallacies we have seen, state how and why.

Example

Andrew (a human) likes to sleep a lot and keep warm, just like a cat. So he should look for a job catching mice.

   i.   PS: Andrew
        A: cat
        TP: job catching mice
        S: sleep a lot, keep warm

   ii. The similarities stated are not the qualities that enable cats to catch mice. Cats catch mice because they are fast and quiet predators with claws. Sleeping a lot and keeping warm, while characteristics of cats, have nothing to do with their predatory abilities. That means that the similarities are not adequate to support the conclusion: they do not give us any reason to believe that Andrew can also catch mice.

Besides, there are no such jobs for humans.

1. Making homosexual marriages legal will undermine the family, and the family is the basis of society. Once homosexual marriages are permitted, what is to stand in the way of group marriages, polygamy, polyandry, until there is nothing left of marriage as we know it?

2. If you have an enemy whom you want to hurt, you should make an image of that person, and then hurt the image in the way you would like to see the enemy hurt. To make the image stronger, you should incorporate into it something belonging to the person, like hair or clothing.

3. A recent advertisement for potato chips shows two people sitting in the middle of a huge empty expanse of ice and snow. There are no other people, no buildings—nothing but ice and snow. One of the people is eating chips. The other asks if he can have a chip. The chip eater refuses. He says, "If I gave one to you, I'd have to give one to everybody else, too."

    The humor of this advertisement relies on its viewers' implicit understanding of a fallacy that we have seen in the chapter. What fallacy?

4. Women too often pay more than men for the same services. At a large local clothing store, which carries both men's and women's clothes, alterations such as hemming trousers or shortening sleeves are done free for men, whereas the same alterations for women cost up to ten dollars. Many dry cleaners charge, for example, four dollars to clean a man's shirt, but five dollars for a similar woman's blouse.

5. Labeling tobacco products and alcohol with warnings about potential harm is good, but why not extend the comparison? If smoking is restricted at sports events, why is there no concern for the people who drink there and then drive home? If there is concern about tobacco sponsorship of sports events, why not about the sports events that are sponsored by alcohol?

6. Whenever I play my computer game of blackjack [a card game], I win big. So if I go to Las Vegas and play blackjack there, I'll win a lot of real money.

7. It is true that steroids are powerful drugs. Using them requires supervision by a doctor. Still, if an informed athlete decides to take steroids, he should be able to make his choice freely. We allow athletes to engage in sports—downhill skiing, for example—in which the documented incidence of death or serious injury is greater than for an athlete taking

some steroids⟧The danger here is treated as just part of sports. Steroids are treated differently not because they are dangerous, but because of politically powerful lobbies against them.

8. If you want your bridge to be strong, it should be stressed from all sides. Similarly, if you want to strengthen your mental and emotional health, you should seek all kinds of stress.

9. Many people seem to believe that animals do not feel pain the way that we do. Farm animals are frequently dehorned or castrated without anesthetic. Pets are usually not given pain-killers after surgery. But it is inconsistent to use animals as models for human physiology, even in testing the efficacy of drugs meant to be pain-killers for humans, while at the same time believing that animals do not feel pain the way that we do. [Adapted from Alan M. Beck, "Is There Intelligent (Animal) Life on Earth?," in *Dogs in Canada Annual*, vol. 85, no. 4 (1994): 144–47.]

10. There are many plausible-sounding arguments for legal assisted suicide for the terminally or chronically ill, despite the fact that suicide would be bound, in many cases, to cause emotional pain to family and friends of the ill person. Still, assisted suicide could never be permitted. Clearly, making assisted suicide legal would remove the prohibition against killing, and then it would be merely a matter of time before wide-scale enforced suicide of the elderly became policy. If doctors are permitted to end a life when the patient requests it, soon doctors will end lives at their own discretion. If society consents in any instance, soon it will be forced to consent in a case where the "right to die" is not so clear.

11. Pornography cannot be defended by using an appeal to free speech. Catherine MacKinnon has argued that even if we agree to classify pornography as speech, it could still be regulated by the government. Many acts of speech are not protected, but prohibited, because of the kind of content that they communicate—for example, "whites only."

12. Many "pro-life" supporters say that abortion should be allowed in cases of incest, rape, or medical necessity. That's not pro-life; that's pro-convenience. If life is sacred, then *all* life is sacred.

13. Film stars and other celebrities can't complain that they have no private lives. These people have hired publicists, issued press releases, ap-

peared on television talking about their private lives. . . . Very often, they are marketing their own personalities. They aren't really in a position to complain when the publicity is not to their liking.

14. It is absurd for Magic Johnson to be a spokesperson for AIDS awareness and safe sex. For years, Magic Johnson ignored safe-sex messages. Then, after he tested positive, he became their spokesperson. This is like someone who goes out and shoots a bunch of innocent people and then becomes a spokesperson for handgun control.

15. In October 1996, there was an outcry after media reports that a diabetic eight-months'-pregnant inmate in a correctional institution had remained chained to a hospital bed for five days. The woman was a first-time inmate, who had been arrested after police stopped a car in which she was riding because it made an illegal U-turn, checked her name, and found that she had failed to pay eight traffic tickets, with fines now totaling over two thousand dollars.

   A spokesman for the correctional institution said that it was customary practice to shackle inmates to the bed. There was, therefore, no other choice but to chain her to the bed.

16. Ludwig Wittgenstein was one of the greatest philosophers of the twentieth century. After completing his first book, he gave up philosophy to teach at an elementary school in rural Austria. His sister tried to dissuade him from this course of action: she said that his teaching elementary school would be like using a precision instrument to open crates.

EXERCISE 8.2 DISCUSSION AND WRITING ASSIGNMENT

I.1. A teacher said to a high-school class:
Don't try to bring a cheat sheet into the exam. People try to get away with this by saying, "Just because I brought it in, doesn't mean I was going to use it." I'm not going to fall for this. That's like walking into a bank with a gun and saying, "Just because I didn't shoot the teller, doesn't mean I wasn't going to rob the bank."

Something has gone seriously wrong with this analogy! What is the problem? Can you determine what the teacher was trying to say, and rewrite the analogy to communicate it?

2. A magazine article argued that claims of abuse by women, and the attention paid to them, were exaggerated. The article cited surveys claiming that men were also abused by women—that spousal violence was more or less equally likely to be practiced by women against their husbands as by men against their wives.

A letter to the editor said this:

> What would happen if we had results of a survey about violence between small children and their mothers? We'd probably find that a much larger number of children are violent with their mothers than mothers with their children. Children often swat and shove their mothers—I've seen it in the checkout line when Mom says "No" to a request for candy. But it is as easy for Mom to restrain the child as it is for most men to restrain their wives.

There are problems with this analogy. What are the problems? Do they affect the analogy that is made, or the conclusion the analogy wants to draw?

II. The following is adapted from David Hume's *Dialogues Concerning Natural Religion.*

"Look round the world: contemplate the whole and every part of it: you will find it to be nothing but one great machine, subdivided into an infinite number of lesser machines, which again admit of subdivisions, to a degree beyond what human senses and faculties can trace and explain. All these various machines, and even their most minute parts, are adjusted to each other with an accuracy which ravishes into admiration all men, who have ever contemplated them. The curious adapting of means to ends, throughout all nature, resembles exactly, though it much exceeds, the productions of human contrivance; of human design, thought, wisdom, and intelligence. Since therefore the effects resemble each other, we are led to infer, by all the rules of analogy, that the causes also resemble; and that the Author of Nature is somewhat similar to the mind of men; though possessed of much larger faculties. . . . [By this argument], we prove at once the existence of a Deity, and his similarity to human mind and intelligence."

1. Identify the four components of the argument from analogy. This may be easier if you first rewrite this argument in language you'd be likely to use in present-day conversation or writing.

2. Evaluate the argument.

3. Construct a similar argument from analogy to prove
   a. that the world came into existence by the same process by which a tree comes into existence
   b. that the world came into existence by the same process by which an animal comes into existence.

4. Identify the four components of the arguments from analogy in 3a and b.

5. Evaluate the arguments you constructed in 3.

6. Which (if any) of the three analogies is strongest? Why?

9 Arguments From Experience

WHEN WE **ARGUE FROM EXPERIENCE**, we use information about things that have been experienced to draw a conclusion about what we can expect from similar things that have not yet been experienced, and may never be experienced. We assume that in significant respects, the future will resemble the past. Without this sort of reasoning, we probably wouldn't survive for very long. We depend on basic expectations about life—for example, that

in the evening we'll find the house where we left it in the morning. There are other, more complicated expectations or predictions that we can make on the basis of experience. For example, if your roommate has failed to pay his share of the rent in the past, he may be likely to fail to pay again. If a political candidate failed to keep most of his promises from the last election, he's not likely to keep the promises he's making now.

It need not be one's own personal experience to which one appeals. For example, the U.S. might have expected problems from their involvement in Vietnam, based on their knowledge of the French government's experience there. If everyone in your family has received poor service from a mechanic, you would be unlikely to take your car to that same mechanic.

Arguments from experience are fundamentally different from the categorical and conditional arguments that we saw earlier. In a categorical or conditional argument, if the premises are true, the conclusion *must* be true. But in an argument from experience, the conclusion might be false even if the premises are true. The more experience the argument is based on, the more likely it is that the conclusion holds. Nevertheless, it is possible that in the present case there are differences between the past and the future that stand in the way of the conclusion. That doesn't mean that there is anything wrong with arguing from experience—it just means that we can expect surprises from time to time.

In this chapter, we'll look at three basic types of arguments from experience. We'll see how the format of the argument from analogy can help us understand these arguments, and we'll look at **statistical arguments** in particular detail.

■ TYPES OF ARGUMENTS FROM EXPERIENCE

There are three types of arguments from experience. Each uses a premise about something that has been experienced to draw a conclusion about things that have not been experienced.

GENERALIZATION. A **universal generalization** uses experience of some members of a class as a premise supporting a conclusion about all members of that class. For example,

> [1] All the daylilies I have ever seen have long spiky leaves.
> Therefore, all daylilies have long spiky leaves.

The conclusion may be qualified, or weakened, as in

> [2] All the daylilies I have ever seen have long spiky leaves.
> Therefore most daylilies have long spiky leaves.

The only difference between examples [1] and [2] is the scope of their conclusions. Example [1] says that the conclusion holds of *all* daylilies, whereas example [2] says it holds of *most*. Weakening the conclusion makes it less likely that your conclusion is simply wrong. While your experience of daylilies is extensive, it is possible that you have somehow missed one type of daylily, which has a different sort of leaf.

GENERALIZATION TO A PARTICULAR. An argument that moves from many experienced members of a class to a single unexperienced object of that kind, is called **generalization to a particular.**

> [3] All the cats I have ever met like to be combed. Lucy is a cat, so Lucy will like to be combed.

The difference between the generalization to a particular and a universal generalization is that the universal generalization draws a conclusion about some objects that you can probably never experience. Support for the conclusion that all daylilies have long spiky leaves will increase as you see more and more daylilies with long spiky leaves, but you'd never be able to see every daylily in the world. The possibility of a different type of daylily would always remain. You could, however, comb Lucy, and argument [3] tells you what to expect when you do.

STATISTICAL GENERALIZATION. The **statistical generalization** begins with knowledge about the prevalence or proportion of a certain property or properties in a group of experienced cases. Then it draws a conclusion that the prevalence or proportion is similar in unexperienced cases.

> [4] Twenty-five percent of North Americans expect an aging parent to live with them someday. Among people 18–34, 38% have this expectation, compared with only 22% of those 35–54, and 3% of those over 55. The survey was conducted on 1,000 adults from across North America.

In this argument, we have information about 1,000 adult North Americans, and we generalize this information to conclude that it's true of *all* North Americans. Again, we could probably never have experience of everyone in North America—even government censuses may miss some people.

The three types of arguments from experience share certain similarities with arguments from analogy. The argument from experience says something like the following:

> The things of this type that I have experienced are similar to other things of this type. This property holds of the things that I have experienced. Therefore, it also holds of the things of this type that I have not experienced.

Since statistical arguments have their own problems and issues, let's leave those aside for the moment and concentrate on the first two kinds. There is some new terminology that we need in order to understand and criticize arguments from experience. Your familiarity with arguments from analogy, covered in Chapter 8, will help you understand these terms.

REVIEW BOX   9.2

Components of an argument from experience

- SAMPLE: the experienced cases (A in analogical arguments)

- POPULATION: the unexperienced cases (PS)

- CATEGORY: the property that is being extended from the sample to the population (S)

- TARGET PROPERTY: the respect in which the sample and the population are similar (TP)

First, the **sample** is the experiential basis of the argument. The sample is composed of the things we know about, the things that we have experienced. In examples [1] and [2], the sample is *all the daylilies I have ever seen.* In example [3], it's *all the cats I have ever met.* The sample in the argument from experience plays the same role as the analogue in the argument from analogy.

The **population** is the subject of the conclusion; it plays the role of the primary subject. The population is the group of unexperienced cases, the things we gain new knowledge about through the argument. In examples [1] and [2], the population is *all* (or *most*) *daylilies.* In example [3], it is *Lucy the cat.*

In an argument from analogy, the similarity between the primary subject and analogue grounds the argument. In an argument from experience, the similarity between the sample and population plays a comparable role.

Instead of speaking of similarities, as we do in an argument from analogy, we speak of the **category**. In an argument from experience, we're talking about a type of thing. In examples [1] and [2], we're talking about *daylilies*; in example [3], *cats*. The sample and the population are similar in respect of being the same kind of thing.

Finally, the **target property**, as in the argument from analogy, is the property that is being extended from the sample to the population. In examples [1] and [2], the target property is *having long spiky leaves*. In [3], it's *liking to be combed*.

There are two concerns in evaluating arguments from experience—the sample and the category. First, we should ask ourselves whether the sample is adequate. For example, if you have only seen a few daylilies, or met one cat, examples [1], [2], and [3] don't have strong experiential premises. In most cases, the more experience you have, the more strongly your argument will be supported. After all, we do keep learning from experience throughout our lives: the more we've seen the more knowledge we have about what to expect.

Second, we should consider what defines the category, and what that defining property has to do with the claim made in the conclusion. To see why this is important, consider an argument with a bad category.

> [5] Every guy named Dave I've ever known has had blue eyes. Therefore most Daves probably have blue eyes.

This is a restricted universal generalization. The problem is that no matter how many Daves I've known, the conclusion is not strongly supported, because the category *Dave* is not the sort of category that supports this kind of generalization. In example [1], the category is *daylily*—a type of plant. The sort of leaves that a plant has is determined by the kind of plant that it is. Knowing what type of plant something is gives you information about its appearance. But a person's name does not give you information about his eye color. Daves are not a genuine type of thing. They only form a category by accident, and if they had different names, they'd still be the same individuals. A person's name is the result of his parents' choice, and his eye color is the result of his parents' genes. So the fact that all the Daves

---

REVIEW BOX 9.3

The form of an argument from experience

1. Sample and population are similar.

2. Sample has target property.

Therefore, population has target property.

Compare this argument form to that given in Review Box 8.2.

I'd ever known—no matter how many—had blue eyes, could only be a coincidence.

Strategies and Conventions

Questions about arguments from experience

• Is the sample adequate?
• Is the category well defined?
• Is the property that defines the category relevant to the conclusion?

(You should answer *yes* to all three.)

What about Lucy the cat? *Cat* names a category of animals. Liking to be combed is a feature of cat behavior. Behavior is partly determined by the kind of thing that you are. The conclusion of example [3] is probably fairly well-supported. Still, as we saw in Chapter 8, determining the criteria by which a thing is said to be of a certain category is a difficult matter. For example, should species membership be determined by observable characteristics, or by DNA?

Asking whether the category is well enough defined to support the conclusion is like asking of an argument from analogy whether the similarities between the analogue and the primary subject are adequate to ground the conclusion. We have to have reason to believe that the target property will be carried over from the analogue to the primary subject. Similarly, we must have some reason to believe that past experience of this type of thing will provide a basis for making a prediction about future instances of this type of thing.

Hasty Generalization

The fallacy of **hasty generalization** occurs when someone argues as if a few experiences are adequate to generalize to a wide-ranging conclusion. Someone who commits this fallacy is sometimes said to be using **anecdotal evidence**. An *anecdote* is a story. So as evidence for a conclusion, the person uses a story or a few stories. These are often stories about the arguer's own life. Naturally, since experience is such a fundamental path to knowledge, one's own life experiences seem decisive. Consider the following example:

> [6] I've known some math professors, and they were real jerks. I wouldn't trust any of them.

Even if the arguer had known truly nasty math professors, one person's experience is unlikely to be wide enough to support a conclusion about all math professors. Yet although the flaw is obvious, people argue this way. You'll notice that the fallacy of hasty generalization is the result of contravening one of the conditions for accepting of premises that we saw in Chapter 6: in hasty generalizations, the arguer provides testimony that goes beyond personal experience. Here's another example:

REVIEW BOX 9.4

Hasty generalization

This fallacy occurs when someone argues as though a few experiences are adequate premises to support a wide-ranging general conclusion.

> [7] There are many reasons that women are underrepresented in science, and I believe that 95% of these are societal. As a woman in fourth-year chemistry, I live with these issues. I've had profs who intimidate women in class, who have made sexist comments to me, and who are not professional enough to see that their beliefs about the appropriate position of women in science cannot be allowed to interfere with their teaching.

What is wrong with this argument? The arguer does not provide a wide enough basis for the conclusion that she draws. She has provided enough information to support the claim that she has suffered from professors' gender bias, but this is all. In order to accept her conclusion, we would need to know that she has experienced a wide variety of professors at many different schools. For most students, such experience simply isn't possible; even those who attend three or four different institutions while earning their degree(s) have a very limited sample. Furthermore, the arguer cannot support the claim that 95% of the reasons that women are underrepresented in science are societal. A conclusion like this could only be the result of wide-ranging research that used respectable methods for gathering statistical data.

It is important to distinguish between anecdotal evidence and examples. Anecdotal evidence is bad evidence. Examples, however, can help persuade the audience. Take this passage:

> [8] A study of two weeks of family-based situation comedies which had a main character who was a child 17 or younger showed that one third of all advice was given by children to adults. An episode of *Growing Pains* showed both parents asking two of their children for advice about how to discipline a third child. [Adapted from Amy Jordan, "The Portrayal of Children in Prime-Time Situation Comedies," *Journal of Popular Culture*, vol. 29, no. 3 (1995): 139–147.]

In example [8], the proposition about *Growing Pains* is not used as evidence to support the conclusion that one third of all advice was given by children to adults. The study that the author mentions would provide that support. Rather, the particular television episode is used as an example to illustrate the sort of advice that is at issue. An example can strengthen an argument by clarifying the issues and making them seem familiar. In the case of example [8], someone might think "I remember that episode," or recall a similar situation from a different TV show. People like examples. Frequently, adding a few particular examples or personal stories can make the issues more real to the audience—composed, after all, of humans, who have a natural interest in other humans' stories and experiences.

This interest may explain why hasty generalization is so often used and accepted. But in examples [6] and [7], the only support for the conclusion is provided by the anecdotes, whereas the conclusion of example [8] is supported by premises about a study. We could look up and evaluate this study. If the particular example were removed, the passage would still contain an argument.

EXERCISE 9.1

Imagine that each of the arguments in this exercise set was advanced by the people in the lists that follow the arguments. Then, for each person,

   i. identify the population, the target property, and the category;

   ii. suggest the likely sample (this may vary depending on who advances the argument); and

   iii. evaluate the argument.

1. X-brand cars are lousy. They have major design flaws. Sometimes their engines fail shortly after you buy the car, either because the company has tried to use one engine design for another purpose—e.g., a gas engine inadequately modified to work as a diesel engine—or because they rushed development on a new engine design. Sometimes there are such rust problems that the car is unsafe to drive for longer than two years. Doors have even fallen off some of these cars before they're out of warranty.
   a. a mechanic
   b. a new car dealer
   c. a used car dealer
   d. a former owner of two X-brand cars
   e. the author of *Lemonaid* (an annual consumer guide providing data collected from drivers, mechanics, and automobile associations on the reliability and safety of new and used cars)
   f. an engineer at the factory where these cars are manufactured.

2. Violence in high schools is increasing. Whereas twenty-five years ago, fights between students were generally easily resolved and soon forgotten, fights today can lead to stabbings and shootings. It is more likely now that fights are caused by drug deals gone bad. Some drugs make people more violent and less able to resolve their differences peacefully.
   a. a high school student
   b. a high school principal
   c. a superintendent of schools
   d. a sociologist
   e. a newspaper reporter

3. Young people in the sixties were more interested in social justice than young people today. Young people are more materialistic and cynical now than they were then. Undergraduates these days are more interested in getting through school and finding a job; they don't care much about real knowledge or issues that affect people outside their own social group.

a. an undergraduate
b. the undergraduate's father
c. someone who was involved in social action in the sixties
d. someone who is involved in social action now
e. an English professor
f. a history professor
g. a demographer

▮ STATISTICAL ARGUMENTS

It's very important to have some basic knowledge of statistical arguments, because they are widely used. Some people find numbers and statistical methods intimidating and they tend to accept any information that is presented as the result of statistical research. Others, who know statistics, may believe that the quality of the statistical argument depends only on mathematical considerations. But as we'll see in this chapter, there are many questions we can ask and many flaws we can identify without doing any math.

Like all arguments from experience, statistical arguments generalize from experienced cases (the sample) to unexperienced cases (the population). They also contain a target property that is extended and require that the sample and population be similar. However, these familiar components have a slightly different meaning for the statistical argument. Let's remind ourselves of the example used above:

> [4] Twenty-five percent of North Americans expect an aging parent to live with them someday. Among people 18–34, 38% have this expectation, compared with only 22% of those 35–54, and 3% of those over 55. The survey was conducted on 1,000 adults from across North America.

The sample is composed of the subjects who provided the data that serves as the basis for the generalization: in this case, one thousand adults from across North America. The population is what we gain new information about—North Americans. Note that the composition of the sample can help you identify the population. In example [4], we have information about North Americans over 18, so we cannot generalize the conclusion to people outside of this group—for example, to Europeans or to people who are under 18.

In example [4], the target property is *expectation that an aging parent will cohabit someday*. In many statistical arguments, as we'll see later, the target property is actually a "family" of properties. Even in example [4], we notice that the target property is broken down by expectations in various age groups.

So the components of the statistical argument in example [4], are, in summary:

> **REVIEW BOX   9.5**
>
> ## Components of a statistical argument
>
> • SAMPLE: experienced cases
>
> • POPULATION: unexperienced cases
>
> • TARGET PROPERTY: usually a "family" of properties, expressed in percentages
>
> • SIMILARITY: the sample is **representative** of the population

[4a] *Sample*: 1,000 people from across North America

Population: North Americans

Target property: expectation that an aging parent will come to cohabit someday: for all North Americans; for those aged 18–34; for those aged 35–54; for those over 55.

As we know, the issue of similarity was important to evaluating arguments from analogy. Likewise, in nonstatistical arguments from experience, there must be a similarity between experienced and unexperienced cases. The issue of similarity in statistical arguments—that is, whether the sample is **representative**—is complicated, and will require a lengthy discussion later in this chapter.

As we'll see, there are two questions to ask about statistical arguments: *What did you count?* and *How did you count it?* First, what you count is, of course, the sample. The composition of the sample itself is one main consideration. Is it big enough? Is it representative? Was it gathered in a legitimate way? In what follows we'll investigate means of answering these questions. Second, the researcher needs some reliable means of determining whether the target property occurs in any given member of the sample. We'll also explore the way in which the researcher determines whether to count a given individual as exemplifying the target property.

What Did You Count?

The first thing we need to determine is whether the sample and the population are similar in ways that matter. If the sample was not selected well, the information gained from it won't accurately reflect the population as a whole.

SAMPLE SIZE. First, we should ask whether the sample was big enough. As we saw with the first two types of argument from experience, the more experience you have, the better your conclusion is supported. In a statistical argument, the bigger your sample (up to a point), the better your conclusion can be supported (because a bigger sample reduces the margin of error). The margin of error is, basically, the amount by which you could be wrong in drawing your conclusion. When example [4] concludes that 25% of North Americans in general expect their aging parents to cohabit, we take that to mean *about* 25%. The range that the approximation covers will vary with the sample size and the confidence level. The confidence level is the probability that the result is true of the population within the margin of error.

Very roughly, on a sample size of 20, your margin of error will be around 20% for a confidence level of .95 and an ideal sample. That means that it's 95% likely that the result is true within 20%. A slightly larger sample of 100 would reduce the margin of error to 8%. Margins of error decrease very slowly as the numbers get larger. For a sample size of 1,000 people, the margin of error is 2.5%, but for a much larger sample of 2,000, it only decreases to 2%.

It is important to recognize that there is no one number that is "big enough," and certainly no formula or simple rule of thumb for assessing this. The way in which the sample was collected and the homogeneity (sameness) of the population are important considerations. For example, imagine that you asked 100 students whether they preferred Option A, being hit over the head with a brick, or Option B, not being hit over the head with anything. Probably 100% of your 100 people would choose Option B. Allowing for the margin of error given above, you can still safely conclude that at least 92% of students prefer not to be hit over the head with bricks. That's a large majority of students, so you have a noteworthy conclusion. In this case, your sample and your population would probably be similar enough in the ways that matter to make your sample representative. The likelihood is that most students, whatever their age, religious beliefs, gender, and so on, would prefer not to be hit over the head. The only thing that would matter in this case is that your sample and your population are both composed of sentient beings, and sentient beings don't like pain.

If, however, your study concerns an issue on which differences among people could be expected to affect the results, the sample must be big enough to reflect any relevant differences. For example, take a study to determine why students at a given college chose their major. At the college, students can enroll in arts, science, or social science. In arts, there are seven possible majors. In science, there are ten. In social science, there are eleven. Thus there are twenty-eight possible majors. A sample of 20 students would not even cover all possible majors. Students may choose a major because it's interesting to them, because their parents expect it, because it's likely to lead to a lucrative career, because their friends chose it, or for one of many other reasons. If we wanted to give the sample the chance to represent all possible combinations of majors and reasons, we'd need a larger sample than we did for the question of being hit over the head, where there were only two options and one relevant human characteristic.

If the subjects are humans, you may often need a fairly large sample just to ensure that enough different kinds of people are represented—differences in age, gender, occupation, social class, education level, ethnic background, religious beliefs, diet, and so on. Some of these factors may be important in the study at issue, others may not.

In the case of the aging parent/cohabitation study in example [4], 1,000 people is a fair size. Because of the differences that could be expected among people on a subject like living arrangements, a reasonably large sample would be required. We probably wouldn't fault the study on the grounds of sample size—at least not on the basis of the information we've been given.

SAMPLE COMPOSITION. Since the question of sample size cannot be separated from the question of sample composition, let's turn to the issue of determining whether the sample is representative of the population in ways that matter. The individuals composing the sample must reflect relevant differences among the individuals composing the population. One way to try to ensure that a sample is representative is to make it a **random sample**. A sample is random if and only if any member of the population has an equal chance of being selected for the sample. (Note: this is an operational definition of *random sample*.)

Strategies and Conventions

Questions for samples

• Is the sample big enough?
• What kind of individuals compose it?

In many cases, a truly random sample is not a realistic goal, because of the time and money that would be required to choose randomly from a large population such as *North Americans*. Consider, for example, a sociologist who has a grant to conduct a study of North Americans—randomness would require that she travel widely to interview the participants; and she may have to pay them for participation. It's likely that instead, she'll look for a captive group of subjects: the undergraduates in her large survey course, for example. These students can be enticed to participate with bonus marks, and they're readily available without travel.

But the problem is that any data gathered about these undergraduates may not be generalizable to North Americans in general. The sample *undergraduates* is, for many target properties, not representative of the population *North Americans*. Students may be North Americans, but they're a certain sort of North Americans. Students are in some respects a fairly homogenous group. They're probably all roughly the same age. There are, of course, mature students who have returned to school, but at most schools they're a minority. Undergraduate students are also similar in terms of education level. There may be a world of difference between what they know in their first year and what they know in their third year, but both the first-year and the third-year students would be classified in the population at large as having "some college education." Moreover, since level of education is likely a correlate of social class, all the undergraduates belong to roughly the same social class. Obviously they all have the same occupation: "student." In summary, the differences that exist between individual students do not outweigh the fact that not all people are students. You should be wary of studies that were performed on the author's students, because this sometimes means that the sample was not representative of the intended population.

One sampling error that has received a lot of publicity in recent years is the fact that many medical and drug studies were performed on huge samples, composed of different sorts of people, of different ages and habits—but all men. The results were generalized to people in general. The rationale for the exclusion of women from these studies was that women might be pregnant, and that women's menstrual cycles might affect the results. Even the mice used in laboratory experiments were mostly male mice.

Strategies and Conventions

Questions for representativeness of samples

- Is the sample composed of individuals representative of the population in ways relevant to the target property? For a good argument, answer *yes*.
- Is the manner in which the sample was collected relevant to the target property? For a good argument, answer *no*.

This mattered. What's a medical study concerned with, broadly speaking? Human physiology. What's a major difference between men and women? Their physiological characteristics. So in some cases, the fairly obvious physical differences between men and women meant that the results of these studies on men could not just be transferred to women. For example, prolonged alcohol use affects women differently from men, because women have a higher percentage of body fat. AIDS-related conditions are differently manifested in women than in men. In fact, several women in the United States had to sue their insurance companies to get coverage for medication in the early years of AIDS, since in many cases the manifestation of their illness was not on the approved list of symptoms. Both the United States and Canada now have legislation requiring that many types of medical studies include women.

Remember that our process of evaluation for arguments from analogy consisted of looking for differences between the primary subject and analogue that would stand in the way of the conclusion. Here, we are looking for differences between the sample and the population that could stand in the way of the conclusion. If the sample is not representative in ways that matter to the properties under investigation, then the conclusion may not follow.

If true randomness isn't possible, you have to use your background knowledge to consider what could affect your results. If you want to know what percentage of the population believes in life after death, you shouldn't conduct your survey on the steps of a church, even a randomly selected one, on Sunday morning. Likewise, if you want to know about people's drinking habits, don't do your survey in a bar on Tuesday afternoon. In both cases, the method of collecting the sample has an effect on the answers you're likely to get. When you evaluate a statistical argument, ask if the conditions under which the sample was collected could influence the results. You should answer *no* to this question.

Another method that researchers use for getting a representative sample is to choose a sample so that it reflects classifications already known to exist in the population. This is called a **stratified sample**. For example, a stratified sample might be composed of roughly equal numbers of men and women. If you were polling your university community and you know that 37% of undergraduates are in their first year, you'd ensure that 37% of your sample, also, was composed of first-year students. And you would represent other classifications in a similar manner.

What can we say about the sampling in example [4]?

> [4] Twenty-five percent of North Americans expect an aging parent to live with them someday. Among people 18–34, 38% have this expectation, compared with only 22% of those 35–54, and 3% of those over 55. The survey was conducted on 1,000 adults from across North America.

The passage says the 1,000 participants came from across North America. That's good, because there may (or may not) be regional differences in expectations about living arrangements with aging parents—North America is a big place. There is, however, no information in the passage about how these 1,000 people were chosen, and that may be important. Ideally, in this case, we'd like to see a stratified sample, taking account of any circumstances that could be relevant.

What circumstances could be relevant to people's expectations concerning whether their aging parents will come to live with them? Income level, certainly. People in a lower income bracket might be more likely to believe that their parents couldn't afford to live on their own after retirement. People in a high income bracket, on the other hand, might be less concerned about their parents' financial security. So unless the sample contained a proportionate number of people in all income brackets, the result would not be generalizable to the North American population.

Strategies and Conventions

A reminder

Look for relevant differences between sample and population.

What about parents' health? People whose parents are in poor health may believe that this condition will prevent them from living alone. That could, in turn, make it more likely that the respondents would expect their parents to cohabit. We'd like to know that these 1,000 North Americans were not interviewed as they waited for their parents in a doctor's office.

Cultural background could also influence people's expectations. Different cultures may have different expectations about intergenerational living arrangements. We'd want to know that all the cultural subgroups present in North America were represented in adequate proportions.

When we ask these questions, we're asking whether there is anything about the members of the sample that might cause them to give a certain range of answers to the questions. Criticizing an argument on these grounds requires background knowledge and creativity, because we must consider every factor that could affect the conclusion.

Since we have no information about any of these factors, we cannot say that the study was a bad one. This is a common evaluation we make of statistical arguments; rather than say that an argument is bad, we often say that we need answers to certain questions before we can fully accept its conclusion. If we were to look up the published study on which example

[4] was based, we would probably find answers to at least some of the questions that we've raised here in our discussion.

Let's consider the sampling in another example.

> [9] A 1989 study reported that 65% of students in Ontario universities are moderate drinkers. However, almost 30% are heavy drinkers, who have 15 or more drinks per week. Among these heaviest drinkers, 18% have 15–28 drinks per week, and 11% have more than 28 drinks per week. The Addiction Research Foundation undertook the study. From four unidentified Ontario universities, 13,200 full-time undergraduates were randomly selected. Questionnaires were distributed by mail. Almost 5,000 responded.

One of the first things to notice is that this study may not give us information about current student drinking habits. Nineteen eighty-nine was a long time ago, and many relevant changes have taken place. Cuts to university funding and student aid mean that students today may have less disposable income than students had in 1989. Many people could drink—even quite heavily—as a social activity. But drinking is expensive. So lack of money could mean fewer people in the bars, and thus less opportunity for social interaction. As a result, people who drank for social reasons might drop the habit. If your study is about people, see when it was done. Some human characteristics remain the same through time, but some wax and wane with fashion and economics.

Second, let's identify our components.

> [9a] *Sample*: 5,000 respondents to the survey
>
> *Population*: Ontario undergraduate students
>
> *Target property*: drinking—how much

To be most fair to the argument, we should take the population to be undergraduate Ontario university students. That's what composes the sample, and we are not justified in extending the information gained through the study beyond the population represented by the sample. This sample may not be representative of people in general, since drinking may play a different social role for undergraduates than for others. It may not be representative of graduate students. Regional differences may mean that it will not be representative of undergraduates outside of Ontario. The principle of charity dictates that we take the population to be the one that could be best supported by the argument (unless the argument claims a wider applicability).

The sample size is certainly adequate. True randomness is also possible here in choosing who received the questionnaire. Registrar's offices, for example, have lists of their students. These lists could have been requested and names chosen by some random algorithm (every twentieth name on the list, for example). Sample composition is the big problem. The four universities surveyed are not identified, and without that information, we can't be satisfied that the results are true of the entire Ontario undergraduate population. Are students at some universities likely to drink more or less than others? Some universities have reputations as party schools. If all four schools surveyed were that sort, our sample would not be representative of *all* Ontario universities. Perhaps students at urban universities are more likely to have access to many kinds of activities, while suburban students are more likely to go to a campus bar.

In general, then, choosing and evaluating a sample means considering it in the context of the target properties being investigated. A badly chosen sample can make the study pointless even before the data have been collected.

How Did You Count It?

After you have chosen your sample, you must carry out your research and collect the data. Your **measurement instrument** is the means by which you measure the occurrence of the properties you're interested in. There are many ways in which research can be conducted. To measure the height of students in your class, for example, you'd use a ruler. Often in the social sciences, you want to measure the occurrence of a certain network of beliefs, habits, or relationships, and for this purpose you might use interviews, tests, written surveys, experiments, or research through records or artifacts.

There are two criteria for measurement instruments: reliability and validity. **Reliability** means consistency, not accuracy. A reliable instrument is one that gives the same results under the same conditions. If my wristwatch is always ten minutes fast, then it's reliable. It does not give the correct time, but it always gives a time ten minutes ahead of the correct time. However, if my wristwatch gains or loses time at odd intervals, then it is not reliable. If an instrument is accurate, then it's reliable. But it is not true that if it's reliable then it's accurate.

> ### REVIEW BOX 9.6
>
> ### Reliability and validity
>
> A measurement instrument ought to be reliable and valid.
>
> • A reliable instrument is one that gives the same results under the same conditions
>
> • A valid instrument measures what it claims to measure

A **valid**[1] instrument is one that actually measures what it claims to measure; that is, valid data are true. A measurement instrument can be reliable without being valid. IQ tests, which we discussed in Chapter 5, are a good example. They are reliable, since they give the same results under the same conditions. But are they valid; do they actually test *intelligence*? As we saw in Chapter 5, the complaint about IQ tests is that they judge as unintelligent some people who might be judged intelligent by other means. This is how validity must be tested: by comparing results from one test to results from a different test performed on the same subjects. You can see the difficulty—the second test must be considered valid. In this case, the colloquial understanding of "intelligent" seemed to be at odds with the quantitative IQ test. But the IQ test was created in order to provide a more precise and reliable method than everyday judgments for determining intelligence.

Sometimes you'll see results measured by what the researchers refer to as "standard tests." These tests are called standard because they're believed to be reliable and valid. If you want to question the reliability and validity of these tests, you'll have to do more research.

There are problems peculiar to various ways of collecting data, which can stand in the way of reliability and validity. Our drinking survey can introduce us to one problem—the self-selected sample.

---

[1]You'll remember that we've also used the term "valid" of arguments. It's unfortunate that there are two different technical meanings for the same word. When you see the word "valid" just keep in mind that the context will determine the meaning.

[9] A 1989 study reported that 65% of students in Ontario universities are moderate drinkers. However, almost 30% are heavy drinkers, who have 15 or more drinks per week. Among these heaviest drinkers, 18% have 15–28 drinks per week, and 11% have more than 28 drinks per week. The Addiction Research Foundation undertook the study. From four unidentified Ontario universities, 13,200 full-time undergraduates were randomly selected. Questionnaires were distributed by mail. Almost 5,000 responded.

Obviously, the method of collecting data here is the mailed questionnaire. What about the fact that of 13,200 surveys sent out, only 5,000 responded? That's a poor response rate—38%. So we should ask whether there is some important reason that *these* people chose to respond rather than others. Is there something relevant to the questions being asked that would appeal to a certain group? There is nothing immediately striking that would associate drinking habits with the low return rate. We could suggest that the heaviest drinkers are too busy drinking to respond, or that the heaviest drinkers have nothing better to do, but neither of these possibilities is particularly salient.

As an example of a case in which self-selection does make a difference, consider a call-in poll on a radio chat show. That poll is unlikely to be representative. Someone who will dial in—possibly encountering busy signals—most likely feels quite strongly about the matter at hand. The participants are more likely to be "for" or "against" than they are to be in the "I don't care" range.

A plausible explanation for the low response rate in the drinking survey is that students are hard to track down—they move, for example, so that the addresses that the university has for them may be out-of-date. Researchers who can afford to do so ought to track down the people who received the survey, and do all they can to maximize the return rate, even going so far as to pay people to participate when necessary. In the case of the student drinking study, the researchers should have contacted as many nonrespondents as possible, obtained their participation by whatever means necessary, and checked whether their answers fall into any particular pattern. The pattern, if there is one, *may* indicate the way in which the return rate affected the results.

The difficulty of returns affects mailed surveys, but another problem occurs in face-to-face interviews, especially for certain types of questions. Imagine that you were being interviewed about your drinking or sexual habits, by an interviewer who looked remarkably like your mother. Would you find it easy to be altogether honest? Or if you were an underage drinker, you might not give accurate answers to an interviewer who looked like an authority figure. Since an interviewer who looked like your mother might elicit a completely different response from you than one who did not, the interview is not reliable.

Neutrality itself may even pose a problem to validity. Michael Root, in *Philosophy of Social Science*[2] says that there is no reason to believe that data collected by a neutral, blank-faced person are valid. What the researcher has learned is how people respond to an impassive, blank-faced person, not how they really are—unless you believe that people's true nature is shown by how they respond to a blank-faced person. And this is hard to accept since it's not a standard human experience to talk, especially about personal matters, to someone who does not react. So the impassivity itself might take the subjects aback.

EXERCISE 9.2 DISCUSSION AND WRITING ASSIGNMENT

If you're planning to go to graduate school, you'll probably need to take a GRE (Graduate Record Examination). This is a standardized test administered by ETS (Educational Testing Service). The skills tested are thought to be the ones most relevant to success in graduate school: reasoning ability, verbal ability, and so on. ETS claims that the GRE is a valid predictor of success; that is to say, the people who do well on the GRE are likely to be the people who do well in graduate school.

The GRE has been accused of racial bias. ETS has defended the GRE against charges of racial bias by pointing out that the GRE is a valid predictor of success in graduate school, and that it is a valid predictor for students of different races.

---

[2]Cambridge: Blackwell, 1993, p. 147, n. 27.

Does ETS's defense show that the GRE is not racially biased? Why or why not? [This exercise was suggested by Michael Root's book.]

Operationalization

When asking *How did you count it?*, another important issue is this: what questions, exactly, were asked? What did the researchers count as exemplifying the properties under investigation? Recall the drinking survey.

> [9] A 1989 study reported that 65% of students in Ontario universities are moderate drinkers. However, almost 30% are heavy drinkers, who have 15 or more drinks per week. Among these heaviest drinkers, 18% have 15-28 drinks per week, and 11% have more than 28 drinks per week. The Addiction Research Foundation undertook the study. From four unidentified Ontario universities, 13,200 full-time undergraduates were randomly selected. Questionnaires were distributed by mail. Almost 5,000 responded.

In this case, it is clear that the respondents answered questions like the following: "How many drinks per week do you have—0–5, 5–10, 10–15, 15–28, over 28?" The respondents could easily determine which category they fell into: they merely had to count the number of drinks per week and fill in the appropriate answer. Compare this with an imaginary questionnaire that asked "Are you a heavy, moderate, light, or non-drinker?" This would elicit responses that differed from person to person. Someone who grew up in a family in which no one drank at all might regard five drinks a week was really fairly heavy; while someone who grew up in a family that drank more might consider 15 drinks a week as moderate. In other words, the second survey would not be reliable—the same number of drinks would elicit different answers from different respondents, depending on the assumptions of the respondent. Moreover, the second survey would not be valid because it would not measure how much people actually drank, but rather, how they perceived their drinking habits.

Any researcher needs to **operationalize** all important concepts so that the respondents are not required to judge for themselves what the concepts encompass. If you think back to Chapter 5, you'll remember that an operational definition is an attempt to give necessary and sufficient conditions for the use of the term that's defined. The researcher has to decide in advance what defines the categories at issue. We have seen the importance of operationalization in cases where terms are likely to have different meanings for different respondents. Operationalization is valuable not only in social science research but also in the natural sciences. For example, when studying a possible cure for a disease, the researcher must decide what will constitute a cure. In cancer research, someone is generally considered cured after he or she has survived without cancer for five years.

Sometimes surveys contain questions that only permit a certain range of responses. As a result, the respondent may find that none of the possible responses are accurate. These are called **loaded questions**, and their relevance to operationalization is obvious: the researcher has failed to allow for likely responses in deciding what constitutes *yes* and *no* answers.

For example, here are two questions from a survey that was sent to all female faculty members at a single university. The survey explained that this was a study to evaluate female faculty members' experiences.

> **[10]** Is your spouse/living partner supportive of your career?
>
> Yes_____ No_____
>
> How does he show his support? _____

This was a poorly designed questionnaire. The first question does not allow for the possibility that the respondent has no spouse or living partner. The researcher could have avoided this mistake by giving a third alternative response, "Not applicable" or "I don't have one." The second question compounds the error. First, it presupposes a "Yes" answer to the first question. This could have been avoided by adding the line "If *yes*, go on to question 2. If *no* or *not applicable*, skip to question 3." Second, it assumes that the living partner is male. These problems with the questionnaire design would render any responses worthless. Someone whose living partner was another woman might be offended by the second question and throw the survey in the recycling bin. Someone who had no living partner would not know how to answer either question. The survey could have been explicitly restricted to heterosexual partnered women, but it was not.

Researching Sensitive Topics

Dependable answers on some topics are difficult to get. Take illegal activities, for example. If you wanted to know how many people embezzle money from their companies without getting caught, do you really think you could find people who had done so and who were willing to answer your question honestly? There are some secrets that people keep from everyone, including social scientists. Besides, if you did get an answer to this sort of question, would you feel morally bound to report the wrongdoer? What if the activity were something heinous, like having sex with children? If you would report a wrongdoer, how could you expect to get an honest answer?

It's not only questions about illegal or immoral activities that may elicit untruthful responses. For example, if someone asked you what you saw on TV last night, you might mention a documentary on PBS, but would you admit that you watched a prurient confrontational chat show? Maybe not. Researchers for the Nielsen television ratings know that people lie about their viewing choices in order to be judged favorably by others. That's why they don't rely on viewer's reports, but instead track the viewing selections by means of a device attached to the TV.

An example of a case in which people may have lied was a huge study of Americans' sexual habits, carried out with a sample size of 3,432. The number of female sex partners reported by men was greater than the number of male sex partners reported by women. If the men and women were having sex with each other, the numbers should have added up. The researchers offered several possible explanations: the men may have been having sex with non-American women who were not included in the survey; there may have been some women, not included in the sample, who had a very large number of sex partners; men and women may have differed in what they called a "sex partner"; or, of course, many respondents may have offered inaccurate reports.[3]

People lie for many reasons, good and bad, so when you see a survey purporting to have collected data on questions you can't imagine answering, consider whether the nature of the questions might have affected the data.

[3]E. Laumann, J. Gagnon, R. Michael, S. Michaels, *The Social Organization of Sexuality* (Chicago and London: University of Chicago Press, 1994).

Ethical Issues in Research

We've seen several ways in which methodology can be unacceptable. Another question that can be asked in evaluating statistical arguments from experience is whether the methodology is unacceptable for ethical reasons.

If you are researching people, you may affect their lives. Professional organizations such as the American Psychological Association and the American Sociological Association, as well as grant organizations, such as the Social Sciences and Humanities Research Council of Canada, often have codes of ethics that proscribe certain research methods that may harm the subjects.

Included among these codes are the following. Informed consent must be obtained, except in unusual circumstances. If the subjects are members of a powerless group, such as prison inmates, employees, or the socially deprived, the researcher, who is in a position of greater power, must not obtain consent by exerting any form of subtle pressure. The subject must be told what sort of privacy and confidentiality are guaranteed. If the researcher is studying a different culture, he must explain his aims and methods in terms that make sense to the subjects, and he must obey whatever strictures the culture places upon its activities. (If he is a man, for instance, he cannot participate in rites which are forbidden to men.) No researcher can make permanent changes to the subjects' beliefs and attitudes.

What kind of unusual circumstances cancel the need to obtain informed consent? They are ones in which informed consent would give the subject some idea what was being studied. The argument is that this knowledge might change the subjects' natural behavior and thus invalidate the data. Deception is not uncommon in social science research. For example, subjects of psychological experiments are sometimes told that they are participating in a study that has a different purpose from the one it actually has. In sociological research, the researcher sometimes deceives the subjects by pretending to be a member of their social group.

The ethical guidelines generally state that deception is permissible when significant scientific knowledge will result, when the harm to the subjects is slight, and when no other methods will work. When deception is used, the subjects are debriefed afterward. That is, the researchers tell them the truth about the experiments and explain why the deception was necessary.

Can such deception be ethical? Some people think that any serious harm is physical harm. They argue that in social science research, no one will be physically harmed by the experiments or research. Thus any risk is outweighed by the knowledge that would result. This criterion of *significant scientific results* amounts to saying that scientific knowledge is more valuable than the participant's autonomy—the participant's ability to give truly informed consent. The criterion of *slight harm to the subjects* is difficult to gauge as well. It is likely that not all serious harm is physical in nature. Consider a case in which a researcher gains the trust of someone by pretending to be a member of her social group and then reveals the deception. To the subject, this may not seem much different from a personal betrayal. You must decide whether an experience in which an individual's trust in other people is diminished constitutes slight harm. Is the harm really slight if the experience permanently alters the subject's beliefs and attitudes?

Opposition to animal experiments is based on a similar argument that the methodology is not justified by the significance of the knowledge that will result. Again, the question is whether there is a means of research that would result in similar data while causing less harm.

Some people think that ethical questions are irrelevant to evaluating the quality of an argument. Other people think that since evaluating statistical arguments consists largely of evaluating the methods of gathering data, anything that makes those methods inappropriate to the subject matter should be part of the evaluation.

EXERCISE 9.3   DISCUSSION AND WRITING ASSIGNMENT

I. A great deal of information was collected in "medical experiments" carried out on inmates in Nazi death camps. At Dachau, for example, people were frozen to death over varying periods of time. These experiments were definitely morally unacceptable—they violated the Nuremberg code on human experimentation. That's not the issue here.

Many of these experiments did not follow scientific standards for experiment design. But if an experiment conducted in this way did follow proper standards and the results were valid, can the data be used? Do they qualify as scientific knowledge?

Some people argue that, although the unethical means of data collection are reprehensible, they do not affect the value of the data. Others argue that ethical considerations should not be excluded in evaluation of data. What do you think? Why?

II. A famous experiment by psychologist Stanley Milgram[4] was intended to investigate how far people are willing to go in obeying authority. Would they contravene their own moral code or harm others to obey someone whom they perceived as an authority?

Each subject was told that the experiment involved only himself and another subject. The second person pretended to be a subject, but was actually a confederate of the researcher. The real subject was told that the experiment was a memory test, in which he was the teacher and the pretend subject was the learner. The researcher explained (deceptively) that the focus of the experiment was on the learner.

During the experiment, the learner (the pretend subject) was strapped into a chair. The teacher (the real subject) sat at a "control panel," which had thirty switches ranging from 15 to 450 volts. Affixed to the panel were handwritten labels which rated the switches on a scale ranging from "Slight Shock" to "Danger: Severe Shock."

The teacher was instructed to read lists of words to the learner. If the learner failed to repeat them accurately, the teacher was told to give him an escalating series of electric shocks.

No shocks were actually given. However, the learner acted out distress whenever the teacher seemed to give a shock. His expressions ranged from a mild grunt, through protests and pleas to be unstrapped, to agonized screams. Finally he fell silent.

The researcher followed a script. If the teacher protested and said he'd prefer to stop shocking the victim, the experimenter said "Please go on." If the subject continued to protest, the experimenter said "The experiment requires that you continue." At the third protest, the experimenter said "It is absolutely essential that you go on." Finally, the experimenter said "You have no other choice, you must go on."

Many subjects protested but carried on after hearing one or more of these statements from the researcher. Many people carried the experiment through till the end, when they were administering shocks that would have been fatal, and all sounds from the victim had ceased. All

[4]*Obedience to Authority: An Experimental View* (New York: Harper and Row, 1974).

subjects became visibly distressed and anxious. (Some subjects said "No, I do have a choice. I'm leaving." But not as many as you'd hope.)

Debriefing consisted of explaining that there were no electric shocks actually given. The debriefing continued long enough to soothe and calm the subject. It also validated the subject's actions, whatever they had been. If the subject had continued with the shocks, he was told not to worry, most people did the same, and any feelings of distress were also shared by other subjects. If the subject had refused to go on, that was also validated. Subjects were told they would receive a copy of the results when the experiment was completed. Follow-up questionnaires were also sent, which asked about their feelings about the experiment.

Was this experiment unethical? You should consider the following questions: Were the subjects harmed? What was learned and could it have been learned any other way? If it could have been learned another way, how does that affect your position on the experiment's ethics?

Evaluating Statistical Arguments

Now that we have explored the questions to ask about statistical arguments, let's look at a few examples. We'll need to combine all of the skills introduced in this chapter. Remember them by remembering these two questions: *What are you counting?* and *How are you counting it?*

> [11] Girls are starting to prefer violent video games, as boys do. In a study conducted on 364 children in fourth and fifth grade in a suburban Ohio school district, a majority of girls disagreed with the statement "Most kids don't think girls should play fighting games." Boys and girls agreed in equal numbers with the statement "Girls should play the fighting games." Boys were only slightly more likely than girls to agree with the statement "Fighting games are mostly for boys."
>
> The researchers fear that instead of boys' adopting female conflict-resolution strategies, girls may become more ruthless and competitive by playing violent video games.

Let's list our components. The sample is *364 children in a suburban Ohio school district.* The population is, apparently, *girls;* we'll assume that whatever *girl* covers it's at least female students in the fourth and fifth grades. The target property is something like *attitude toward violent video games.*

First, what did the researchers count? Example [11] is adapted from a newspaper report of a study, so we don't have all the information we'd want. The sample size is not very large and has a margin of error of about 6% to 7%. However, we have not been given actual numbers of "agree" and "disagree" responses. That means that any issues of sample size and its margin of error cannot be raised. We also would like to know how many of these 364 kids were girls and how many boys.

But it's probably more profitable for us to concentrate on who made up the sample—children in a suburban Ohio school district. Is the sample representative? How similar is a suburban Ohio school to, say, an inner city urban school? Or to a suburban California school? (Ohio has some pretty harsh winters—is that when these kids were playing video games? Would they much rather be out on their skateboards, if only the weather permitted? If so, the sample is not representative of children in areas without similar exigencies.) A single school district may have other peculiarities: Perhaps students have access to video games in the cafeterias; or maybe the schools are located in neighborhoods where there is a high concentration of video arcades. So we'd almost certainly want a wider-ranging sample.

When we ask how the researchers conducted their research, though, we notice even bigger problems. According to this report, the researchers asked whether girls should play violent video games, whether others thought that girls should play violent video games, and whether fighting games are mostly for boys. These questions could not reveal anything at all about whether girls prefer these games, much less whether they play them (as the main conclusion—that girls may become more ruthless and competitive by playing these games—requires). In fact, the responses could be interpreted more plausibly to show a commendable lack of sexism—girls should play whatever games they want. In other words, the means of collecting the data are not valid. This study, as reported here, does not show what it purports to show.

Moreover, the researchers' fears—as stated in the second paragraph—are totally unsupported by the research. We won't cover causal arguments fully until the next chapter, but it's obvious that there is a missing premise in the final paragraph—that playing violent video games causes ruthless and competitive behavior. That's a significant missing premise. At the very least, we'd want to see a citation to a respectable causal study before accepting this premise.

Someone could read example [11] in the newspaper, believe it must be true (it's in the paper; it's the result of a study; there are numbers), and worry that her daughters will be enticed by *Mortal Kombat*. However, that would be an unjustified response since there were problems with both the sample chosen and the questions put to the respondents. The study is not a compelling one, and we can determine that without doing any math at all.

Here's another example, taken from a book called *How to Lie with Statistics*.[5]

> [12] The United States Navy used to recruit people with the following argument. During the Spanish-American War, the death rate in the navy was nine deaths per thousand people. However, during the same period in New York City, the death rate was sixteen per thousand. This shows that it's safer to be in the navy than out of it.

Here, the difficulty involves the similarity between the sample and the population. Quite apart from the issue of whether New York City is representative of the rest of the country, consider who's in the navy and who's living in New York City. The navy is made up of people healthy enough to pass a thorough physical examination. The population of New York City, on the other hand, includes people who are old, sick, or physically unfit. The correct comparison would have been between people in the navy and young, healthy people who are not in the navy. Certainly the death rate outside of the navy could be expected to be far lower than nine per thousand.

Obviously, the navy wanted to slant the statistics in a way that would facilitate recruitment. Newspapers and magazines, too, will often report the results of studies so as to have the most dramatic impact. For example,

> [13] Women aren't as happy in their careers as men think. In a *Fortune* magazine survey of its subscribers, 61% of men thought that women were satisfied with the overall status of women in the workplace, but only 44% of women agreed.

[5]Darrel Huff (New York and London: W. W. Norton, 1954, 1982), p. 83.

First, you'll want to consider the sample. How many people were polled? How many men and how many women? Such questions are always relevant when a sample is broken down into sub-groups. The survey could have had 1,000 respondents, but if only 75 of these were women, it's likely that the data would not permit a generalization to all women.

Next, look closely at the wording. The dramatic first sentence claims that women aren't that happy in their careers. But the respondents were asked a question about the overall status of women in the workplace. These are not the same thing at all. It's easy to imagine that many women are happy in their own careers but remain concerned that other women aren't treated fairly.

Before we close this chapter, we'll look at a different sort of report— one that's taken from a professional journal, and not from a sensationalist newspaper blurb.

[14] A study was conducted on two college campuses between 1985 and 1988. Its goal was to compare the frequency with which students use college versus general slang and to use this information as a means of classifying conceptions of undergraduate life. Undergraduate slang is made up partly of slang terms from the culture at large, and partly of college-specific slang terms. The latter, in turn, is composed of both nationally used terms, and local, regional, or institutional terms. College slang provides a means of expression for undergraduate conceptions of college life itself.

The study focused on slang terms that students use to characterize their peers (e.g., *keener*, *babe*). Such terms are numerous, and permit students to categorize others according to their social and personal attributes.

There were two samples of slang usages collected. The primary one came from Holy Cross College, a small liberal arts school in Massachusetts, with an enrollment of 2,500 students. Eighty percent of the students lived on campus, and the remainder lived nearby. The secondary sample came from the

University of California at Davis. At the time of the study, UC Davis enrolled 16,000 undergraduates, of whom 95% were from California. Fewer than one third of the students lived on campus.

During 1985 to 1988, 137 students from seven introductory sociology classes volunteered to conduct peer interviews and act as participant observers as part of a research paper assignment. They completed a minimum of four interviews using a standard interview form. The subjects were required to be different in gender and academic class. They asked students to suggest labels used to characterize other students, and to suggest definitions for these labels. They also spent a day observing slang usage among their peers and recording the results. At Davis, 51 undergraduates in a 1988 social psychology class were asked to list and define terms that were commonly used to label others. Four hundred sixty-five slang terms were collected at Holy Cross, and at UC Davis, the students suggested 239.

Of the terms collected at Holy Cross, 27.7% were general slang, while 72.3% were classified as college slang. At UC Davis, 45.2% of terms were general slang and 54.8% were college slang. The means of classifying general versus college slang was this: terms listed in the *New Dictionary of American Slang* with meanings identical or similar to the ones collected were classified as general slang; while terms that were not listed at all, listed but identified as college slang, or listed with a radically different meaning, were classified as college slang.

It is possible that the more cohesive, exclusive nature of the small residential college permitted more elaboration and transmission of the student subculture. [Adapted from David M. Hummon, "College Slang Revisited: Language, Culture, and Undergraduate Life," *Journal of Higher Education*, vol. 65, no. 1 (1994): 75–95.]

First, let's try to clarify who composed the sample. At Holy Cross, we know that 137 researchers were required to conduct at least four interviews each—that means at least 548 interviews took place. But we do not know whether there was any overlap. The published study did not indicate whether the interviewers were required to ask subjects if they had been previously interviewed. So we don't know how many individuals were interviewed. It is unlikely that the designer of the study wouldn't have considered this, so let's give the study the benefit of the doubt and assume that at least 548 individuals were interviewed. We have no information about how many Holy Cross students were observed as opposed to interviewed. At Davis, we know that the sample comprised 51 students in one class.

So far, what can we say? For one thing, there's a reason that the researcher called his Davis sample the *secondary* sample. Fifty-one individuals is not many at all—especially to represent the population at a large public university, where the students, though mostly Californians, may be quite diverse in other ways.

A sample of 51 people would give us a margin of error of 10% to 12%. The numbers for college slang versus general slang were 45.2% and 54.8%, respectively. That means that the number could range from, say, 35.2% to 55.2% for college slang. These figures are probably still far enough below the Holy Cross numbers to permit the inference that the researcher draws. But they are based on the assumption that we have a perfect sample, and this sample probably isn't perfect.

The surveyed Davis students came from a single class; this could mean that they were all in the same academic year. What if these students were from the first-year class, during September? Then the lower reported usage of college-specific slang terms might have resulted from the students' unfamiliarity with such terms. A differently chosen sample, composed of students who had attended Davis long enough to learn the full campus idiolect, might have approached the 72.3% usage rate found at Holy Cross.

The Holy Cross sample is potentially a fairly good one. If the researcher required that his volunteers not reinterview people who had been previously interviewed, it's possible that at least 20% of the student body was interviewed. That does not guarantee representativeness, but the additional requirement that subjects differ in academic class probably resulted in a good cross-section of students.

Now that we have considered *what* was counted, let us address *how* it was counted. At UC Davis, students were asked to volunteer slang terms. I think we've covered the problems there. At Holy Cross, students collected terms by two means. First, there were interviews. Were they valid? We're told that the researchers used a standard interview form, so we know that the same questions were asked of the subjects. But we do not have any information about the precise wording of the questions. We are told that the researchers asked the subjects to suggest labels used to characterize other students, but that's all we know. Some standard interview forms instruct the interviewer to probe more deeply in certain circumstances or clarify the question. Maybe the forms suggested types of terms. If so, that could have partially determined the results. There may be other reasons to account for what terms were volunteered. For example, a male student being interviewed by a female might be less likely to suggest derogatory terms used for women. If this happened often, and if the derogatory terms were largely college *or* largely general slang, it could skew the results.

Another difficulty is that the observers were students, observing student behavior. Would they have noticed things that an outside observer would notice? Or would some terms pass them by, because of their familiarity?

The classification of terms into college and general slang was effected with the help of the *Dictionary of American Slang*. Without any knowledge of that book, we'll have to accept the classification provisionally.

Are there any ethically objectionable aspects of the study? There do not seem to be. No deception was involved. The interviewer was in all likelihood free to explain that he or she was working for a professor who wanted to explore the use of slang terms.

Should we reject the study on the basis of the questions raised here? No. The most customary result of evaluating a serious statistical argument is to raise questions we'd like to see answered. (Of course if we raise many questions, or exceedingly serious ones, we'd reject the study outright). Raising questions is valuable. The next time you write a paper for any course dealing with statistical arguments, you'll be able to provide a more detailed and careful analysis. Moreover, if you participate in setting up a study, you'll have some background against which to compose an acceptable sample and means of data collection.

▌ SUMMARY

The basis for any argument from experience is, of course, experience. Thus it is important when evaluating such arguments to consider the extent and the quality of the experience. Ask yourself whether the sample was both large enough and representative in ways that might matter. The definition of the target property is another important consideration. In the case of statistical arguments, we must remember to ask whether the means of data collection was reliable and valid.

We have not yet finished our discussion of study design. The causal arguments that we will consider in the next chapter use methods similar to those employed in arguments from experience. So we will combine our use of the skills learned in this chapter with some new ones introduced in Chapter 10.

LEMUR Exercise 9.1

EXERCISE **9.4**

For the following arguments, identify the sample, population, and target property. Then consider any relevant issues such as sample composition, sample size, data collection, measurement instrument, reliability, validity, and ethical difficulties.

Example

In 1992, *Seventeen* magazine conducted a survey of its readers to discover the extent of sexual harassment in schools. The study was conducted by means of a questionnaire that was included in an issue of the magazine. The questionnaire was preceded by a story about a girl who had been so mistreated by her peers at school that she took legal action. The story closed with a statement about the need for more caring schools.

There were 4,200 responses. *Seventeen* has 1.9 million subscribers. Among the results were these: 89% reported unwanted suggestive jokes or comments; 10% reported that they were forced to "do something sexual."

The sample is 4,200 respondents to a survey in *Seventeen* magazine. The population is *students*, or *people in schools*, or *girls and young women in schools*. We do not know whether the goal of the study is limited to students; it may encompass teachers as well. We also do not know if it is limited to girls and women, or if it encompasses boys too. Most readers of *Seventeen* are probably teenage girls. The target property is *sexual harassment*.

A sample size of 4,200 respondents would be adequate, if the researchers had randomly selected 4,200 members of the population. But readers of *Seventeen* may or may not be representative of girls and young women in general, and it is doubtful that they are representative of all students. Moreover, the sample is self-selected. There were at least 1.9 million people who had a chance to respond, so the 4,200 respondents represent a 0.2 return rate. Any self-selected sample can be problematic because the people who feel most strongly about the issue are the ones most likely to respond.

The survey was preceded by a story about an extreme case of harassment. This might have biased the results by putting the respondents into a negative mood immediately before they filled out the questionnaire.

We don't have enough information about operationalization here. However, we can reject the study based on the fact that the sample was self-selected and thus probably isn't representative. [This exercise is adapted from Christina Hoff Sommers, *Who Stole Feminism?* (New York: Touchstone, 1995), pp. 181–183.]

1. In example [14] we considered a study which investigated slang terms that students use to characterize their peers. Holy Cross students collected 465 slang terms and UC Davis students collected 239. In the following exercise, the sample and means by which the data were collected is the same as in example [14]. This passage focuses on the way in which the slang terms might provide a classification of undergraduate life.

At Holy Cross, the 465 terms were suggested a total of 1,416 times. Some terms were suggested only once; some were suggested 50 times. At Davis, there were 405 reports of the 239 terms. The frequency with which the term was suggested is taken as an indication of how often it is used.

Some terms shared the same meaning. The number of different terms available to communicate the same aspect of undergraduate life was taken as an indication of that aspect's importance.

Slang that identified students in terms of their academic life constituted 7% of terms and 13% of usages at Holy Cross, but only 4% and 5% respectively at Davis. Most of these fit the college rather than general slang classification.

Slang that identified students in terms of extracurricular life was, once again, more common at Holy Cross (17.5% of terms and 24% of usages) than at Davis (4.6% and 6.4%). Terms for athletes were most common at Holy Cross; terms for fraternity involvement were most common at Davis.

Slang for peer social life and leisure activities was comparable at both schools: 9% of terms and 8% of usages at Holy Cross and 9% and 7% at Davis. At both, there was a large number of terms for people who frequently party.

Slang describing the personal attributes of others was more common at Davis, where it accounted for 40% of terms and 38% of usages. At Holy Cross, such slang constituted 28% of terms and 21% of usages. Many of these terms were derogatory. They often identified students in terms of personality and social interaction. Also common were terms to locate others in social groups according to their gender identity, sexual habits, social class, and physical appearance.

Campus slang is, relative to general slang, much richer in terms for academic life. Often, the terms insult students who work hard at their studies and thereby reinforce student values. The number of terms that apply to the personal and social identities of others may show the extent to which conformity to norms is valued, and deviation stigmatized.

2. There seems to be evidence against the notion that the aging population will lead to a crisis in health care. The Manitoba Longitudinal Study on Aging (MLSA) provides information about individual use of the health-care system. The study found that fewer than one quarter of Manitoba's older population stay in a hospital during a given year. Only 5% of this older population uses 59% of these hospital days. Five percent of older people who died between 1971 and 1981 used 20% of all hospital days used by older people.

Older people make only 1.7 more visits to the doctor than people in the 15–44 age group, and only 0.9 more than people in the 45–64 age group. The very old (85+) use more home care, nursing homes, and hospitals than younger groups but make the same number of visits to doctors as people aged 65–69. [From Mark Novak, *Aging and Society* (Scarborough: Nelson Canada, 1993), pp. 202–203.]

3. A study was conducted to investigate the relationship of liking one's names to self-esteem and social desirability. Fifty-nine male and 108 female students in a general psychology class at a state university in the southern United States rated their first, middle, and last names on a

seven-point Likert scale. (From 7, like very much, to 1, dislike very much.) They also completed standard self-esteem and social desirability tests. People who scored higher in self-esteem tended to like all their names—first, middle, and last—better than people who scored lower. Previous studies had shown this correlation only between first names and self-esteem, or between middle names and self-esteem. This may be because these studies were conducted in different countries with different naming practices, or possibly because they used different measures of self-esteem. Higher social desirability was found to correlate positively with greater liking for one's first and last names. [From Charles E. Joubert, "Relationship of Liking One's Given Names to Self-Esteem and Social Desirability," *Psychological Reports*, vol. 69 (1991): 821–822.]

4. *European Car and Driver* (October 1996, pp. 104–107) conducted a test of brake pads in which researchers tested six types of brake pads by measuring stopping distance. They also gathered information on pedal feel, noise, and dust.

Braking distance was measured, to within one foot, on ten consecutive 60 to 0 mph stops for each set of brake pads. The same car (a 1986 Volkswagen GTI with stock 9.4-inch vented front brakes and 9-inch rear disc brakes, and no ABS) was used for testing all of the brake pads. Each set of pads was tested with a new set of rotors. Testing took place over two days, during which weather conditions were similar, on the same stretch of road. The same type of brake fluid was used for each set of brakes, and the brakes were bled between each test. The same already-worn Toyo tires were used during the course of all the tests.

5. A study was conducted to gain information about the distribution and seasonal movement of juvenile (sexually immature, age 0–3 years) herring in the southern Gulf of St. Lawrence. Echosounders were used to locate the fish, which were then caught by trawling with nets of various kinds. Researchers measured, weighed, and estimated the ages of the fish.

The largest winter catches were obtained by trawling within two meters of the mud bottom, in the western half of Chaleur Bay. Nearly all herring caught were less than a year old. However, bottom tows of areas in which there had been no traces on the sounder yielded various fish, including juvenile herring. [From H. M. C. Dupuis, S. C. Courtenay, E.

M. P. Chadwick, "Distribution of Juvenile Atlantic Herring in the Southern Gulf of St. Lawrence," *Canadian Technical Report of Fisheries and Aquatic Sciences 2141* (Moncton: Department of Fisheries and Oceans, 1997).]

6. A study was conducted to determine what residents of the geographic American South consider its boundaries. A questionnaire and an outline map of the United States that included state boundaries were distributed to students in introductory geography classes at universities located within the Census South (Delaware, Maryland, Virginia, West Virginia, North and South Carolina, Georgia, Florida, Kentucky, Tennessee, Alabama, Mississippi, Arkansas, Louisiana, Texas, and Oklahoma). Limitations on time and resources limited the testing to half of these states. An attempt was made to included every second state. Within each state, roughly 125 maps and questionnaires were sent to a university.

   Only students who answered "yes" to the question, "Do you consider yourself a Southerner?," and who identified themselves as residents of the state in which they attended college were included in the sample. Those chosen were asked to outline on the map "the region you define as the South." A total of 278 usable maps were returned.

   Respondents from each state were found to have different images of the South. Each, with the exception of those from Maryland, included their own states wholly within the South. Only those from Texas and Arkansas included significant parts of Texas and Arkansas.

   The results of this study may suggest that an understanding of a region's geography should take into consideration the perception of those who live there and who dominate it culturally. [From James D. Lowry and Leo E. Zonn, "Cognitive Images of the South: An Insider's View," *Southeastern Geographer*, vol. 29 (1989): 42–54.]

7. Many Canadians believe multiculturalism has been taken too far, a recent survey shows. Nearly 75% of Canadians believe new immigrants should try to adapt to Canadian ways. It was emphasized that the study included Canadians of many different ethnic groups.

8. A university dean who wanted to introduce a new series of small, discussion and research based, first-year seminars sent questionnaires to all current first-year students. He described the projected seminars, and asked students to answer "yes" or "no" to this question: "If such courses had been available to you when entering, would you have taken them?"

Five hundred questionnaires were sent out; 184 were returned. One hundred twenty-eight of the returned questionnaires (about 70%) answered *yes*. On this basis, the dean concluded that 70–80% of incoming students would take the courses when they were introduced. Was he justified in drawing this conclusion?

10 Causal Arguments

IN CHAPTER 9, we studied arguments that used statistical research methods to generalize a property or set of properties from a sample to the general population. In this chapter, we'll extend the skills learned in Chapter 9 to causal arguments. The sort of **causal arguments** that interest us here draw a conclusion that one class of things or events lead to or result in another class of things or events—for example, "Eating a high fat diet causes heart attacks" or "Poverty causes people to commit violent crimes." Clearly, this is an important kind of inference to be able to make. Sometimes we want to know the cause—for example, why are all these people getting sick? Sometimes we want to know the effect—will this drug cure them? In either case, a causal argument is required.

The causal arguments that we'll consider are generally statistical arguments—that is, they generalize from samples to populations. Thus to evaluate them, we need to consider the means of collecting the sample, the similarity of sample to population, and the operationalization of the terms employed. We'll also learn new techniques specific to causal arguments.

In this chapter, we'll begin by considering what is required for causal relationships. We'll go on to consider test and control groups, which are essential in making causal inferences, and then look at types of causal studies. Finally, we'll unify all the skills we've gained in order to evaluate causal arguments.

▪ CAUSE AND EFFECT

Two things are true of every causal relationship: 1) the cause cannot come after the effect and 2) cause and effect are correlated— that is, they are associated, or found together. Both of these are necessary conditions for concluding that there is a causal relationship between A and B. In other words, if A occurs after B, then A cannot be the cause of B. Likewise, if A and B are not correlated, there cannot be a causal relationship between them.

These are necessary, not sufficient, conditions. Neither the temporal order of events nor correlation is enough to allow a conclusion that a causal relationship exists. In fact there is a fallacy associated with taking either condition as sufficient. We'll look first at the issue of temporal order, since correlation will require a fair bit of discussion.

> **REVIEW BOX 10.1**
>
> ### Necessary conditions for causal relationships
>
> • The cause cannot come after the effect.
>
> • Cause and effect are correlated.

Post Hoc Fallacy

The ***post hoc* fallacy** arises from taking the temporal order of events as sufficient evidence for a causal conclusion. (The fallacy's full name is *post hoc ergo propter hoc*, which means "after this, therefore because of this.")

Here is an example:

> [1] You did really well in school until you started hanging out with Max. He's a bad influence. It's his fault you're failing chemistry and math.

This is clearly a causal inference that concludes that Max caused the decline in your grades. It could be that Max *is* a bad influence, but there's nothing in example [1] to prove this; the argument's only premise says that your grades were good before Max came into your life. The temporal order of events would not rule out a causal connection between Max and the lower grades, but it cannot establish one either.

Here is another example of a *post hoc* fallacy. If a woman who has had breast implants develops connective tissue disease, she may associate the one new or unusual occurrence, the disease, with the other unusual occurrence, the introduction of the silicone. That's a natural way of thinking, and it's one that enables us to be creative in discovering causes. But considering everything that *might* be relevant is only a first step. Again, the temporal order of events indicates that it's possible the implants caused the disease, but since the disease developed after many events, not just the insertion of the implants, temporal order alone cannot be enough to establish a causal connection.

Superstitious beliefs, too, are often based on *post hoc* reasoning. For example, if you wear your favorite hat to an exam and do well on the exam, you may become convinced that this is your lucky hat, and wear it to every exam thereafter. If we assert a causal connection between two events, we should have some notion of what sort of mechanism could connect them. It's true that if the hat gives you confidence, you may be more likely to do well. But in that case, it's your mental state, and not really the hat, that is causing your success.

The Fallacy of Jumping from Correlation to Cause

REVIEW BOX 10.2

Correlation

Two properties are correlated if and only if occurrences of, or changes in, one are accompanied by occurrences of, or changes in, the other.

The second condition necessary for causal relationships is more complicated. Let's begin with a clear definition of **correlation**. Two properties are correlated if and only if occurrences of, or changes in, one are accompanied by occurrences of, or changes in, the other. Correlation can be positive or negative. Whenever A and B are positively correlated, there are more occurrences of A among the members of B than among the non-Bs. For example, if more drinkers than nondrinkers smoke, there is a positive correlation between drinking and smoking. Whenever X and Y are negatively correlated, there are fewer occurrences of X among the members of Y than among the non-Ys. For example, if fewer men than women have eating disorders, then being male and suffering from an eating disorder are negatively correlated.

Correlation can be difficult to establish, as we'll see below. Before we look at this issue, though, let's look at what correlation cannot do for us—what inferences correlation alone cannot support.

Correlation, like temporal sequence, is necessary but not sufficient for causation. Even if two things are found together all the time, it is wrong to jump to the conclusion that there is any causal relationship between them, let alone that the relationship is of a particular kind.

There are three reasons we cannot infer correlation from causation. First, consider the discovery of a positive correlation between drug use and poverty—poor people are more likely to use drugs, and drug users are more likely to be poor. It could be that poverty causes drug use: people who are poor may have few opportunities for advancement, have little chance of higher education, live in bad neighborhoods and have few role models, etc., so they take drugs to escape the hopelessness of their lives. Or it could be that drug use causes poverty: people may spend all their money on drugs, or they may be unable to hold down a job as a result of their drug habit. Either possibility is plausible, and the discovery of the correlation does not help us decide between them. Thus, in any correlation between A and B, it's possible that A caused B or that B caused A.

Sometimes the temporal order of events can help us decide whether A caused B or B caused A. For example, further investigation might show that the drug users were poor long before they started taking drugs. Then, since the cause cannot come after the effect, it would not be possible for drug use to cause poverty. That would still not prove that poverty causes drug use, though, since other possibilities have not yet been ruled out.

To see the second reason we cannot infer cause from correlation, consider the following argument:

> [2] I know two men who were completely happy in their marriages until their wives started working. Within a year, both were getting a divorce. That just shows that when women abandon their traditional roles, marriage and the family are destroyed.

Example [2] suggests that the divorces were caused by the fact that the women took jobs. Of course, we'd reject this argument anyway because it is based on anecdotal evidence of the sort we saw in Chapter 9. Two people's stories do not constitute a good sample. The suggested causal connection, though, is also suspect. There is a third causal factor that could account for both correlates: it is possible that the women were unhappy in their marriages and that this unhappiness caused both the jobs and the divorce. For example, they may have taken the jobs in order to be able to pay for the divorce. In any correlation between A and B, it may be that A neither causes nor is caused by B: the correlation may result from a third factor that caused both.

Discovery of a correlation can inspire you to investigate whether there is a causal relationship between the two correlates. But correlation alone cannot establish that such a relationship even exists, let alone determine what form it takes.

The third reason that we can't infer cause from correlation is that the correlation could be a coincidence. Here's an obvious example:

> [3] Last year everyone who got an A in this class had a name beginning with the letter "A." There are 18 names on my class list beginning with "A," so I can expect to give out 18 As this year.

No one would argue this way. Students' names have nothing to do with their grades. The notion that there is some plausible mechanism connecting cause and effect in example [3] is obviously farfetched.

Sometimes, however, the move from correlation to cause seems more plausible when the correlation could be nevertheless a matter of coincidence. What if we had evidence that people who lived near a certain factory experienced an unusually high incidence of cancer? This might mean nothing at all. There are sometimes random series of events: we saw this when we considered the gambler's fallacy in Chapter 7. It could be that chance alone resulted in a higher rate of cancer among a group of people who happened to live near one another and near a factory. The fact that factory emissions can be dangerous does not mean that they always are.

Coincidence can be very difficult to rule out. In the case of this example, we would need to locate other factories manufacturing the same products by the same processes, and investigate the incidence of cancer among people living near those factories. If the correlation was discovered to hold in other similar cases, the probability of coincidence would be reduced. Unless that further step was taken, though, the possibility of coincidence would remain.

Control Groups

Let's reconsider the example of a woman who develops connective tissue disease after receiving silicone breast implants. Clearly, the fact that one woman developed a disease following her implants does not prove anything. But what if we had a much larger sample—for instance, 10,000 women who developed connective tissue disease after receiving breast implants? The larger sample would still not prove that the implants were the cause. We'd need to know that the incidence of connective tissue disease was higher among women who have had breast implants than among women who have not had them—that is, we'd need to begin by establishing a positive correlation between implants and connective tissue disease. Since correlation is a necessary condition for causation, if there is no correlation, there is no cause either.

We can prove correlation only by comparing two groups: a **test group** and a **control group**. The control group and test group should be as similar as possible, with one exception: members of the test group should possess one of the properties we're interested in—for instance, breast implants— and members of the control group should not possess that property. After identifying test and control group, we measure the occurrence in members of each group of the property under investigation. So if we discover that the occurrence of connective tissue disease is significantly higher in the test group than in the control group, we can assert a correlation between implants and connective tissue disease.

Let's look at an example of a study that tries to establish a correlation. During the 1980s, the popular roleplaying game *Dungeons and Dragons* inspired controversy. Teen suicides and homicides were attributed to playing the game, and the media also suggested that players experienced feelings of alienation and detachment. This study investigates the relationship between playing and feelings of alienation.

[4] The subjects were 70 student volunteers from a single college, who were given full information about the study. Thirty-five subjects (25 men and 10 women) were students in a psychology course which gave them bonus marks for participation. They reported never having played *Dungeons and Dragons*. Their mean age was 20.3 years. The other 35 subjects (30 men and 5 women) were players found in a campus game club. Their mean age was 21.2 years.

Subjects completed questionnaires, which included questions about age, sex, and general game activities (e.g., number of years played, time spent playing, level of skill, and amount of money spent). To measure alienation, which was defined as a feeling of detachment from the social environment, subjects answered questions consisting of three standard scales for measuring six types of alienation (powerlessness, meaninglessness, normlessness, cultural estrangement, social estrangement, and estrangement from work). The questionnaires also contained "filler" questions which were not scored.

The questionnaire defined "meaninglessness" as a lack of a sense of purpose. Fewer players than nonplayers reported feelings of meaninglessness. There was a positive correlation between feelings of cultural estrangement and playing: seventeen subjects who had played the game, or 49%, reported feelings of cultural estrangement, compared to eight subjects (23%) who had not played. "Culture" in the study was narrowly focused on media forms of entertainment such as television, movies, and magazines. Fewer players than nonplayers expressed interest in the media.

No reliable differences were found in the rest of the alienation conditions. [Adapted from Lisa H. DeRenard and Linda Mannik Kline, "Alienation and the Game Dungeons and Dragons," *Psychological Reports*, vol. 66 (1990): 1219–1222.]

The authors of this study wanted to determine whether gameplaying and feelings of alienation are correlated. Let's begin our evaluation by identifying the components of the argument. The sample is 70 student volunteers from a single college, who had full information about the study. This sample was divided into a test group and a control group. The test group was made up of 35 players drawn from a campus gameplaying group. The 35 members of the control group, none of whom had ever played *Dungeons and Dragons*, were drawn from a psychology course. "Alienation" was defined as a feeling of detachment from the social environment and operationalized by means of three standard scales. You'll recall from Chapter 9 that standard scales or standard tests are separately created and researched tests, believed to be reliable and valid. The result of this study is that there is a positive correlation between gameplaying and feelings of cultural estrangement, and a negative correlation between gameplaying and one alienation condition, meaninglessness.

How shall we evaluate this study? First, we might note that the sample is small. In correlational or causal studies, as in noncausal arguments from experience, a big sample is better at representing differences among people. The sample in example [4] is fairly homogeneous: all members are students at the same college. That means that we can't really extend the results to gameplayers who are not students, or even to students at a different type of college. When studying people, sample size can affect representativeness. However, since the causal or correlational argument works by a comparison between test and control groups, a significant result can still be achieved with a small sample. So even though extending this result to all students may be inappropriate, we may still be able to claim that the correlation genuinely holds for these students and others like them.

The researchers were looking for a **statistically significant difference** in the occurrence of a property between the control group and test group. "Significant" has a mathematical meaning in this context, which we don't need to explore too deeply. In nontechnical terms, a significant difference between the two groups is one that is greater than would be likely by chance. (Like the margin of error, statistical significance is based on an ideal sample.) You can see why a rather small group need not make a causal inference shaky. The precise numerical value of "significant" will vary with the sample size. With a large sample, a small difference will count. With a small sample, a larger difference is required, but if the large difference is present, that can prove a correlation. For example, if you fed arsenic to 10 people (your test group) and they all died quickly, while no member of the control group died within the same period, wouldn't you feel fairly comfortable with asserting a 100% correlation between arsenic and death? Sometimes a difference in a small group will not be significant, but it will be close enough to significance to indicate that redoing the study on a larger number of subjects could be valuable. You do need to pay attention to whether a nonstandard meaning of "statistically significant" was used. Sometimes researchers who are eager to prove something will decide that a smaller difference will count. In these cases, take the result with more than a grain of salt.

Let's return to the evaluation of example [4]. In correlational or causal arguments we need to question not only the similarity between sample and population, but also the similarity between control group and test group. Are there relevant differences between the test and control groups in example [4]? There is a difference in mean age: 20.3 years for the gameplayers, and 21.2 for the nonplayers. That may matter; since older students are likely to be closer to completing their programs and realizing their career goals they may feel a greater sense of purpose.

The authors of study [4] do not attempt to draw a causal conclusion from the results. In fact, in their published paper they give many reasons why a causal connection cannot be supported by the evidence. Let's look at some of those reasons and consider whether new studies could be set up to establish a causal connection.

What causal conclusions might be possible? One is that gameplaying causes lower feelings of meaninglessness. The gameplayers were found to have lower feelings of meaninglessness than nonplayers. Another possible causal conclusion is that gameplaying causes people to feel culturally estranged. Fewer gameplayers than nonplayers expressed interest in media.

Now let's look at the potential problems with these conclusions. First, even if we are willing to jump to the conclusion that there is a causal relationship, there is no information about which way the causal arrow points. Consider the claim that gameplaying causes lower feelings of meaninglessness. It is possible that playing games causes people to feel less meaningless because the game provides a sense of purpose. But is also possible that the people who participate in gameplaying feel less meaningless in the first place. Maybe their sense that life is meaningful allows them to enjoy roleplaying, competition, and the social aspects of club membership. Consider the conclusion that gameplaying causes people to feel culturally estranged. It is possible that gameplaying leaves people with less time to devote to cultural activities and thereby increases the potential for feelings of estrangement. And it is just as possible that people who already have little interest in cultural activities are more likely to seek other leisure pursuits. It would be difficult to determine the direction of the causal arrow, although establishing the temporal order of events could help. For instance, we might conduct a long-term study which identified people as feeling meaningless or culturally estranged, and then tracked them to see whether they took up gameplaying.

> **REVIEW BOX 10.4**
>
> ## Control groups
>
> All causal arguments must have control groups. The control group should be as similar as possible to the test group, except for the presence or absence of the causal factor being studied.

In any case, we cannot assume a causal connection between gameplaying and meaninglessness or cultural estrangement. There are several plausible third causal factors that could account for both correlates. First, as the authors of the study suggest, the negative correlation between gameplaying and feelings of meaninglessness might be explained by the fact that the gameplayers were drawn from a campus gameplaying club. Perhaps any club membership gives people a sense of belonging and thereby a sense of purpose. To determine whether it is the club membership, rather than the club's particular activity, that is the causal factor, we could compare people from other groups based on common interests with a control group of people who do not belong to any club. Second, it may be the case that any recreational interest leaves little time for media pursuits. We could compare people who are committed to other recreational pursuits—for example volleyball or swimming—with a control group of people who have no such commitment to discover whether people who are committed to any recreational activity feel more culturally estranged than those who are not. Third, it is possible that the geographic location of the college from which the sample was drawn somehow contributed to the subjects' feelings of estrangement. If the school was in a remote area, students may have felt culturally isolated, and this may have provided them with incentive to create their own culture. This could be ruled out by performing the same study on students at many different kinds of colleges. Finally, in this study "culture" is very narrowly defined as interest in media; a broader definition may not show a correlation.

In general, this is a very responsible study in its refusal to draw dramatic conclusions to support the media frenzy. During the 1980s many young people were forbidden to play *Dungeons and Dragons*. If their parents had evaluated the evidence in example [4], isn't it likely that a different decision would have been made?

Are you beginning to despair of ever establishing a causal relationship? That's good, because it is very difficult to do; particularly in a case like example [4], which involves people's habits and personalities. Some skepticism about claims of causal relationships will do you no harm. Evaluate the evidence and make your own decision.

Even large, respectable studies make methodological errors leading to dissimilarity between control group and test group. One such error was exposed by David Plotkin in an article published in *Atlantic Monthly*.[1] Plotkin wanted to determine if mammography facilitates early detection of breast cancer in women and thus reduces their risk of death from the disease. This led him to investigate several breast cancer studies.

In his article, he discusses one historically important study that was conducted on 60,696 women who were between 40 and 64 years old. The subjects were enrolled in the study between 1963 and 1966 and were tracked for as long as 15 years. They were randomly assigned to the test group and control group, alternately in order of signing up. The members of the test group received regular mammograms and clinical breast exams, while the members of the control group received only ordinary care from their doctors. So far, this is an excellent example.

But the composition of the test group posed a problem. Two questions were asked of the women who were assigned to the test group: "Are you pregnant?" and "Have you ever been treated for breast cancer?" If a woman answered "yes" to either question, she was removed from the study. The pregnant women were removed because a fetus can be harmed by exposure to X rays. The women who had been treated for breast cancer were removed because giving mammograms to women who had already had breast cancer would not test mammography as early detection. Altogether, 434 women were excluded from the test group as a result of their answers to the two questions. Given the study's age range it's likely that few women were excluded because they were pregnant. It seems probable, therefore, that most of the 434 women were excluded because of previous breast cancer. The women in the control group were not asked these questions, and none were excluded from the study.

For five years, the women in the test group were given mammograms and breast exams. The number of women who died of breast cancer in each group within ten years was tallied. The control group had 193 deaths; the test group 147. (Since the sample size is large, a small difference counts.) You can see the problem, though—those 434 excluded women may have made the difference. Maybe the control group had a larger number of deaths because the women who already had breast cancer were not excluded. The excluded women would be enough to account for the difference in death rates.

Strategies and Conventions

Questions for correlational or causal studies

Are there differences between control group and test group other than the presence or absence of one of the properties being investigated?

In Chapter 9, we saw why it is important to look for differences between sample and population. Causal arguments are also arguments from experience, in which knowledge of a sample is generalized to a larger population. Thus differences between sample and population can also be important in causal arguments. In the discussion of the *Dungeons and Dragons* study, we mentioned that since the study was conducted at only one college, the results may not be generalizable to nonstudents or to students at other types of colleges. In causal arguments it is also important to look for differences between control group and test group. If there are differences between these groups other than the presence or absence of the suspected causal agent, we have no reason to believe that the suspected causal agent, rather than one of the other differences, accounts for the presence or absence of the other property.

EXERCISE 10.1

Describe how you might set up a study to support or refute each of the following causal arguments. In your description, be sure to explain how you would select the sample, operationalize the terms, and select the control group.

1. Studies show that intelligent parents tend to have intelligent children. Clearly, intelligence is an inherited trait. Unfortunately, this means that there is no way to greatly improve a child's intelligence.

2. There is a higher incidence of liver disease among smokers than among nonsmokers. This indicates that smoking is damaging to more than just the lungs.

3. People who receive degrees from high-profile universities such as Princeton or the University of Toronto generally earn more money in their careers than people who receive degrees from less prestigious institutions. This shows that the best way to ensure a good income is to attend a high-profile school.

4. It's obvious why certain people live in poor, ugly, and dangerous inner-city communities. The performance of children from these communities on standardized tests is much lower than the national average. And since earning enough money to afford living in a better community requires intelligence, these people just don't belong elsewhere.

Types of Studies

"Look for differences" is an easy enough instruction to remember, but there are many ways these differences could be manifested. There are three ways to set up a causal study. Recognizing the type of study can help you determine what questions to ask. A study may involve correlational research, a controlled laboratory experiment, or a control group / test group experiment. The fundamental difference between research and experiment is that in research, the researcher does not control any conditions, whereas in an experiment the researcher controls at least one condition.

CORRELATIONAL RESEARCH. In **correlational research**, the researcher does not control any conditions, and only collects the information. In many cases, people have already sorted themselves into the test group and control group—some people are exposed to the suspected causal agent because of their beliefs, habits, places of residence, jobs, etc. Sometimes, if a causal agent is suspected to be harmful, research is the only possible means of investigation.

For example, what if you wanted to know whether cellular phones cause brain cancer? You cannot give cell phones to people and say "Come back in a year and we'll see what happened." If you have some idea that this agent may be harmful, you cannot expose people to it to see if it really is. You must construct your test group from already-existing users of cellular phones. Those existing users constitute the test group. The control group is constructed by matching the members of the test group with people who are as similar as possible, apart from the use of cellular phones. Diet, physical activity, and stress levels at work are some factors that might affect people's health and thus their susceptibility to cancer. So the members of the control group ought to match members of the test group in at least these respects.

> **REVIEW BOX 10.5**
>
> ## Types of studies
>
> - CORRELATIONAL RESEARCH: the researcher does not control any conditions
>
> - CONTROLLED LABORATORY EXPERIMENT: the researcher controls all conditions
>
> - CONTROL GROUP/TEST GROUP EXPERIMENT: the researcher controls the presence or absence of the causal factor

CONTROLLED LABORATORY EXPERIMENT. Whereas in correlational research, the researcher doesn't control any conditions, in a **controlled laboratory experiment**, the researcher controls *all* the conditions. Controlled laboratory experiments are performed with animals, not humans. An example of a controlled laboratory experiment is a study to determine if artificial sweetener causes cancer in laboratory rats. The rats are divided into control group and test group, and fed the same food (apart from the causal agent). Rats from the same family are used so that any particular susceptibility to cancer is ruled out. The researcher can be reasonably certain that no other possible causal factors have crept into the test rats' lives. The rats are not free to go out and do things that the researcher doesn't know about. With human subjects, there is always the possibility that they might fail to mention activities, habits, behavior, etc., that could be relevant. Since all the phenomena are under the researcher's control, the single difference between control group and test group must be the one that makes the difference.

Although the differences between the control group and the test group are minimized in controlled laboratory experiments, there can be other problems caused by dissimilarity. In some cases, dissimilarity between animals and humans can prevent generalization of results from animal experiments to humans. No one really wants to know whether saccharin causes cancer in rats; rather, the researchers look for results in rats in order to generalize the results to humans. Animal studies are based on an analogy between the animal and the human. The animal is the analogue, and humans are the primary subject.

The analogy can be questioned, as any analogy can, by asking whether there are relevant differences between the analogue and the primary subject. First, a suspected causal agent may not be given to animals in quantities that would be equivalent to an ordinary human exposure to the agent. In any case, the agent could not be given over the number of years that a human would likely be exposed, because the life spans of most laboratory animals are shorter than the lifespans of humans. So the agent is given in high concentrations of the agent. One question that can always be asked is whether this difference in quantity matters. Consider the example of saccharin. Is it harmful to humans, or is it just harmful if taken in doses in excess of a kilo a day? Second, physiological differences between animals and humans may undermine the analogy. Saccharin was banned some years ago, because it caused bladder cancer in rats. But it is now thought to have caused the cancer in rats because it interacted with rat urine in ways that would not affect humans. Humans and rats—or any other animal—are similar, but different species may always be different in ways that matter.

CONTROL GROUP/TEST GROUP EXPERIMENT. In a **control group/test group experiment**, the researcher provides the causal factor—that's why it's called an experiment—but does not control all other conditions. Subjects are sorted into groups; one group is exposed to the suspected causal factor, the other isn't. These experiments can be performed on people when the causal factor is harmless, or when the people have volunteered with full knowledge of the risks. An example of the harmless kind is sometimes seen in psychology experiments. Consider an experiment to discover whether people perform better on reading comprehension tests taken in a blue room or a white room. Subjects are separated into control group and test group. One group is sent into a blue room, the other into a white room, and both are given an identical test. No one is being harmed by this experiment. An example of an experiment in which people volunteer knowing the risks is a group of terminally ill people who are willing to try any new drug to recover. Generally, the trial drug is tested first on animals, to ensure that it's not immediately fatal; then there is a stage of trial on humans who must be fully informed.

In all control group/test group experiments, the sample is chosen to be representative of the population in ways that might matter. Then subjects are randomly assigned to control group and test group. This helps ensure that if there are factors that could be assigned a causal role, they are split equally between the two groups. Since any possible causal factor works the same way in each group any difference in results could be assigned to the controlled causal factor. The breast cancer study mentioned above was an example of a control group/test group experiment. The researchers provided the causal factor, the mammogram.

There are two further considerations when evaluating a causal study: replication and blindness. Replication is important in all experiments. We have seen that a reliable test is one that generates the same results under the same conditions. A reliable experiment is, similarly, one that yields the same findings when performed by different researchers. The importance of replication is shown by the fact that there are entire journals devoted to replication of various experiments.

Unlike replication, blindness is only important in certain types of experiments. In **blind** experiments, the subjects do not know whether they are members of the control group or of the test group. Some experiments are done **double-blind**. In a double-blind experiment, neither the subjects nor the researchers with whom they have immediate contact know who is in the control group and who is in the test group. Blind and double-blind experiments are useful because they prevent the subjects' and researchers' expectations from influencing the results.

Consider an experiment to test the efficacy of a drug. The members of the test group are given the drug, and the members of the control group are given something that appears to be the drug but is actually inactive. This is called the **placebo**. Even the people who are receiving the placebo may report improvements in their condition. (When people believe they are getting a certain treatment and act as though they are getting that treatment, we call this the **placebo effect**.) If the researchers know who is receiving the placebo and who is receiving the real drug, their observations may reflect their desire to prove that the drug is effective. So such an experiment should be performed double-blind. Even though both subjects and researchers may succumb to wishful thinking—the subjects want to improve their condition, and the researchers want to achieve an important result—the effects of this wishful thinking will be neutralized by being spread equally between the control group and test group. Obviously, animals used in medical research will not be prone to the placebo effect, but the people who study them might be. If you see a medical experiment that is not blind or double-blind, be very skeptical of the results.

In the last chapter, we saw that some experiments rely on deception. The use of deception is an attempt to avoid an analogous placebo effect for factors such as behavior and personality. Recall Stanley Milgram's study on obedience from Chapter 9 (p. 256). In this study, the researchers deceived the subjects about the focus of the experiment and about the role that the subjects would play in it. If the subjects had known the truth about either of these two issues, they might have acted differently and thereby influenced the results. This experiment was blind; it would be difficult to conduct the experiment double-blind, since the researchers must present subjects with the right cues at the right times.

▌ EVALUATING CAUSAL ARGUMENTS

We have considered causal relationships, seen the value of test and control groups in research, and discussed three different types of causal studies. Now let's put this information to use by analyzing a few causal arguments. Remember to ask the following questions: What is the causal claim being tested? What is the sample, and what is the population? What type of study is involved? Are the control and test groups similar? How are the results measured? We'll begin with an argument taken from a newspaper report.

> [5] Reports of a high rate of stillbirths and deformed babies among women who worked at computers while pregnant led researchers to study the possibility of a link. They exposed 600 pregnant mice to levels of magnetic field similar to those that come from computer monitors. After a year, researchers found no significant differences between the exposed mice and a control group.

First, what causal claim is being tested? Whether working on computers causes harm to the baby during pregnancy. The sample was *600 pregnant mice*, plus the mice in the control group (we have no information about the numbers there). The population was *women*. This is a controlled laboratory experiment, and thus is based on an analogy between mice and women.

Strategies and Conventions

Questions for causal arguments

• What is the causal claim being tested?

• What is the sample?

• What is the population?

• What is the type of study?

• Are the control groups and test groups similar?

• How are the results measured?

The mice were probably exposed to a magnetic field rather than a computer monitor to ensure exposure. But if there is some feature of the monitor other than its magnetic field that could account for the stillbirths and deformed babies, the study would be invalidated. We have no information on how the concepts were operationalized or how the results were measured. Certainly the pregnancy problems that counted would need to be clearly defined. A stillbirth is easy to understand, but defining *deformed* would require some thought. An adequate definition ensures that the researchers consistently included the same types of cases in the category *deformed*.

Is there any obvious basis on which to criticize example [5]? Yes. Mice are pregnant for a very short time. Women are pregnant for nine months. The difference in the exposure time could make a difference. Since the study design may not have been able to test what it claimed to test, the argument's conclusion is not valid.

Is there a better way to conduct such a study? Correlational research might provide a more valid result. If researchers found pregnant women who worked at computers, matched them with a control group who had little or no exposure to computers, and then collected the results when the women gave birth, the analogy between mice and humans would not pose the problem we identified. Clearly, a control group/test group experiment with humans would not be an option, since if there is some suspicion that exposure may cause harm, it would be unethical to supply that exposure.

Here is another study that was reported in the newspaper.

> [6] Pop music may help schoolchildren pass exams. In a nationwide British study, 11,000 students in 250 schools were randomly split into three groups. They listened to either Mozart, the pop group Blur, or a radio chat show, while taking a test on spatial reasoning. The students who listened to the pop group scored 56%; the other two groups, 52%. The difference approached significance. The author of the study cited a California study in which adults performed better on a similar test while listening to Mozart, and said that this may show that adults process music differently.

This is a control group/test group experiment, although of a slightly different kind—any two groups serve as controls for the third. The researcher supplied the causal phenomena—the music and the tests. The sample is the 11,000 students in 250 schools, and the population is probably *students*, though we have no information on their age range. Results were measured by performance on the spatial reasoning test.

The sample is probably adequate, since 11,000 students and 250 schools is large enough to encompass all different kinds of students and schools. However, we have no information concerning its composition.

The most important thing to notice is that the study was designed without a *silence* condition (the most common "real life" condition). So although it could show that students test better when listening to pop music than when listening to chat shows or Mozart, it can't tell us whether they test better than when they are not listening to anything at all. If people must be exposed to noise while taking an exam, it might be the case that they prefer listening to music with a familiar beat. This doesn't mean, however, that they will perform better than if they took the same test in a noiseless environment. Moreover, notice that the subjects were only tested on spatial reasoning. So before we could accept the study's conclusion, we'd need to know that performance on spatial reasoning tests can be generalized to performance on tests involving other skills such as reading comprehension or multiplication.

Strategies and Conventions

Look for the differences

In causal studies, look for differences

• between sample and population.

• between control group and test group.

Besides, the account claims that the difference *approached* significance. In other words, it is not significant, and so we do not have adequate evidence to support the conclusion that pop music may help schoolchildren pass exams. The difficulty probably isn't that the researchers used an inadequately small sample. A sample of eleven thousand should achieve a significant result. It may simply be the case that there is no significant relationship between music and passing exams.

Finally, the study offers no support for the researcher's claim that adults and children may process music differently. Adults may be more familiar with Mozart than with the pop music that was chosen, but that has nothing to do with "processing" music. Based on the newspaper report, this appears to be a poor study; it is always possible, though, that the report didn't do the study justice.

We'll end this chapter, like Chapter 9, by examining a study taken from a professional journal.

[7] A study was conducted to find out whether counseling helps people to recover from their grief following the death of a spouse. The researchers located 78 men and women whose spouses had recently died of cancer. Of this group, 20 were randomly selected as controls. These participants filled out questionnaires at the beginning of the study and again one year later.

Of the remaining 58 people, 36 agreed to take part in group therapy for bereavement. The control and experimental groups were similar in sex, mean age, and the length of time that the spouses had been dead. Ninety-five percent of the original sample participated in follow-up questionnaires one year after the study began.

A standard scale with high reliability was used to measure depression and anxiety. A five-item scale was used to measure frequency of drug and alcohol use. Four characteristics of mourning developed in a previous study were tested. (For example, the frequency with which the bereaved person thought of the dead spouse.) Psychological well-being, coping, and self-esteem were also measured by standard tests with high reliability. The strain experienced in occupying a single role was measured on a 14-item scale with high reliability. The subject's feeling of social stigmatization was measured by a 12-item scale, with a lower, but adequate, reliability.

After one year, the control and experimental groups both showed less depression and anxiety, less abuse of alcohol and drugs, more well-being, higher self-esteem, improved feelings of control, lower grief, and reduced perception of social stigmatization. There were statistically significant differences only in self-esteem and single role strain.

It seems that group therapy does not have a significant effect on recovery from bereavement. However, this study provides no information about whether the effect of therapy would be greater for the bereaved who actively seek treatment than it is for those who participate only after being approached. [Adapted from Morton A. Lieberman and Irving Yalom, "Brief Group Psychotherapy for the Spousally Bereaved: A Controlled Study," *International Journal of Group Psychotherapy*, vol. 42, no. 1 (January 1992): 117–132.]

The causal claim being tested in example [7] is whether group therapy helps people get over the death of their spouses. The sample is the 95% of the original 56 people who participated. (There were 20 in the control group, and 36 who agreed to become part of the test group by entering therapy; 95% of these completed the study.) The population is meant to be *people whose spouses have died*. This is a control group/test group experiment, because the researcher provided the causal factor—group therapy. Recovery from grief was measured by standard tests.

Let's begin by considering the similarity between sample and population. There are two issues to raise: the fact that the members of the test group were approached by the researchers to enter therapy, and the fact that all spouses had died of cancer. We remember from Chapter 9 that sometimes the composition of the sample can serve as a guide to determining the population. In this case, we might prefer to restrict the population, and take it as *people whose spouses have died, and who have been encouraged to enter therapy*. This restriction still leaves us with a useful conclusion, since if we believe that people who are encouraged to enter therapy do not significantly benefit from it, we might be less likely to recommend such treatment to bereaved friends and family. Furthermore, health professionals might not target the bereaved for counseling, and public funds could possibly be diverted from counseling the bereaved. The researchers acknowledge that the fact that people were approached could have influenced the results. By ignoring this we would make our evaluation a straw person argument.

Now let's turn to the fact that the spouses of the participants all died of cancer. This could matter. There is a difference between death from cancer and, say, death from an accident. The latter comes as a shock, whereas death from cancer tends to occur slowly and may allow the surviving partner time to adjust. The opportunity to explore and express feelings through group therapy may or may not be more valuable to people whose spouses died suddenly. On the researchers' behalf, we could choose to restrict the population to people whose spouses had died of cancer. Since many people die of cancer, the sample would still be representative of a sizeable population.

We have no information about the age range of the subjects, only their mean age. This could also matter. There may be important differences between people in their 40s whose spouses have died, and people in their 70s whose spouses have died. Younger people are less likely than older people to have experienced deaths among their cohort and thus less likely to have observed peers dealing with grief. This means they have probably had fewer models for how to behave. Were all ages represented in the sample?

Finally, let's turn to the similarity between test and control groups. There are few problems here, since we are told that subjects were comparable in sex, mean age, and the length of time the spouse had been dead. We also know that all of the spouses died of cancer. The controls were selected randomly. Thus any other factors that could cause subjects to recover more quickly (for example, a supportive network of friends and family, church membership, or an absorbing career) or more slowly (for example, social isolation) would ideally be distributed equally among the groups and thus neutralized.

On the whole, this study has no obvious flaws of the sort that we saw in examples [5] and [6]. We can restrict the population to *people whose spouses have died of cancer, and who have been approached to enter therapy.* This restriction is suggested by the researchers' comment that the study does not show whether the effects of therapy would be greater for people who sought treatment themselves. The restricted population can still yield useful information; we know that people who are encouraged to enter therapy do not recover from their grief more quickly. The primary difficulty we have with example [7] involves the age range of subjects. We cannot tell whether the sample is representative of the population, and whether the control and test groups are similar in age.

▌ SUMMARY

The first thing to notice about any causal inference is whether it commits either of the two fallacies discussed at the beginning of the chapter. The *post hoc* fallacy results from taking the temporal order of events as sufficient evidence to establish a causal relationship. The fallacy of jumping from correlation to cause results from taking correlation as sufficient.

Causal arguments must be evaluated using the skills learned in Chapter 9. Identify the sample and population, and evaluate their similarity. Ask how the data were collected, and how results were measured. Additionally, ask what causal claim is being tested and whether the test group and control group are similar.

LEMUR Exercise 10.1

EXERCISE 10.2

For each of the arguments below, identify, where possible, the following features:

- the causal claim being tested
- the sample
- the population
- the test group and control group
- the type of study
- the measurement instrument

Evaluate the argument.

Example

Divorce and remarriage is a mortal sin. But since not everyone believes this, we should discourage divorce by pointing out that it is harmful to health and decreases life expectancy. More divorced men than married men die of cardiovascular disease. The death rates of white divorced men from pneumonia are four times greater than for married men; from suicide, seven times greater. Divorced women lose 50% more work time due to illness and injury than married women. Children of divorced parents are more likely than children of still-married parents to have mental and emotional problems, to live in poverty, and to commit suicide.

The causal claim is that divorce causes harm to health and decreased life expectancy. The author has mentioned several studies, but gives us little information about them. We do not know how many people composed the samples or how they were chosen. Apparently the control groups were composed of married people, since each premise compares divorced and married men and women. The married and divorced people would need to be similar in all relevant respects other than marital status, but we do not know whether control and test groups were similar. There is no information at all on types of studies or measurement instruments.

The premises jump from correlation to cause. Third causal factors can be imagined in almost every case. For example, cardiovascular disease may be more common among heavy drinkers. Did the drinking cause both the divorce and the disease? Pneumonia is a common cause of death among AIDS sufferers. Some AIDS sufferers got the disease due to promiscuity or intravenous drug use. Thus it may have been the promiscuity or drug use that caused both the divorce and the disease, which in turn caused the pneumonia. The men who committed suicide may have suffered from severe depression; perhaps this depression caused both the divorce and the suicide. The premise that divorced women lose more work time due to illness and injury than married women also jumps from correlation to cause. The women may have been ill or injured before their divorces; in that case the illness or injury may have caused both the divorce and the lost work time after the divorce.

The premise that children of divorced parents are more likely to have mental and emotional problems also jumps from correlation to cause, since it is just as possible that the child's mental and emotional problems caused the divorce.

We should reject this argument on the basis of the incomplete information provided here. It is possible that the studies mentioned could answer our questions satisfactorily, but there is nothing in the argument presented to support the causal conclusion.

1. In an Australian study, a group of 78 young people were asked why they thought they were at present unemployed. Subjects, who described their current status as unemployed, were aged 18 to 20, roughly half men and half women. They were given four possible responses: lack of ability, lack of effort, the economic situation, or bad luck. The first two responses attribute the reasons for unemployment to factors internal to the individual (failings on his or her part), while the second two responses attribute the unemployment to external factors beyond the individual's control. The subjects also responded to questions on a self-esteem scale and a hopelessness scale (both scales valid and reliable).

   The individuals who attributed their reasons for unemployment to one of the external factors (i.e., either bad luck or bad economy) showed significantly greater self-esteem than the individuals who attributed their unemployment to one of the internal causes (lack of ability or lack of effort). Those who attributed the unemployment to external causes also showed significantly lower hopelessness. [Lower hopelessness score = less hopeless, or more hopeful.]

2. In the 1950s, men went to work and women stayed at home. There was no shortage of goods and services. Jobs were more labor intensive. Now, with technological advances, it is even less likely than it used to be that society can provide work for both women and men. In Japan and Switzerland, women stay home to provide the only proper care for their children, who are much better behaved than children in this country. Feminism has been successful in the countries that are now experiencing the worst decline. This is hardly coincidence.

3. A study shows that two-day-old infants whose mothers spoke either English or Spanish preferred their native language. The subjects were 16 infants between 25 and 56 hours old. Eight had English-speaking mothers and eight had Spanish-speaking mothers. The infants heard speech through headphones. They sucked on a nipple connected to a sensor which was attached to a computer. The computer recorded the infants' sucking patterns and controlled what they heard through the headphones. Recordings of the voices of eight Spanish-speaking women and eight English-speaking women were used. Each Spanish voice was randomly matched with an English voice of the same loudness and roughly the same pitch.

   The auditory stimuli were presented for 18 minutes. In cases where the infant stopped sucking for more than two periods of 45 seconds the data were excluded from analysis. One researcher monitored the recording equipment. The other held the nipple in the infants' mouth. The second researcher could not see the equipment and could not hear the stimuli.

   The sounds were presented during sucking bursts. A sucking burst was defined as a minimum of three consecutive sucks, and the voice began during the third suck. The voice continued during the entire sucking burst and stopped whenever one second passed with no sucking. During the final six-minute period, the infants responded to their native language with significantly longer sucking bursts. This sucking behavior is interpreted as a preference by infants for their native language. The infants changed their sucking patterns so that they could hear the native voice for longer periods than they heard the foreign voice.

   Certain voices were preferred by the infants. Four of the 16 infants responded with longer than average bursts while hearing a voice that was speaking a foreign language. Other infants who heard the same voice speaking their native language responded with even longer sucking bursts. This shows that even a voice that appealed to all the infants appealed more when it spoke the native language.

It is possible that the infants' exposure to their native tongue during the two days between their birth and this experiment accounts for their preference. However, it seems more likely that they gained experience sufficient to form this preference prior to their birth. More data would be required to support this claim.

4. Testosterone has been shown by some studies to have links with aggression, dominance, sensation seeking, lower occupational achievement, drug use, fighting, and arrests. It would seem then that testosterone may also have a negative effect on marriages. Testosterone is a hormone present in many other animals as well as plants, so the circumstances under which marriage could influence it are fairly limited.

Testosterone is likely to affect socioeconomic status, possibly because testosterone-linked antisocial behavior prevents people from doing well in school. As a result they end up in lower-status jobs. Testosterone may affect men's performance at their jobs early in their careers. People of lower socioeconomic status are also more likely to divorce. Thus it is possible that the association between testosterone and marital quality could be accounted for by social status.

There are correlations between high levels of testosterone and irregular work histories, trouble with the law, and alcoholism. Factors like alcohol abuse, trouble with the law, and unemployment also have a negative effect on marriage. Thus the relation between testosterone and marital quality could be accounted for by male behavioral problems.

To determine the relationship between testosterone and marital quality, a study was performed on 4,462 former servicemen, who were part of another study. They were representative of the United States population in race and education. The study showed that testosterone had a consistent negative relationship with all aspects of quality of marriage. These aspects were defined as follows: whether the man had never married; had ever divorced; had, while still married, spent time separated from his wife due to relationship difficulties; had, while married, experienced sex with at least three people other than his wife; and had hit or thrown things at his wife. [Alan Booth and James M. Dabbs, Jr., "Testosterone and Men's Marriages," *Social Forces*, vol. 72, no. 2 (December 1993): 463–477]

5. A study reports that children who attend day care over a long period may have problems with aggression and overactivity. The test group involved 42 white, nonhandicapped urban children, born in 1980. The children had attended group day care continuously, 30 hours a week, for at least 4 years, from at least 18 months of age. The control group consisted of 42 white, nonhandicapped children who had never attended day care. The controls were matched individually for difficult temperament score (based upon a standardized test-scale) at age three, and factors such as maternal education, father's absence, number of siblings at age six, sex, and month of birth.

   The children who attended day care were significantly more aggressive and active. Their behavior was judged by the mothers, and the validity of the mothers' judgment was supported by an independent rating by teachers of a subsample. [Christopher Bagley, "Aggression and Anxiety in Day Care Graduates," *Psychological Reports*, vol. 64 (February 1989): 250.]

6. In 1982, Ronald Reagan launched the "war on drugs" in the United States. The fact that he did the right thing is shown by the increase in drug related offenses, despite the war on drugs. There are more Americans in prison today for marijuana offenses than at any other time in American history. Perhaps penalties should be stiffer. Marijuana must be stamped out. It is responsible for the slovenly unmotivated nature of today's young people.

7. Day care is dangerous for infants. Studies conducted on children in war refugee camps and wartime orphanages during and after the Second World War show that these children were likely to suffer permanent damage. Experiments on baby monkeys, who were deprived of their birth mothers and given "substitute mothers" constructed of wire-mesh, showed that the monkeys suffered severe emotional distress. [Adapted from Susan Faludi, *Backlash* (New York: Crown Publishers, 1991), pp. 43–44.]

Glossary

abusive *ad hominem* a counterargument that attacks the arguer's personality rather than his argument

***ad hominem* (abusive or circumstantial)** a counterarugment that attacks the arguer rather than the argument

ambiguity an ambiguous term has more than one definite meaning

analogue in an argument from analogy, the thing to which the primary subject is being compared

anecdotal evidence using a few personal experiences to support a wide-ranging conclusion (also known as the fallacy of *hasty generalization*)

antecedent the sufficient condition; the first part of an *if . . . then* sentence

appeal to ignorance an argument that uses the fact that there is no evidence against *p* as a premise in support of *p*

appeal to the majority an argument that a proposition is true because "everyone" believes it

appeal to the select few an argument that a proposition is true because not everyone believes it

appeal to tradition an argument that a proposition is true because it has "always" been believed

argument an attempt to prove a proposition by giving reasons to believe it

argument from analogy an argument that draws a conclusion about one thing by comparing it with another thing

argument from experience an argument that uses experienced cases in the premise(s) to draw a conclusion or make a prediction about cases that have not been experienced

assert   to assert a proposition is to claim the proposition is true

assumption   a missing premise; a premise that is not stated explicitly, but is required for the logic of the argument

authority   a person who knows more about a topic than most people

begging the question   assuming the conclusion of an argument in the premises

blind study   a study in which the subjects do not know whether they are part of the control group or the test group

categorical statement   a statement asserting that all or some members of a subject class belong or do not belong to a predicate class

categorical syllogism   an inference from two categorical premises

category   the type of thing something can be said to be

causal argument   an argument that draws a conclusion that one class of things or events leads to or results in another class of things or events

circumstantial *ad hominem*   a counterargument that suggests that there is something about the arguer's circumstances that accounts for his holding the position he does

common knowledge   beliefs likely to be shared by most members of a culture or subculture

complement   for every class, there is a complement, made up of everything that does not fall within that class—for example, *dogs* and *nondogs*

conclusion   what an argument is trying to convince you of

conditional statement   a statement that asserts that one thing is necessary or sufficient for another thing

consequent   the necessary condition; the second part of an *if . . . then* sentence

contradictory statements   statements that cannot both be true and cannot both be false

contraposition   in a categorical statement, the result of switching subject and predicate terms, and exchanging both subject and predicate terms for terms that name their complement classes

contrary statements   statements that can both be false and cannot both be true

control group   in a causal study, the group in which the causal factor is not present

control group/test group experiment   a causal study in which the researcher controls the presence or absence of the causal factor, but no other conditions

controlled laboratory experiment   a causal study in which the researcher controls all conditions

convergent premises   independent premises that give independent reasons to believe a conclusion

conversion   switching the subject and predicate terms of a categorical statement, valid only for *E* and *I* statements

copula   *is* or *are*, used to join subject and predicate in a categorical statement

correlation   two things are found together; it cannot be immediately inferred that one is the cause of the other

correlational research   a causal study in which the researcher does not control any conditions

counterargument   an argument that tries to refute another argument

counterconsideration   a negatively relevant proposition included in an argument in order to anticipate an objection

counterexample   a counterexample to a claim is a thing or situation that would prove the claim false

deductive argument   an argument whose structure dictates that if the premises are true, the conclusion must be true; a categorical or conditional argument

dichotomy argument   an argument that uses an implicitly restricted disjunction as a premise; one or more additional premises rule out all but one disjunct

disjunction   a statement that offers two or more alternatives (disjuncts); usually an *or* sentence

distributed term   in a categorical statement, a term that makes a claim about all of the members of the class named by the term

double-blind study   a study in which neither the subjects nor the researchers know whether a given subject is part of the control group or the test group

emotionally charged language   a term that carries additional emotional force

equivalent   equivalent propositions say the same thing in different ways

equivocation   a fallacy that occurs when an argument contains an ambiguous term; the conclusion appears to follow only because the meanings of the ambiguous term are conflated

euphemism   a term that attempts to gloss over warranted emotional force

explanation   gives reasons why something is true, without trying to convince you that it *is* true

fallacious appeal to authority   an appeal to someone that contravenes one of the criteria for proper use of authority

false dichotomy   a fallacy that occurs when a disjunctive premise falsely suggests that it exhausts all possible alternatives relevant to the conclusion

gambler's fallacy   the belief that a run of random events has to change, when the past events cannot have any bearing on predicting the future events

generalization to a particular   an argument that moves from many experienced members of a class to a single unexperienced object of that kind

hasty generalization   a fallacy committed when someone argues as if a few experiences are adequate to generalize to a wide-ranging conclusion.

immediate inferences   inferences that yield equivalent propositions

indicator words   words that can help identify or standardize an argument by giving clues of the logical relationships between propositions in the passage

invalid   an argument that is unacceptable because of its logical form

irrelevant premise   a premise that counts neither for nor against the conclusion

linked premises   interdependent premises that work together to support the conclusion

loaded questions   questions that presuppose, or only allow for, a certain response or range of responses

major term   in a categorical argument, the predicate of the conclusion

measurement instrument   the means by which a researcher measures the occurrence of the target property

middle term   in a categorical argument, the term that connects the major and minor terms

minor term   in a categorical argument, the subject of the conclusion

modus ponens   an argument that affirms a sufficient condition

modus tollens   an argument that denies a necessary condition

necessary condition   one that is required

negatively relevant premise   a premise that works to disprove the conclusion

obversion   the result of changing a categorical statement from affirmative to negative or from negative to affirmative, and replacing the predicate term with the term for the complement of the predicate class

operational definition   a definition that prescribes an operation, the result of which determines whether a given object can be called by the term defined

operationalization   giving operational definitions for terms

particular affirmative statement   a categorical statement that asserts that some of the members of the subject class belong to the predicate class; an *I* sentence

particular negative statement   a categorical statement that asserts that some of the members of the subject class do not belong to the predicate class; an *O* sentence

persuasive definition   a disguised stipulative definition, where the term defined has a central role in the argument

placebo   given to the members of the control group in a causal study, it appears to be the causal agent, but is actually inactive

placebo effect   the fact that if people believe they are exposed to a certain causal agent, they will act as though they have been

population   in an argument from experience, the subject of the conclusion

post hoc **fallacy**   results from assuming that since *B* happened after *A*, *A* caused *B*

positively relevant premise   a premise that works to support the conclusion

predicate term   what a sentence or proposition says about the subject term

premises   reasons for believing a conclusion

primary subject   in an argument from analogy, the subject of the conclusion

principle of charity   interpreting a passage so that it makes the most sense—giving the author the "benefit of the doubt"

proposition   a sentence or part of a sentence that expresses one and only one complete thought, which can be true or false

random sample   in a random sample, any member of the population has an equal chance of being selected

relevance   a relationship sometimes present between premises and conclusion; see negatively relevant premise, postively relevant premise, irrelevance

reliability   a measurement instrument is reliable if and only if it gives the same results under the same conditions

replication   an attempt by different researchers to obtain the same results using the same study design

representative   information is generalizable from sample to population only if the sample is representative

sample   in an argument from experience, the cases of which you have experience—the subject of the premise

scope   how many things a proposition is about—all or some

shifting the burden of proof   an attempt to prove a conclusion by showing that the opponent cannot disprove it

similarities   arguments from analogy are based on similarities that are known to hold between the primary subject and analogue

slippery assimilation   a fallacy committed when someone ignores that fact that several insignificant differences can add up to a significant difference

slippery precedent   a fallacy committed when someone argues that an action, while acceptable on its own, will set a precedent for further unacceptable actions; but the precedent would not in fact be set because of relevant differences between the cases

statistical generalization   an argument that uses a premise about the prevalence or proportion of the target property in a group of experienced cases to draw a conclusion that the prevalence or proportion is similar in unexperienced cases

standardizing   clarifying the relationships among propositions contained in an argument

statistical significance   a significant difference between control and test groups is one that is greater than would be likely by chance

stipulative definition   a definition that makes the meaning of a term more precise for a particular purpose

stratified sample   a sample composed such that it reflects other classifications that are already known to hold for the population

straw person   a counterargument that substitutes another position for the one actually at issue

subargument   an argument that is embedded in a larger argument, giving reasons to support one of the premises of the larger argument

subcontrary statements   statements that can both be true and cannot both be false

subject term   what a sentence or proposition is about

sufficient condition   one that is enough to result in the consequent

target property   the property that is extended from the analogue (in an argument from analogy) or the sample (in an argument from experience) in the premises to the primary subject or the population in the conclusion

test group   in a causal study, the group in which the causal factor is present

testimony   an account of someone's personal experience

truth-value   to know the truth-value of a statement is to know if the statement is true or false

tu quoque   a counterargument that suggests that the arguer holds a position that contradicts his actions

two wrongs   a fallacy committed when someone argues that if one case is bad, and permitted, another case that is similar in being bad should be permitted too

undistributed term   a term that makes a claim about some but not all members of the class named by the term

universal affirmative statement   a categorical statement that asserts that all members of the subject class belong to the predicate class; an *A* sentence

universal generalization   an argument that uses experience of some members of a class as a premise supporting a conclusion about all or most members of that class

universal negative statement   a categorical statement that asserts that all members of the subject class do not belong to the predicate class; an *E* sentence

vagueness   a vague term has no definite meaning

validity [of arguments]   if the premises are true, the conclusion must be true; used to evaluate the logical structure of a deductive (conditional or categorical) argument

validity [of measurement instruments]   a valid instrument is one that measures what it claims to measure

Index

307